Cheers for *Chance to*

MW01198867

"*Chance to Change: A Midlife Resurrection* is a moving and powerful expression of the transformational journey at the heart of us all ... the soul's awakening to authentic purpose and limitless possibilities. With creative mastery, Amy Thornton not only shares her remarkable path of unfoldment with amazing vulnerability, she also gifts us with an exquisite and beautiful book that is a joy to read, a treasure for anyone's library. I am certain that you'll be deeply blessed by reading and sharing this book."

— *Dr. Roger Teel*, Senior Minister, Mile Hi Church,
Author of This Life is Joy

"*Chance to Change* sheds a personal light on the powerful changes available to us when we acknowledge our past wounds and tell the truth about them. Amy Thornton shares her own journey in such a unique way, may it open doors for others to find deep and profound changes in their lives."

— *Pia Mellody*, Best-Selling Author, Original Staff at
The Meadows, Arizona

"Amy Thornton shares her transformational memoir with a lively, creative flair that invites the reader to embrace possibilities for change. Thornton's unique sensitivity to language leads to the awareness that each change in perspective can fuel the energy of personal empowerment. Deeply probing one's consciousness has never been so exhilarating!"

— *Claudia Abbott*, RSCP, Former Editor-in-Chief,
Science of Mind magazine

"We all have our unique *song* to *sing*. Amy's journey offers the opportunity to celebrate and expand what that is for each and every one of us."

— *Lannie Garrett*, Singer, Entertainer, Owner of
Lannie's Clocktower Cabaret

"Amy Thornton found a way to revolutionize her outlook – and her life – one letter at a time. Her charming book – the perfect blend of sass, spunk and spirituality – invites us to explore a similar adventure."

— *Victoria Moran*, Author, Creating a Charmed Life
and The Good Karma Diet

"In today's fast-paced world, Amy Thornton's insights and ideas in *Chance to Change: A Midlife Resurrection* are refreshing and transformative."

— *Debra Fine*, International Speaker, Trainer and
Best-selling Author, CEO of DebraFine.com

"Amy Thornton writes in a style that is truly original. Her creative word play, honest self-reflections, and cameo storytelling combine with the luscious illustrations to sweep you with her on her personal journey. The decluttering chapter made me laugh hard; other parts moved me; the whole work is a quirky narrative spiced with wisdom and fresh insights."

— *Dr. Sue Allen*, *Director of* Allen & Associates,
Rhodes University Foundation Scholar

"Amy Thornton's 'take' on midlife crisis is fresh, insightful, full of wit and wisdom ... and educational. This is a very engaging read that really pulls the reader in! As another bonus the artwork is spectacular!"

— *Art and Shelly Volkman*, The Volkman Group,
Executive Search

"Chance to Change: A Midlife Resurrection is a poignant and unique look at personal transformation and healing. With impeccable respect for the power of words, Amy courageously and honestly infuses wit and memorable 'isms' into her auto biographical masterpiece. At first glance these are simply playful, yet as you read on they become profound and memorable touchstones for healing. Blending humor and such serious personal topics is an art form and Amy Thornton delivers with warmth, hope and clarity! After reading the book, we will forever view *retirement* as '*revirement*' and will smile at the shift."

— *Linda McDonald and Ron Benson*, The McDonald
Group; *former Board Members of Mile Hi Church*

"Moved by an innate passion for transformation, Amy Thornton takes us on her personal journey into a simpler and more meaningful way of life – through the power of words, inspirational stories, clever insights and the great desire to return home ... to her true self. Engaging, thought-provoking and just plain fun!"

— *Cindy L. Chadwick*, *Marketing Director*, Life
Healing Center, *Santa Fe, New Mexico*

"In *Chance to Change: A Midlife Resurrection*, Amy Thornton encourages all of us to tell our stories in a unique way."

— *Kathy A. Wells, M.A.*, *Quantum Psychology*
Psychotherapist

"Chance to Change offers many keys to opening the doors of transformation. To truly reap its rich rewards, this book should be savored and read over time with space to reflect and integrate its seemingly simple wisdom. Amy Thornton shares a powerful tale of reclaiming personal power that can lead to a rich and aligning sense of being."

— *Carol Ratcliffe Alm*, *Executive and Personal Coach,*
Business Strategist, and Presenter

"*Chance to Change* is a book with so many new and creative ways to expand consciousness that it has its own glossary. Author Amy Thornton recreates language and uses it to recreate her very self. She has taken a center-of-life crisis and spun gold from it. Rather than wallow in self-pity, Thornton brings her skills as wordsmith, artist, and graphic designer to share her inner – and outer – resurrection. A fast-paced exploration into the mind of an extraordinarily creative person, *Chance to Change* takes us on a journey of self-recreation loaded with brilliant art and even more brilliant word play. The book is a tsunami of ideas all aimed at helping us navigate the waters of life."

— *Patrick Soran*, Editor, Creative Thought *magazine*

"Amy Thornton has beautifully applied her gifted artistic background and crafted a most unique and thought-provoking book, *Chance to Change: A Midlife Resurrection*. Amy's message of creative inspiration comes to us in a beautifully presented package filled with rich word crafting and visual impact, best embraced one chapter at a time, one insight at a time. The V-inspired photography at the close of each chapter celebrates the deeper layers of awareness available to us through Amy's creative journey."

— *Carl Studna*, *Visionary Photographer, Psychotherapist and Award-winning Author of* Click! Choosing Love, One Frame at a Time

"Amid the '**Thorn-isms**' lie the roses. Thought blooms such as pay attention not only to WHAT you think but HOW you think, or remember to define what having *IT* means to you, and the fabulous concept of *Revirement*. Amy Thornton digs deep into her inner garden and wants you, her reader, to reap the harvest ... weeds and all."

— *Karyn Ruth White*, *Motivational Speaker, Comedian and Author of* Dream Droppings: How to Turn Your Crappy Days into Rich Compost and Grow Your Dreams.

"In *Chance to Change: A Midlife Resurrection*, Amy Thornton takes a very creative look at aging with grace. Her own story and revelations lead the reader to thought-provoking contemplations."

— *Cynthia James*, *Author of* What Will Set You Free *and* Revealing Your Extraordinary Essence

"With rich insights and colorful stories, Amy Thornton brings an infectious enthusiasm and encouragement to the rich potential found in reinvention. A true artist expanding her vision from paint to words, keep writing Amy, I can't wait for the sequel!"

— *Debbie Taylor*, Taylor Made Events & Speakers

Chance to *Change*
A Midlife Resurrection

AMY THORNTON

Artists don't get older ... they get better.

— Pablo Picasso

May we all shine as artists of our lives.

Published by Go(o)d Works Publications, an independent publishing house in
Denver, Colorado. **www.goodworkspublications.com**

Available from Amazon.com and other retail outlets.

Library of Congress Cataloging-in-Publication Data available upon request.

For more information, please email: **amy@amythornton.com** or visit: **www.amythornton.com**

Printed in the United States of America
Cover and interior design: Amy Thornton
Special photography: Carl Studna and Michelle Elm
Interior art photography and illustrations: Amy Thornton

Dedicated to ...   *Eternal Life, Amy Thornton*

Contents

Prologue: The *IT* Itch   i-vi
A lifelong search for *IT* culminates in midlife despair.

P A R T   O N E · *SEEING* ·───────

1. Shoot-Out in the *Not-OK Corral*   2
Meeting my own worst enemy, shrinking thinking.

2. Painting with Words   7
My passion for words leads to midlife salvation.

3. Secrets of Life   14
Answers aren't hidden; they're *right-in-front-of-me.*

4. First *JOLLI* Jolt   18
The French word *reVirement* turns me all about.

5. All about Change   30
A Boomer AHA: I'm already good at change.

6. Power of Words   38
Words can change *worlds.*

7. **Think about Thinking**   46
   Deciphering the power of my thinking.

8. ***Stalk* My *Talk***   54
   Turning self-talk in the right direction.

9. **OverITs and NexITs**   67
   Getting good and over *IT* before the next *IT* arrives.

10. **A Quantumesque Life**   78
    Quantum leaping from *old* to *bold*.

PART TWO · *DOING* ————————————————

11. **Vhorizon of Perspective**   90
    The V drives perspectives to a high way.

12. **Clear the Magnet**   102
    What prevents the magnetization of a bold life?

13. **Tough on Stuff**   110
    Tactics for getting through too much stuff.

14. **My Second Vepiphany**   124
    Another *T-to-V* switch expands the path to reinvention.

15. **Reviewing the RoughStuff**   135
    Getting to the *root* of all *loot* for an inner turnabout.

Contents

16. **Matter of Mattering**   146
    Life as I know *IT* ends as I dive *in* to *win*.

17. **Getting My Enoughness**   154
    Pivotal practices for more turning about.

18. ***ON NO* Switcheroo**   162
    Discovering the mysteries in all **MyStories**.

19. ***Selling* or *Telling?***   171
    Telling the truth changes everything.

20. **A *RealDeal Heal***   178
    A renaissance arrives from *DOING* to *BEING*.

PART THREE · *BEING* ·

21. **My Third Vepiphany**   188
    A third *T-to-V* shift inspires a brighter vision.

22. **Bookending My Life**   195
    Writing the next life-book to *sing* my *song*.

23. **Garbagegems, Dollishops & Pioneergypsy**   203
    Childhood holds clues for midlife rebirth.

24. **Top Three P's**   213
    Principles emerge from the past for paradigm shifts.

25. It's All Go(o)d   224
The good, bad and ugly seem divinely directed.

26. A V.O.D. Experience   235
A writing retreat brings on a V-overdose.

27. Finding *IT IS*   246
Turning *IT* about with what *IS*.

28. *Vow* to *Wow*   253
Higher love is the very reason I have come.

29. I AM Ammo   261
Empowerment comes from "I AM" insights.

30. A *JOLLI* Finale   268
Celebrating the V-journey.

Epilogue: Living Life *AsIS*   278
A life event tests all my theories.

Acknowledgments   281
Tanks of *thanks* to oh-so-many.

About Amy Thornton   282
Particulars about the author.

To Connect   283
Please stay in touch.

Glossary   284
Reference guide for **Thornisms**, *JOLLIs* and phraseology.

I have been a seeker and I still am, but I have stopped asking the books and the stars. I have started listening to the teaching of my Soul.

— Rumi

The *IT* Itch

"Amy, you're so old and fat!" I sucked in my bulging waistline and fumbled to lock the airline seat belt. A heavy sigh pushed me back into the cramped seat as I settled in for my return flight to Colorado.

While the flight crew scurried about preparing for takeoff, I reached for electronic escape and began flipping through digital vacation snapshots. One image revealed a pleasantly plump picture of myself dressed all in black—my wardrobe fix for a growing middle-age middle. In the photo, I forced a grin, as though hoping to hide a secret dread.

My chest gripped tight. With reader glasses, I zoomed in to more closely inspect my waistline and vanishing chin. *"Wow, Amy, you're not even fifty and already you are reeeally old."*

With one swift click, I blackened the camera screen and jammed the camera into the bag under my seat. My vacation photos brought despair rather than joy. One negative thought opened a mental hatch, waving in others. *"I hate this. You're old, fat and have no idea who the hell you really are. What have you done with the first half of your life? None of IT is enough. What is IT you're missing?!?"*

The *"Big 5-0"* towered ahead, casting an eerie shadow over the first half of my life. That secret

One photo launched a sweeping life review.

dread I'd hoped to ignore came flooding forth with the pressure to figure out what *IT* – my life and all I'd done so far – was all about. I'd always raced towards satisfaction, reaching for all the right stuff in education, experiences, relationships and jobs. I constantly searched for some invisible reward. My incessant over-achieving boiled down to one simple two-letter word — *IT*.

A midlife "dis-ease" burned through me as a mental *IT* itch, leading me to an uneasy conclusion. My life had raced from *IT* to *IT*.

Strapped into the tiny plane seat, I wallowed in a midlife muddle. A succession of empty-ended *IT* questions ensued. What was *IT*? Where was *IT*? Who had *IT*? When would I get *IT*?

The pilot's voice disrupted my inner *IT* debate. "Afternoon, folks. We've hit turbulence. Please fasten your seat belts."

As the plane jerked, my mind lurched onto its own bumpy ride.

Memories of a wildly creative and busy childhood flashed by. Prompted by artistic and frugal parents, our Thornton family alma mater encouraged a "do-*IT*-all" attitude. With straight-A fervor, I grew into a whirling dervish, steadily spinning through a series of multi-talented accomplishments.

I performed in talent shows, competed in art shows and was chosen prom queen. Memories merged into one symbolic vision of me hunched over a grand piano on stage. My cramped fingers pounded out the "Hallelujah Chorus" in accompaniment to my high school's senior chorale in the finale of Handel's *Messiah*.

The week of high school graduation, I won a citywide writing contest to live and travel in Brazil. A crash course in Portuguese allowed me to impress my host family, who found my unbridled enthusiasm and American independence daunting.

My *IT* accolades had just begun. Four years of liberal arts education culminated in a *summa cum laude* degree as I graduated the top art student in my class and was listed in the coveted *Who's Who in American*

Colleges and Universities, but my prestigious honors were cloaked with insecurities. I secretly celebrated graduation with a bulimic sugar spree. All of *IT* left me feeling like a fraud. And yet my *IT* drive surged ahead with progressive urgency to find *IT*.

Armed with a Bachelor of Fine Arts degree and a Eurail pass, I traveled through the capitals of Europe to view the great masters of art and their *IT* artistry.

Unfortunately, this unwinding backpack adventure screeched to a halt under the Albert Bridge in London. My *IT* searches had also fueled a host of vices that eventually unraveled out of control. While staring into the cold, night waters of the River Thames, I contemplated suicide.

The utter despair of that surrender launched a stream of unforeseen incidents leading to decades of recovery from multiple addictions; the course of my life changed completely.

A rumble in the plane's aisle woke me from my mental review. The snack cart pulled up beside me. "Something to drink, Ma'am?"

I placed a steaming cup of tea on the wobbly seat tray, reached for my reliable Pilot pen and listed my many *IT* searches on a blank airline napkin. Colliding flashbacks revealed the depth of my *IT*-focused life in a shocking and bewildering *IT* list.

My job résumé boasted successful careers as a contemporary artist and award-winning creative director. From London's Kings Road to New York's Madison Avenue, I had vied for a multitude of *IT* triumphs. However, this professional *IT* list brought no inner satisfaction.

Hunting for *IT* in the land of love, I'd hoped romantic relationships would provide *IT*. A youthful marriage ended in disappointment and divorce. I then spent decades in domino romances, searching for unrequited *IT* love and connection. Yet, by midlife, no man had fulfilled my *Mr. IT* list of requirements.

I'd seen therapists and attended decades of personal growth seminars. Why hadn't any of these delivered lasting emotional *IT* answers?

Once, in an extravagant ceremony, I was submerged in a hot tub while breathing through a snorkel to replicate a rebirthing. The birth of my true, inner *IT* never arrived. Journeys to the center of myself introduced me to my inner child. Why hadn't this integrated *IT* self lasted?

The yearning for my intangible *IT* had led me out there to in here to everywhere. As I turned the napkin over and continued to scribble my list, more elaborate *IT* searches from my history unfolded.

Skydiving from a plane at 30,000 feet, I'd dived into my fears to embrace an authentic *IT* life. That *IT* high lasted less than a week. In Sedona, Arizona, I concluded a seven-day fast – complete with coffee enemas – by jumping off a 50-foot waterfall into a vortex of invisible energy. Surely, I should have found *IT* there!

A move to Manhattan promised an exciting *IT* life. When the skyscrapers failed to lift me to *IT* heights, I returned to the natural summits of Colorado to find *IT* there.

Materially, a vast array of *IT* possessions stuffed my small Denver home. My closet held multiple outfits with matching shoes for every *IT* occasion. Since the age of twelve, a minimum of two jobs had financially supported the accumulation of all my *IT*s. But alas, no stash of cash could have bought my missing *IT*.

I traversed Europe a couple of times and visited almost all fifty of the United States; I still hadn't found *IT*.

In my twenties, I trekked to the Gulf of Mexico on a 15-speed bike with my ex-hubby. In my thirties, I survived a harrowing shipwreck in the Atlantic Ocean. In my forties, I marveled at Kilauea's flowing lava under a moonlit sky. Extreme adventures brought short-lived relief and only fueled my conviction to find *IT*.

Many spiritual searches paralleled my life's journey. In college, I diverted from my Lutheran upbringing to be "born again". When this failed to supply *IT*, I chanted "Om" in ashrams and stretched into *IT* with yoga and meditation.

Profuse reading of well-known authors on the leading edge of "New Thought" fell short of *IT*. Harnessing the powers of "now" vanished as the "now" refused to remain still long enough for me to find *IT*.

I'd managed early-life addictions with daily practices and meetings. For over two decades, I practiced the steps of recovery and received great relief. But, as my midlife *IT* itch burned inside, I sensed that my recovery efforts had fallen short of providing the inner authenticity I craved.

I hunched over my list and rubbed my forehead. *"What on earth is wrong with you?!? Why hasn't any of this been IT?!?"* The enormity of my *IT* list seemed unbelievable. And yet, I still asked what *IT* might be next.

My whole life looped around an invisible *IT* racetrack, vying for the next *IT* move to make. With increased despair, I realized I was all out of *ITs*. My mental trip ended as the plane touched down on Denver's runway and I landed in one massive state of over-*IT*.

"Was IT a different job, an unknown man, an extravagant experience?" I hungered for an exit from the *IT* rat-race, but how?

Internal unrest continued for weeks after that bumpy ride. I itched to understand the enormity of my baffling *IT* list. Why had none of my vast and impressive *IT* pursuits ever stuck to my bones?

The urgency of my query must have triggered some great universal or mysterious powers because something unexpected soon happened. In the middle of the night, a verbal antidote came to my rescue with a simple *"Just-One-Little-Letter-Insight."*

My *IT* answers unfolded through creative word plays. By changing just one little letter in words to make other words, I arrived at inspired insights. Shifts like *know* this *now,* or *there* is *here* held clues to my puzzlements. One particular letter – V – emerged as my verbal heroine. It provided the creative impetus for all that followed.

A *revolution* of *evolution* brought *bold* spins on *old* themes. Infused with renovated answers, my elusive and irritating *IT* itch soothed into silence as I transformed from a searching human being into a *RealDeal* human being. The process delivered a vital midlife resurrection beyond any *IT* I could have imagined.

Transpiring over half a decade, my life-changing saga wove together conflict and resolution for mega-metamorphosis. Like the life of a butterfly, my tale of transformation unfolded in a three-part journey presented here as *SEEING*, *DOING* and *BEING*.

Similar to the way a caterpillar's legs scurry it along a course of discovery, the letter V was leading me to uncanny awareness via surprising insights. As it spun me into a cocoon, I dove *in* to *win*. From there, a refreshing alignment arrived. Akin to the wings of a butterfly, an inner freedom burst forth, flying me home to myself.

My body, mind and spirit lost pounds of excess baggage. Ultimately, I reached my own version of enlightenment after falling madly in love with the *"I"* at the front of *IT*.

A powerful and brilliant *chance* to *change* progressed from the inside out. *IT* became the ultimate discovery of *IS*.

SUMMARY> The *IT* Itch

SEEING

Shoot-Out in the *Not-OK Corral*

- *Fuel* to *Duel*
- *Piece* by *Peace*
- Eye-Peelin' Talents

The *Big 5-0*, a common phrase describing the launch of midlife, triggered an exploding mind field within me. Internal *IT* searching created a fiery *fuel* for the *duel* going on in my mind. A colorful memory from childhood illustrated my mental struggle.

On a hot August day in 1966, the Thornton family of four visited Tombstone, Arizona, site of the shoot-out at the O.K. Corral between Wyatt Earp and Doc Holliday. As a nine-year-old, I was fascinated by the historic photos of grizzly bandits with scarves hiding their true identities. Cowboys, blurred in sepia tones, told hidden stories of dueling conflicts.

Recalling that trip forty years later, I teetered on what I feared might be the precipice of my own tombstone. I faced hidden stories told by negative inner bandits. The duel was fueled by a shoot-out taking place in my internal *Not-OK Corral*. A wild bunch of Amy Brain Bandits fired bullets of doubt from all directions, shooting holes in my life's story:

> BANG: *"Who do you think you are?"*
>
> POP: *"Amy, who are you, reeeeally?"*
>
> KaPOW: *"Why haven't you found IT yet?"*
>
> WHAM: *"Why don't you feel good about anything you've accomplished so far?"*
>
> ZaPPP: *"Why aren't you happy? What's missing?"*

POW: *"What is IT you're still looking for?*
Why can't you find IT?"

And the final KABANG: *"Amy, when are you finally*
going to get IT together?!?"

The dodging doubts kindled despair at my inability to find *IT* after almost five decades. *IT* joined forces with the *Big 5-0* and a private war battled away. I carried on life's appearances, but no matter what I did, my internal *Not-OK Corral* remained. I could not stop wondering what *IT* would fulfill life's purpose and prove my life counted. What uncovered *IT* would finally be *IT?*

Piece by *Peace*

Along with our summer vacations, my family spent many long weekends at my grandparents' tiny mountain cabin in southern Colorado. Grandpa Byron worked a State services job and Grandma Beulah ran her single-chair beauty shop for over forty years. Every saved penny went to the purchase of their pride and joy, a three-room nature retreat they lovingly called *The Holiday Cabin.*

Every summer, Grandma Beulah unfolded a brown leather card table in the corner of the main room by the wood-burning fireplace. My older sister, Julie, poured out the summer's

Family photos from my grandparents' mountain retreat, The Holiday Cabin.

scenic jigsaw puzzle. Piece by piece, a colorful masterpiece emerged as the curvy edges were locked into place. I strategically placed the cover of the box on the red brick mantel, allowing the beautiful photo to guide our puzzle-piecing treasure hunt.

After the last curvy piece found its place, Grandpa Byron carefully slid the cardboard patchwork onto a sturdy board covered with white Elmer's glue. Once dried, the puzzle reinvented as a painting was framed and passed along to one of my grandparents' many friends.

That memory reflected my midlife expedition out of my *Not-OK Corral*. My many *IT* puzzlements finally came together, falling into place. Piece by piece, a deep peace locked within me. And from my internal battleground, a beautiful picture assembled. A masterpiece emerged worthy of framing in this book and passing along to my friends.

Increased awareness allowed me to *SEE* things from a new angle. For this *SEEING*, an extra-strength knack for looking beyond the obvious surfaced. A knack birthed from adventures at *The Holiday Cabin*.

Eye-Peelin' Talents

When dusk settled into the valley, Grandpa would jingle the keys to the olive-green station wagon, signaling the start of another deer-peering escapade. Family and friends piled into the long Buick.

As the youngest of the family, I crawled deep into the cargo area, where the half-opened back window provided prime viewing range and allowed me to enjoy the scents of mountain sage that filled the dusty

All of us enjoying eye-peelin' nature.

evening air. Grandpa or Dad belted out the familial command for these evening expeditions, *"Okay, everyone ... keep your eyes peeled for deer!"*

We scouted for hidden fauna-treasure. I poised, both hands gripping the window's metal edge. The rush of cool air blew my short-cut bangs aside as I imagined my eyes peeling wide to open my sights. With my extra strength – vision – I could easily spot a camouflaged elk or doe.

From my perch, I'd screech out, "There's another one!" and the family's response, "Great eye-peelin', Amy!" would fill me with triumph. I became the best eye-peeler of the family.

Years later, as the journey out of my *Not-OK Corral* progressed, I brushed off my talents for opening my sights to an expanded vision as I embarked on the first part of my journey: *SEEING*. This brought the essential awareness necessary to launch my *chance* to *change*.

I couldn't *DO* anything about my baffling *IT* obsession until I'd opened my ability to *SEE*. With my extra-strength inner sights peeled to look deeper, I could *SEE* the life-changing insights that would usher in a host of actions. Change would come, percolating from the inside out.

SEEING opened the gates for *DOING* and, as a result, my entire state of *BEING* would find renewed alliance. By the end, I would conquer my dueling Brain Bandits and walk arm in arm with them out of my *NOT-OK Corral*. Striding off into a second-half-of-life sunset, I would find peaceful resolutions to my elusive *IT* searches.

To light the path of this expansion, I turned many times to my inventive childhood, where a long-time fascination with words began.

SUMMARY> Shoot-Out in the *NOT-OK* Corral

CHAPTER 2

Painting with Words

- Thornton Creative Gumption
- Making up Words
- *Streams of Mind*

I grew up in a western suburb of Denver, Colorado, during the Baby Boom era. Although my family's middle-class financial status teetered on lower-class, our neighbors and friends never knew it. A combination of extreme frugality and lively innovation birthed a creative family life, rich with plenty.

My parents' do-it-ourselves attitude overcame any material lack. With endless curiosity, spirited initiative and unbridled resourcefulness, we embodied creative spunk. We lived at a nonstop, get-up-and-go pace. One word – gumption – described the Thorntons to a "T".

Early life produced the perfect training ground for gaining skills needed to find, make and go for any *IT* imaginable — no *IT* was too large or too small to be conquered, conspired and created. Unfortunately, this would add to my hefty midlife frustration at still not finding *IT*.

My mom, Marge, captain of our shining epitome of a Boomer mother ship, steered us all forward, filling her days with preparations. Cooking meals, sewing clothes, doing laundry, ironing, knitting, making ceramics, teaching Sunday school, baking bread and preserving jams to go on the bread were but a few of her versatile talents. Every night, she highlighted the day's events in five-year, leather-bound diaries, her logs of our family's journey.

From her Minnesota farm background with its prudent Scandinavian influences, Mom provided the foundation for Dad's creative exuberance. My dad, John, excelled as an artist, art director, printer, antique refinisher, travel director and chief project-starter.

They formed a dynamic duo building, sewing and inventing whatever was needed during those pre-Home Depot days. They transformed our small, three-bedroom home into a creative caldron for endless concoctions. Refinished rooms in the concrete basement provided various domains for our family's creativity.

Mom's kingdom reigned at the north end of the basement. Her sewing room bulged with shelves of fabrics and antique tins stuffed with buttons, zippers and ribbons. A millinery closet stored colorful netting, miniature silk flowers and supplies to create our yearly Easter hats. We frequented Goodwill and Salvation Army stores to forage for supplies. I stitched my first machine-sewn apron by age six. We rarely bought anything new. The unspoken Thornton rule: Make everything! But I'll never forget the thrill of using precious savings to purchase my first store-bought dress in eighth grade.

Showing off 4-H projects and a favorite first-day-of-school dress.

From clothes to crafts and camping, life evolved in a flurry of nonstop activity. Next to the sewing room, Mom's laundry room doubled as her ceramic studio. Amid shelves brimming with rows of glazes and molds, a small kiln fired ceramic gems for household use and special gifts.

The other two basement rooms housed Dad's creative domain. His workshop buzzed with saws and tools that had been passed down through generations. Adjacent to the stairwell, Dad's art studio provided the space for him to create landscape watercolors and oil portraits.

An avid calligrapher, Dad penned names at ten cents a letter on certificates. His Old English creations helped fund our summer vacations.

When I turned twelve, Dad purchased an antique letterpress. As his print-shop apprentice, I earned a whopping dollar an hour on projects; my babysitting days at twenty-five cents an hour quickly vanished. Years of parental lessons taught Julie and me how to plan, sew, paint, assemble and invent anything our eager young minds conjured.

If I wasn't painting pictures of the rose bushes lining our front walk, I was building troll-doll castles and designing Barbie doll evening gowns. The main room in the basement flourished as center stage for many an original Watusi dance. Inspired by *The Dean Martin Show*, where dazzling dancers swirled around in sequined hot pants, I pushed all the furniture to the walls and choreographed original dances for hours.

The long credenza along the east wall housed our Sony reel-to-reel tape player. I taped imaginary interviews, changing my voice to suggest pretend guests. Johnny Carson's *The Tonight Show* provided the incentive for a wide range of stunts, including stuffed animal visits from the wild.

Making up Words

In August, 1964, Walt Disney introduced us to Mary Poppins. The mesmerizing songs from the movie soon flowed from our living room's Spinet piano. The classic tune etched into my musical brain was the super-strength tongue twister "Supercalifragilisticexpialidocious".

Poised on the piano bench, I belted out the magical notes. Julie and I word-dueled over who could rattle off the fourteen-syllable tongue twister faster. I spent the rest of August memorizing the word and, when September classes resumed at Russell Elementary, impressed everyone with my precocious verbal "expialidosciousness".

At about this same age, I spent hours memorizing a favorite fable about a roly-poly Asian boy who was stuck in the village water well.

His long name delayed his rescue because none of the town folk could remember its rambling meter. I still recall the impact this playful name made: *Nicki-nicki-tembo-oh-so-rembo-oo-mah-mochie-gama-gama-guchi*. Throughout my life, from cars to friends, I would thrive on coining clever nicknames—though they were never quite that extensive.

It wasn't long before Dad and I started making up our own words. We called them **Thornisms** (thorn•isms; Thornton-invented words). Soon our Siamese kittens became **supercatas** and the antiques Dad refinished were labeled **fragilistic**. While we engaged in some activity or lively debate, a new word, misspelled, mispronounced or a combination of both often leapt from our imaginations. Excited glances were exchanged with verbal high-fives and joyous exclamations of, *"Yay, another* **Thornism***!"*

Although playfully creative, the **Thornism** approach to expressing myself took a toll on my grammar and spelling. In my various professions as graphic designer, creative director and author, I'm known for my **typoknackabilities** (typ•o•knack•a•bil•i•ties; the knack for typos) and **grammarring** (gram•mar•ing; marring grammar).

My youthful enthusiasm for words spread everywhere. Whether learning calligraphy, hand-setting type on our antique letterpress or conversing with guests on my imaginary talk show ... I *loved* words.

Life went along, creative and plentiful as always, when tragedy suddenly struck.

Streams of Mind

When I was a junior in high school, my mother died from a short, invasive battle with breast cancer. This was a tough blow to our family as Mom's influential glue bonding us together immediately dissolved. The influence of her can-do approach to life, combined with her limitless focus on fixing everything, left me ill-prepared to cope with my grief.

No amount of Thornton creative gumption could cure my pain, so

I buried the agony by adapting into an image of a dependable adult, hoping to make my missing mom proud. I grew up overnight, replacing Mom as caretaker for Dad, who had fallen apart. Unconsciously, I developed a separate private self to hide my pain and confusion, which would ultimately escalate into dangerous addictions by age twenty.

While I was drowning in emotional tidal waves, my adolescent confusion conspired with denial and a "life-goes-on" cover-up. I found some relief when my creative writing teacher, Miss Hardesty, suggested I pour out my thoughts and feelings into a spiral notebook.

I soon discovered that fervent journal writing helped **nagivate** (nag•i•vate; navigate nagging aggravation) my internal mental rapids. Unrestrained writing allowed the streams of my mind's negativity to change course as a magical flow of deliverance steered me towards safer inner shores.

I'll never forget the day I opened my first spiral diary and, without any forethought, wrote out the title: *Streams of My Mind*. It was a phrase I would continue to illustrate on the first page of my countless journals

First two journals, Streams of My Mind, *from the seventies.*

over the next forty years. Of the hundreds of journals I've filled, I cherish the first two from 1974 and 1975 the most.

The insights I discovered by rowing through unrestricted writing cleared my murky mental questions, delivering much **soulace** (soul•ace; solace for my soul).

My *Streams* journals (short for *Streams of My Mind*) proved to be steady *Verbal Best Friends Forever.* They patiently listened to me and advised me throughout a lifetime of twists and turns. When I was emotionally and mentally capsized in a current situation, my writing would impart new currents of awareness, allowing reinvigorated *SEEING* to guide me onto new routes of *DOING* towards revitalized states of *BEING*.

It's not surprising that the resolution to my duel with the *Big 5-0* and my *IT* Brain Bandits began on the pages of *Streams*. Thanks to my **Thornisms** and **typoknackabilities**, my midlife despair gradually found a tranquil harbor. My pen often poured insights to page as if it were an oar rowing me upstream to safety. Verbally primed from a lifetime of **nagivations**, my journaling saved the day and ultimately led me to an exit from my *Not-OK Corral*.

I wondered: Had Mary Poppins or some other magical goddess played a supercalifragilisticexpialidocious hand in bringing about my resolution? For words to propel so much power, something mystical had to have been involved.

A slight revision to a favorite Olympian allegory from ancient times revealed a striking parallel.

SUMMARY> Painting with Words

◆ The Thorntons generated a creative gumption of going for *IT*.

◆ Dad and I made up our own words and call them **Thornisms**.

◆ A lifetime of journaling **nagivated** the currents of my mind

Chapter 3

Secrets of Life

- Mount Olympus Story
- Answers in AHAs
- *Look* of *Book*

At the beginning of time on Mount Olympus, after eons of labor spent helping the Earth and its life forms, the gods and goddesses steered their sights on the curious human evolution unfolding. Entrusted with the Secret of Life, they agreed that IT needed protection from human tampering. They argued about where to hide IT.

Zeus, king of the gods and ruler of Mount Olympus, pointed to the Himalayas. "Let us hide IT on the tallest mountain; they can't possibly climb that high; they'll never find IT there."

Aphrodite, goddess of love, replied, "Humans have insatiable curiosity and ambition. They have proven to be more tenacious than we ever imagined. They will eventually climb the tallest mountain to find IT."

Poseidon, lord of the seas, pointed his mighty fork towards the waters of the world. "We should hide IT at the bottom of the deepest ocean."

"You don't understand," said Hermes, messenger of the gods, balanced on a cliff overlooking them all. "Humanity has boundless imagination and potent desire to explore the world. Sooner or later, they will reach IT even in the greatest ocean depths."

Finally, the goddess of wisdom, Athena, spoke up with the solution. "Let us hide IT in the last place humans would ever look, a place they will find when all other possibilities are exhausted and they are finally ready to see IT."

"And where is that?" the others asked in unison, to which Athena replied, "We will not hide IT at all!"

Olympians of Mount Olympus

Answers in AHAs

After four-plus decades of my climbing the highest heights and diving to the deepest depths, my elusive *IT* search finally revealed its secrets. As my revolutionary expedition into midlife unfolded, tough answers emerged like silent typos that had been *"right-in-front-of-me"* all along. My eye-peelin' talents revealed a host of AHA (common acronym I call: Awareness Has Amazement) moments, allowing me to change.

Satori, the Sanskrit word for instant awakening, became a favorite description for the deep understanding that unfolded, often in a matter of mere moments. This **wholographic** sense (whole•o•graphic; a holographically inspired wholeness) inspired resounding inner shifts. My *chance* to *change* transformation emerged as *evolutionary* moments with *revolutionary* proportions.

Any fleeting skepticism in the power of coincidence and serendipity vanished. As my story unfolded, powerful forces surfaced with *right-in-front-of-me* evidence for renewed *SEEING*, which shifted everything.

I experienced unexplainable, yet ever-present, sources of power that merged in and through my journey, a journey that became a **godyssey** (god•ys•sey; an odyssey to finding my own version of God). My hidden *IT* was often unveiled in such simple and surprising ways, I surmised that ancient Olympians had secretly placed me right in front of *IT!*

Look of *Book*

Although this story may border on the lines of a self-help book or memoir, it is flooded with experiential examples. I have dedicated myself to the phrase *walk* my *talk*.

I have also devoted this book to the number three. A longtime fan of "three", I see the number as an inspiring force behind a range of diversity and divinity. The Father, Son and Holy Ghost shared a supreme order in my mother's religion. Primary elements of the earth, sky and sea represented nature's holy three. Human beings combine body, mind and spirit. Even the word "trinity" hinted at a sense of unity.

Threes shaped the crafting of this book. Whether I was curbing creative impulses or organizing content, three reigned supreme. For starters, thirty chapters each contain three primary themes introduced with three bulleted phrases.

If titles couldn't condense to three words, they became divisible by three. And, playfully, three remains the only single number that rhymes with my verbal champ, the letter V.

A photographic page summarizes each chapter, highlighting its three main themes. The reflecting photos visually celebrate the letter V. Invisible blessings and affirmations are typed into their backgrounds. A list of these blessings are available upon request.

Typographically, **Thornisms** are displayed in bold with definitions following their first use within the body of text. Occasionally, a typo sheds light on another way of *SEEING*. These few **O.P.T.s** (o•p•t•; acronym for *On-Purpose-Typo*) are highlighted with a squigggle line.

On occasion, nicknames protect the identities of those who instilled tougher lessons as in Ms. Had*I*Tall or Mr. Hotartist. The use of all CAPS expands the meaning of some words or names, as in finding *IT* or being inspired by Dr. WAYne Dyer.

An alphabetical glossary on the last pages of the book defines **Thornisms**, nicknames and phrases.

All *JOLLIs* (jol•li; acronym for *Just-One-Little-Letter-Insight*) stand out within the text in italics, as in my *old* was soon to find *bold*.

But I'm getting ahead of myself ... onward to the V!

SUMMARY> Secrets of Life

CHAPTER 4

First *JOLLI* Jolt

- Dreaded Retirement Options
- Farewell, Tired Word
- My *JOLLI* Epiphany

On June 12th, I counted down seven months to my fiftieth birthday. Once again, a band of dueling Brain Bandits filled my mental *Not-OK Corral*. Meeting with a financial advisor, I received depressing news about my finances. The bleakest aspect of turning fifty for me involved my lack of financial planning for retirement, which suddenly seemed right around the corner.

For most of my life I'd simultaneously worked at two or more jobs in order to fund my unending *IT* escapades, successfully ignoring any serious retirement planning. But, finding myself lassoed by my *Big 5-0* and *IT* Brain Bandits, I despaired I would be down and out by the time I reached retirement age.

I pictured some of my more successful friends at sixty-five, hatching their carefully laid nest eggs. With gleaming smiles, they gallivanted out of their *OK Corrals* into golden sunsets. While cruising the Caribbean and making toasts on exotic islands, they savored the lifestyles their financial *IT* eggs served up. All while I continued to search for some *IT*, with no *IT* egg to even sit on, let alone incubate and hatch.

Slumping away in my *Not-OK* state of mind, I wrapped my arms around my growing, middle-age middle, imagining my January birthday. Emotionally and financially unprepared for the second half of my life to begin, I faced down that scary word "retirement". All options my mind explored appeared to be hopeless.

I grabbed my current *Streams* journal and started to row rapid sentences through my mental **nagivations**. Four options offered possible escape from my retirement *Not-OK Corral*.

Retirement Option #1. Marry Someone Rich.

The simplest, most obvious option unraveled first. I just needed to get my *IT* together and find a man who also had *IT* together. Around the next *IT* corner, Prince Charming would surely arrive to save the day. Sweeping in on his horse and shooting down my mental Brain Bandits, he'd pull me high into his lap. Off we'd gallop out of my *Not-OK Corral* into our own retirement sunset.

Unfortunately, no amount of Walt Disney *mix* would *fix* this option. After a young-age divorce, a heart-crushing broken engagement, years of therapy and many books and classes about relationships, I knew better. This **d'illusion** (dil•lu•sion; the delusion of an illusion) generated immediate realistic understanding. No Mr. *IT* could transform my *Not-OK* to *Now-OK*. This I knew with certainty, disqualifying option #1. Next up:

Retirement Option #2. Become a Nun.

Hmmm. This inspired a transcendent idea. Why not do the world some good on exotic missions to Africa while fulfilling worthy causes? No more mortgage payments. My antiquated vision of a nunnery found me within the secluded walls of a tiny convent room.

No more fashion or home decorating needs as I nestled into life at the abbey. No more wardrobe worries with plenty of camouflage for my expanding middle. Goodbye trendy hairstyles, makeup and image management. This could be *IT*. Throw myself into religion and sidestep the whole prospect of grappling with worries of retirement.

Well, almost immediately, this option failed as well. My **thornistic** (thorn•is•tic; having Thornton tendencies) creative constitution would likely lead to trouble the first months. I couldn't ignore my quest towards manifesting a life of my dreams: creating my art, achieving authenticity and helping others. Could I walk away from all previous efforts? Could I ignore the longing to discover my elusive *IT*?

Once I failed to become the next Mother Teresamy, I would probably slump into a bigger ... holy ... *Not-OK Corral*.

Options with more desperate measures came to mind.

Retirement Option #3. Commit a Crime.

I thought to myself: *"Come on, Amy, get creative. Surely there's a crime you could commit that won't harm anyone and would only damage your own reputation and pride. Surely you can conjure up a felony— something like a failed bank robbery. The slim likelihood of you pulling this off would surely land you behind bars. As long as you got a life sentence, you'd have IT made."*

No more financial responsibilities or future retirement to stress over and figure out. In a forever-orange wardrobe, I could spend time beefing up my biceps, studying in the prison library and decorating my half of the 6 x 8-foot cell. Never having to wonder which way to go or what to do next, I would find all my retirement problems solved in a single-file lineup. My *IT* would be completely taken care of for the rest of my days.

This option triggered more sobering thoughts, *"Come on, Amy, get real. You know you'd rebel, big time. At the first chance, you'd end up stabbing either yourself or someone else with your lunch fork!"*

Desperate, I arrived at my last option:

Retirement Option #4. Just Die Young.

The grim reality of my options sank in. Without my *IT* answers or financial nest egg to hatch, all seemed hopeless. The only remaining choice seemed to be to kick the whole *IT* bucket list aside and check out of life before retirement starts.

It wouldn't be the first time I'd considered death as my only option. In my twenties, I suffered suicidal-strength depressions. Memories flashed back to decades earlier, when contemplating suicide had filled many hours.

Now at midlife, even though decades of recovery and therapy had brought relief, I spiraled down into frightfully dark thinking. I recalled an astonishing article I'd read about the rising number of Boomer suicides occurring in the United States, and wondered if I might become another of these tragic losses.

A twisted rope of despair cinched from my gut to my heart. Was death truly the only feasible option for my retirement? Such a permanent solution to my temporary problems would put an end to me ever achieving *anything* else.

"*Reeeally, Amy?*" I asked, thinking through my suicidal thoughts. "*How could you pursue this option without messing up someone else's life? Someone would have to arrange your funeral and figure out what to do with this house stuffed with all of your stuff. Could you really depart without a trace?*" I wished for an instant vaporizer to complete the job.

Suddenly I flashed on the memory of a friend's smiling face and my heart ached at the thought of never again embracing the things I loved about life. The finality of my suicidal solution sank in as I considered never sharing another *smile* or *mile* with any of my wonderful friends.

Suicide ended all possibilities for any future. Absolutely all my options would abruptly end and any chances of ever finding *IT* would be over, for good. This fourth awful idea ended *all* my options—quickly eliminating it as a viable option!

The finality of this sudden realization allowed a pause for my humor to return. Then again, I joked, if reincarnation kicked in, a return to the bottom of the *IT* food chain could be in store for me. Reincarnated as a grasshopper or a cow, I would be forced to engage in yet another perpetual search for the next tasty *IT*.

Clearly I needed a fifth retirement option. Bad.

Farewell, Tired Word

Before going to bed, I returned to my trusty journal, *Streams*. Grabbing my favorite blue Pilot pen, I launched into my **nagivations** about retirement. They read something like this: "*Really, Amy, just what* *are you going to do about retirement? What options do you have? You're totally missing IT, what are you going to DO about your retirement?"*

Ugh! The word retirement stared back at me from the pages as my *Big 5-0* approached. A few months earlier, like other Americans turning fifty, I had begun to receive a plethora of snail mail from retirement associations and investment firms.

As if they were laced with anthrax, I'd thrown the mailings away. By opening just one of those envelopes, I assumed I would come down with some deadly aging illness as symptoms of retirement infiltrated my lungs. Not any part of me wanted to identify with that word—retirement.

If I could eliminate all aging evidence as quickly as possible, maybe the whole issue could be sidestepped. But, alas, wouldn't I just be floating down that infamous river of **de'Nile** (de•nile; denial as long as the river Nile) that ran through me?

Thick and heavy, the word retirement loomed in the gloom of my thoughts. My clever options had failed to deliver answers. The more I poured out my *fears*, the more *tears* flowed and exhaustion pinned me down. In a fit of complete despair, I scrawled the word in two-inch letters across my *Streams* page:

RETIRE

"What?" I thought as I paused to look again.

"What's that?" I reviewed the letters before me.

"Hmmm, why haven't I seen that before?"

Suddenly I saw the word in a whole new light: Re-Tire.

A big AHA hit as I realized why fatigue returned every time I thought or spoke about retirement. Not only was "re-tire" asking me to get tired, but the "re" in front of it actually <u>required</u> me to repeat getting tired, over and over again.

The word retirement yelled out as if to say, *"Come on, Amy ... let's figure out your options on how to get good and tired—then let's hit 'repeat' and do it all over and over again! Then let's* cement *the whole repeating tired-deal by calling it retirement!"*

My body slumped as my emotions landed in an inner dump. The fears and frustrations around my lack of planning to get tired over and over swallowed me and I arrived in one gigantic ball of "tired" as the truth now broke free.

I sat in bed, staring at the pages in my lap, considering that one simple word – retirement – the word everyone used to describe the final years of life. Why hadn't I seen this before? Was I too lost in my own retirement woes to notice? Locked into a hypnotic haze of verbal habit, had I been just too tired to *SEE* it?

I felt like I'd been induced into a mass-population tired-trance where subliminal messaging chanted, over and over again, *"Amy, you're getting sleepier and sleepier ... tire, Tire, TIRE!"* Was this why some folks expire shortly after they retire? Maybe they decide not to get tired over and over again. The word reeked of old.

On the verge of expanding into my greater potential, I desperately needed inspiration. If I only knew what *IT* was. I'd just begun to ask the right questions about who I came here to *BE*. On the verge of finding my elusive *IT*, easing into "tired-ville" just couldn't be the answer. And my four retirement options – creative as they sounded – were *sooo* not *IT*.

Unexpectedly, a renewed surge of energy ignited a flame of *SEEING* inside me. For decades, I'd experienced the power of my thoughts and words. And I'd long believed the adage: *You are what you think*.

Without hesitation, Amy Thornton decided <u>*not*</u> to be hypnotized into the retirement trance ever again. Not now, no how, no way, not ever. I surged forward towards something unknown.

I vowed to eliminate the tuckered-out retirement word from my vocabulary forever. When hearing or seeing the word in the future, I would remind myself: I am *not* getting tired over and over again.

Exhaling a huge sigh, I leaned back, **amyazed** (amy•azed; Amy is amazed) that banishing one word from my inner kingdom could release such exhilarating effects on my fatigue and future outlook.

I felt a revitalized hope on my second-half horizon. One huge puzzle piece had locked into place. I understood why I felt so dang tired. This brought comfort to my discomfort, and soon I fell into a deep sleep.

> **A proclamation sidebar:** Henceforth, the word retirement is banned from this book. It will be referred to as the **tiredword** (tired•word; **Thornism** for the word retirement) and will be used as reference only ... no need for its tired, old energy here.

My *JOLLI* Epiphany

A few hours later, around four a.m., I awoke with a start and sat straight up in bed. I could have sworn someone in the other room had shouted a single word to wake me up: *"ReVirement!"*

The word echoed again in my sleepy thoughts: *"ReVirement, Amy. ReVirement."*

"What's that word?" Where had I heard it before? I wasn't sure. I jumped up, dashing into my home office. I jiggled my Mac's mouse to wake up my screen and launched a search. After typing in the word *reVirement*, I made the discovery that would change my life forever.

ReVirement was the French word meaning reversal, change of direction, turnabout ... even revolution. Jolting up in my desk chair, I swiveled about, completely awestruck by my verbal discovery. Now *THIS* was something I could get very <u>*untired*</u> about!

The definitions of *reVirement* illuminated yet another new insight:

 reVirement when expeditions heading north suddenly make a turnabout and head south; when race cars zoom around a track, competing for the win, and suddenly the underdog upsets the race and pulls from the outside lane into the inside track, turning about the entire race, crossing the finish line for the victory.

Instantly I proclaimed, *"Why couldn't I cross life's second-half finish line with this new word? Why couldn't I replace the worn out* **tiredword** *with* reVirement?"

The dictionary remained open on my Mac. I looked up the **tiredword**'s definition and shook my head in mild disgust at its meaning:

> **reTirement** from the French word *retirir* meaning to go off, withdraw from, pass into seclusion, go out to pasture.

"Really? You've got to be kidding me," I thought. This didn't match what I'd envisioned for my search to a meaningful second-half. Working my buns off for decades to be heading out to pasture? I didn't think so!

The word *reVirement* described more aptly the positive passage through the midlife tunnel I hoped to find. Enraptured at what a powerful AHA this discovery had brought, I considered its simplicity. Changing *just-one-little-letter* to invent a new word was almost too easy.

I'd only replaced the *"T"* in the **tiredword** *reTirement* with a *"V"* to make the word *reVirement*. Simple. Yet strong enough to brighten up my puzzling, midlife *IT* searches. Was I just talking *semantics-shemantics?* Could changing a letter in a word really make a big difference?

The simplicity of it settled in as I considered the Olympian gods' tendency to place answers *right-in-front-of-me*. The magic within one letter created a life-changing moment. A *Just-One-Little–Letter-Insight* had resulted from a simple *"T-to-V"* switch. I jotted down its acronym, *JOLLI*, and thought in a British brogue, *"Jolly good, Amy."*

Could I now speak of *reVirement* instead of the **tiredword** for my second half of life? Would this now encourage me to seek out what the French had inspired for centuries, a more jubilant perspective on life, a *joie de vivre* (joy of living)?

Could I possibly launch a *JOLLI* revolution, *reVirement*, and turn about all of America's **tiredword** woes? Reigning in my racing-revolutionary thoughts, I realized the need to *pause* my *cause* for a moment and remind myself, *"Slow down,* **Amyzon** (Amy•zon; an Amy nickname inspired by the second-longest river in the world, the Amazon; the name aptly describes the over-excited momentum that can run me at times). *Let's not try to change the whole world by seven a.m."*

Breathing deeply, I considered that, at the very least, I could launch a personal revolution starting with me. Perhaps I could turn about all my bouts of doubt with the motto: *reVirement.* Would this one word help me eliminate the dueling *IT* Brain Bandits fighting within me?

Then I implored, *"Amy, why not start a bigger revolution?"* The energy I felt from *reVirement* revitalized as it resonated. This verbal designation enhanced and changed everything. The **tiredword** only stumped my jump toward fifty. Maybe I could convince my other Boomer friends to join a *reVirement* revolution with me.

A way out of my *Not-OK Corral* arrived as a reinVigorated, V-victorious word saved the day. By eight a.m. I'd reached such a V-vibrant V-voracity that I grabbed my *Streams* journal and a river of insights flowed. How could all of this be emerging from a simple *JOLLI?* I drew a big letter "V" across the page.

Setting *Streams* aside, I jumped out of bed to get a glass of water. As clear liquid poured into my drinking glass, I sensed the clarity brought about by my V-inspired discovery. I quickly returned to write more ideas as they bubbled to the surface. *Streams* lay sideways on the bed, and the big V I'd drawn switched directions. Leaning to the left, the V suggested an arrow shape, pointing in a whole new direction. I added a

line to the middle, making an arrow, and smiled at the change in directions this one letter and word, *reVirement*, had inspired. How could just one little letter open up my whole perspective on such a previously dreary topic?

The V translated into a **varrow** (var•row; V-inspired arrow), snapping open my old *narrow* perspective with renewed hope. Already I sensed an integral turning-about—just as the internet definitions had predicted. *ReVirement* often involves a winning underdog; this reminded me to change lanes and upset my own *IT* race by crossing another finish line, a revolutionary *reVirement* finish line.

Instead of dying young as my fourth dreary option had suggested, I visualized myself running a new life marathon. Emerging from despair, I could enter a revitalized human race. A bright smile would spread across my face as I broke the ribbon across the finish line, my fingers stretched up in vibrant *"V's for Victorious!"*

Crossing a reVirement *finish line.*

Rushes of energy swept down my arms. This *reVirement* path had brought the hope of a reinvented mental environment within me, one I wanted to race towards.

The letter V had heralded in a renewed V-vision for my life. I didn't know what would happen next and it didn't matter. I stepped out of my *Not-OK Corral* and moved quickly ahead towards a *Now-OK Corral*. A revitalized vista stretched out ahead, holding the promise of untold revolution.

During the days, months and years following my *JOLLI* discovery, the letter V continued to marvel and inspire me. If my *reVirement* spirits sagged, the V showed up

in the oddest places, reminding me to do a turnabout. A simple hand
gesture for *"victory"* or *"peace"* randomly burst forth
when renewed inspiration was needed. A fallen V-tree-
branch might land beneath my steps, reminding me to
change directions. Little did I know a culminating
V-explosion would one day bring spiritual
recalibration.

At many points along my expedition, I
reminded myself, *"Amy, stop everything! This
is not the direction you want to be going in.
Remember the V and reVirement. Change
directions. Revolutionize. Turn yourself about."* And *voilá!* (said with a
French accent, of course), my *SEEING* would shift, pivoting me in a new
direction of *DOING* towards another renewed state of *BEING*.

On that June morning, I heralded in a whole new life, a midlife
metamorphosis that lit up my body, mind and spirit.

From the sidelines of my life marathon, I silently heard the
encouraging motto, *"Viva the V, Amy!"* *Viva* is the Spanish word for
living, alive and alert.

My life started to turn about, leading me into a re-wired,
re-fired, and re-attired *reVirement*. Within one year of my **vepiphany**
(ve•pi•phan•y; a V-inspired epiphany), I lost thirty pounds and celebrated
my fiftieth birthday with a bash. I resigned from my advertising art
director job to fulfill a lifelong dream of doing art full time, which would
lead to more life-changing conclusions.

I also discovered the unimaginable. My lifelong *IT* list unraveled
and the secrets to solving *ITs* elusive mysteries continued to unfold
right-in-front-of-me.

SUMMARY> First *JOLLI* Jolt

◆ The dread of retirement suggested four dreary options.

◆ I banned the **tiredword** from my inner kingdom forever.

◆ *ReVirement* ignited a change of directions and revolution!

CHAPTER 5

All about Change

- All about Turnabouts
- William Murray's Quote
- The Inside Lane

As the verve of *reVirement* took hold, I wondered: *"How could generations of Americans have decided on using the* **tiredword** *for the second half of life?"* Not one of my Boomer friends was getting tired over and over again. If anything, they passionately embraced a reinvented **reVi:rementality** (re•vire•men•tal•ity; the mentality of *reVirement*).

However, if 80 million Boomers embedded their thoughts with the **tiredword**, I wondered about all that "tired" going around. Seemed like it was time for a revolutionary change. One thing I knew about myself and other Boomers is that we're *all about change*.

Where to begin with that short phrase—*all about change?* Boomers have forged multiple innovations. We launched the technological evolution in a progressive lineup starting with a room-sized computer. Boomer computer wizards continued to reinvent and revise technology, creating handheld devices so advanced and multi-dimensional they now prevail as extensions of our very selves.

Boomer women fought for equal rights, with some moving up the corporate ladder to run multi-million-dollar corporations. Some Boomer men broke the male-code, giving the term "household engineers" a whole new meaning. We got smart about our planet by serving and conserving and began recycling our garbage. We perfected our morning rituals and don't even order our coffee like any previous generation!

Everything Boomers have accomplished celebrates change. It's inherent to our booming nature. Maybe we need an upgraded word like *reVirement* to ignite a revitalized vision for us all.

I smiled, considering the Boomers who'd invented the clever name "streaking" for running around naked. If we could invent a word for this, surely we could embrace a simple *T-to-V* switch that resulted in a fresh word like *reVirement* for future generations to use.

William Murray's Quote

During the first year of my *reVirement,* I kept my excitement to myself. Frankly, it almost seemed silly; the simplicity was *so right-in-front-of-me*. But the effects of my *JOLLI* could not go unnoticed.

My eye-peelin' talents allowed me to *SEE* a threshold of old ideas that needed to be put to rest about turning fifty and entering *midlie* (**O.P.T.** – oops, I'd meant to type "midlife"; that's an interesting typo as my ideas around *midlife* have mostly turned out to be lies*)*.

From my revitalized vantage point, *reVirement* shifted all my notions about aging, allowing me to regenerate the giddy, *get-up-n'-go* gumption of my youth. I reconsidered dreams set aside for years. With a rewired **reVirementality**, I commenced *SEEING* new venues.

One big *IT* had chased me for a very long time. Since college days, I'd dreamed of living as a full-time artist. Although I'd painted and exhibited my artwork for decades, art always seemed to take the back seat to whatever bread-winning job paid the bills.

A luring *IT* hovered over my artistic dreams. Fueled with revitalized ambition, I became convinced an **artIT** (art•it; turning art into an *IT* to get) was the *IT* I'd always yearned for. I allowed *reVirement* to pave a new mind-track to a new **artIT** race, with permission to go for *IT*.

Within a year of my June **vepiphany**, my *reVirement*-inspired savings allowed me to leave my job and paint full time for a year.

While I geared up to leave a steady paycheck and launch my *reVirement*, bouts of doubt flooded in. As if on cue, "change" opened the door, welcoming in unwanted guests cloaked in hesitancy. But I soon learned that a decision succeeded by unwavering commitment – a **wholistic** understanding – delivered a no-turning-back quality.

While I considered two key ingredients necessary to launch lasting change, a classic quote crossed my path. It fueled my decision to keep turning about in new directions. I'm most **greatfull** (great•full; full of great gratefulness) for its conviction; it emerged as the guiding masthead as I embarked on my *reVirement* expedition.

Often linked to William H. Murray, who encouraged his men on a Himalayan scouting expedition in 1912, this quote's origins actually evolved from the 18th century and the German politician Johann Wolfgang von Goethe:

"Until one is committed, there is hesitancy, the chance to draw back. Concerning all acts of initiative and creation, there is one elementary truth, the ignorance of which kills countless ideas and splendid plans: that the moment one definitely commits oneself, then Providence moves, too. All sorts of things occur to help one that would never otherwise have occurred. A whole stream of events issues from the decision, raising in one's favor all manner of unforeseen incidents and meetings and material assistance, which no man could have dreamed would have come his way. Whatever you can do, or dream you can do, begin it. Boldness has genius, power, and magic in it. Begin it now."

> — Attributed to William Murray,
> The Scottish Himalayan Expedition, 1912
> (originally from Johann Wolfgang von Goethe)

I drove away from my secure job, breathing in my decision to embrace an artist's life on a full-time basis. Within days, all manner of unforeseen events and people began to appear, all unplanned. With *reVirement* as my manifesto, I discovered a revitalized boldness infused with power and magic as my daily decisions to go for my **artIT** allowed the next steps to emerge.

The Inside Lane

I began sharing *reVirement* with my friends and expanded my vision. Hoping to confirm its common, everyday usage, I needed a French interpretation from someone fluent in French.

I called Heather, my niece, to confer with her husband, Jacques, a native of France. Seeking the full *reVirement* scoop, sans any back story, I asked him the popular meanings and common usage for the word.

Initially, Jacques failed to recognize my pronunciation. Of course! I phrased *reVirement* to resemble the English **tiredword**. After spelling out the word, I heard Jacques on the other end of the phone, rephrasing the French pronunciation, which sounded like "ru-veer-mon."

He said the term was most commonly heard at the racetrack. Jacques recalled summaries of sports' stories when announcers described a close race. During the last speeding moments around the track, an underdog pulled a fast one, moving from behind to the inside winning lane.

ReVirement described the underdogs' sudden shifting of lanes and the race's sudden change in direction. The "switching" ignited unexpected change, similar to the way banning the **tiredword** had shifted everything for me.

As Jacques described this, I doodled concentric circles around a letter V on a yellow sticky note. My race, newly inspired by the V, circled towards another AHA. I secretly grinned, thanking him for more **vevidance** (vev•i•dance; dance of V-evidence).

I pictured myself turning from the outside track in a new direction. Could a decision to commit allow unforeseen incidents to materialize? Had I spent my life racing around an invisible outside *IT* track? Reaching for answers whizzing by, had I sped around an outside *IT* lane, making pit stops to fill up on external *ITs* to complete me? Maybe the race to a brilliant second-half required shifting to another track—the inside lane.

A veer into this inside lane of my mental racetrack suggested freedom. An upset on my current mental track could pivot and shift spinning thoughts towards a new route. My renewed **reVirementality** promised *IT* answers to be discovered from within, in the inside lane. Yet most of my life's previous focus had been spent on the outside.

My Pilot pen raced with more journaling to uncover the best route to my interior. Could I really win from the inside lane? Retracing the tracks of my first half of life led to a vital **vortext** (vor•text; whirling vortex of text). Layers of old ideas screeched to a halt as I began *SEEING* them and putting them down on paper. My whole *IT* search was unraveling before my eyes.

The first half of my life – jam-packed with much *trying, prying* and *crying* – had also been full of my attempts to coerce a host of *ITs* to stay in one place long enough so I could get *IT,* whatever *IT* was. Now I wondered if my *IT* existed smack-dab in the middle of the constant whirling state of change. In retrospect, I could *SEE* that I had been riding a cosmic roller coaster of empty *IT* hopes and dreams. And while focused on the exteriors of life, authentic living had passed me by.

A **vortext** of spinning questions penetrated my *IT* race. If I allowed the outside lanes of change to speed by me, could I live a centered life from the inside lane? What if this constant pivoting movement of changing directions and turning about was the only *IT* there was? What if my *IT* was *right-in-front-of-me* ... in the middle of *IT* all? What if there was no more *IT* to get?

This shook up all my current ideas about change. My tenacity led me to resist change as much as I craved it. If *reVirement* proved to be *all about change*, I would have to befriend change.

Could I really *live* a *life* not based on any *IT* obtainment? I couldn't deny that my very best *IT* searching had left me empty-*IT*-handed. I had to ask myself, *"Amy, what do you have to lose? What if there's a whole new you waiting on the other side of that elusive* IT *finish line?"*

What if <u>all</u> my turning-about leads to the inside lane, where no outside *IT* exists? What if my *IT* can only be found inside? What if it's <u>all</u> an inside *IT* job?

My life's vision cracked open and started shifting. I began to challenge outdated ideas about finding *IT* and resisting change. One life-altering question emerged: What if my real *chance* to *change* meant getting out of the *IT* rat-race altogether?

This didn't make sense—at least not based on the sense I knew then. There were *ITs* to do, *ITs* to go to, *ITs* to succeed at. Could I possibly let go of all of *IT* and live without an *IT* steering the Amy-race?

This internal questioning filled the backdrop of my emerging **artIT** life. I'd poured my heart, finances and energy into becoming a successful, contemporary artist. But a continuous stream of doubts and questions threatened to derail my **artIT** race.

When a great opportunity came to exhibit my colorful paintings in a one-woman art show, my **artIT** questioning increased in velocity. A grand plan unfolded through which I would prove to myself that my *JOLLI* inspirations could inspire bold results. I envisioned myself as an artistic emblem of how powerful a V-revitalization could be. I steered towards a successful outcome across my **artIT** finish line.

But the more I painted, framed and promoted my art show, the more I clamored to find sweet success. Something churned from deep within, begging me to change. But if I failed to accomplish my own **artIT** dream, how could I inspire others to embrace their *chance* to *change?*

Hesitation and uncertainty continued to challenge my efforts, hoping to shoot down any previous enthusiasm. *"Amy, you're just an artist. You can't possibly influence changes for an entire nation with just one simple letter. There are too many things wrong with the world as it is. How could your just-one-little-letter-insight idea really make a difference?"*

And yet, I remembered what my good friend Scott Friedman had once said: *"Amy, if your dreams don't scare the socks off of you, then they're not big enough!"*

As my **vortext** of spinning explorations continued, they traversed a trepidatious route, traveling back and forth from the inside lane. The challenge of changing directions and switching from the outside in faded thanks to Scott's encouragement to dream big. Soon my V-visions of starting a *reVirement* revolution from the inside out would become so big, my socks would officially be blown from Denver down under to Melbourne, Australia. ~ Thanks, Scott!

A dream big enough to blow my socks off.

As though I'd signaled to the Universe that I was ready for more **vevidance**, another friend – Debra Fine – invited me to a luncheon with a very famous guest speaker, Gloria Steinem.

SUMMARY> All about Change

- ◆ I already belonged to the turn-about generation of Boomers.

- ◆ Decision and commitment were essential for inner changes.

- ◆ I pulled from the outside track into the inside lane.

CHAPTER 6

Power of Words

- My *JOLLI* **Shero**
- Change *Your Word* to *Our World*
- *Old* or *Bold?*

I jumped at the chance to join a powerful group of women to hear the iconic Gloria Steinem speak at a Denver luncheon. I wondered what I might say to her, given the opportunity.

Online searches generated many results for Gloria's vast accomplishments and her contributions to the women's liberation movement starting in the sixties and seventies. While airing my bangs with the blow dryer, I was hit with another *JOLLI* insight. *"Hey, Amy, you're about to meet a woman who changed an ENTIRE nation with just-one-little-letter!"*

In 1972, Gloria and her team dropped the "r" in Mrs. to name their magazine *Ms.,* popularizing the term that provided an emblem for generations of women to recognize their independence. She motivated everyday women to embrace revolutionary change. The new title, *Ms.,* became a personalized symbol for the women's movement.

For me, Gloria's *JOLLI* example held powerful **vevidance** that a *just-one-little-letter-insight* could indeed change everything. *Ms.* also signified a shift in the term *Mrs.* and being one of *Mr.'s* belongings.

By headlining her magazine *Ms.,* Gloria helped millions of Boomers forge equanimity. This two-letter title is so accepted only a few decades later, we rarely *pause* to consider the *cause* that inspired its destiny.

The term *Ms.* had existed for a few hundred years in association with the suffrage movement. *Suffrage*. Hmmm, isn't _that_ an interesting word used to describe the historic sweep of women's coming of age—the uniting of the words *suffer* and *rage?*

I wondered if, at the luncheon, I might say, *"Thank you, Ms. Steinem, for inspiring such a powerful JOLLI. You changed generations forever! You're my* **shero**!" (she•ro; she version of hero)

I arrived at the banquet room, which was filled with women equally excited to hear Ms. Steinem speak. Many women had brought daughters, granddaughters and other female friends. The large room buzzed with a lively *Mzzz–Buzzz*.

At the table of ten ladies I joined, my friend Debra shared that she and her sisters had read all of Gloria's books. Ms. Steinem had inspired Debra to set her sights on anything she wanted—including becoming a successful entrepreneur and international speaker.

I admired Debra Fine as a shining example of a go-getting Boomer passionate about the power of change. Enlisting Debra into my silent *reVirement* revolution, I made a mental note to chat with her later about her uncanny ability to always flourish with the changing times.

After brunch, Ms. Steinem stood to speak. She eloquently delivered a powerful talk filled with encouragement. Towards the end of the question-and-answer session, a long pause gave me courage. Shaking a little in my boots, I raised my hand. I stood and looked deep into her eyes and asked my question, "Ms. Steinem, I'm the only female in my immediate family who not only received a college degree but has lived to age fifty. Now that I'm here, after years of searching, I'm just now discovering who I am. With your multitude of accomplishments, what keeps you moving forward? What drives you on?"

With a penetrating gaze as if she were looking right into my soul, Gloria Steinem exclaimed, "You!"

Surprised, I jerked back as if a jolt of cool air had whisked through a side door. Although she'd meant the collective "You" she held my gaze, bold and strong. A galvanizing shiver ran up my leg as I felt the power behind her one-word response.

With that one word – "You" – reminded me to grab hold of my bold decision to turn about from the inside out and leave my *IT* chasing in the past. Maybe my ideas about an American *reVirement* revolution weren't so far-fetched.

Gloria further explained that what continues to drive her forward is the hope of increasing change in our world. She added that some of her greatest achievements and satisfactions unfolded well after she reached fifty. She stood before me, a shining pinnacle of what I hoped to embrace in my second-half. I lowered myself into the banquet chair, deeply encouraged by Ms. Steinem's words to persevere in my dreams.

Change *Your Word* to *Our World*

Just when I thought the questions had ended, a small voice came from the back of the room. Tanya, a young girl, asked Gloria, "But, Ms. Steinem, I'm just a twelve-year-old kid. What could I possibly do to change the world?"

Without skipping a beat, Gloria rolled out a response that resonated with everyone in the room—and in my own **reVirementality** room.

Gloria asked Tanya to think about anything she deemed unfair. For instance, had she complained about the amount of funds and space used by the school for sport activities that only a few students could use?

All heads turned towards the back of the room to see Tanya nodding her head. We witnessed the idea sinking in as she began linking her thinking back to the question "What do I think is unfair?"

Gloria encouraged her: "Whatever you find in your world that is unfair, let *THAT* be the light to guide you toward creating change in your world. As you change *YOUR* world, the bigger world will change!"

"Hmmm ...." I began linking my own thinking. *"That's JOLLI brilliant, Gloria!"* Digging into my purse, I retrieved my Pilot pen to jot down the word *our* on a cocktail napkin. Then I added the letter "y" to the front. The word *our* became y*our,* a *JOLLI* filled with meaning.

It sounded so simple, making a difference in *your* world for *our* world. Could the influence of *just-one-little-letter* change the power behind *words* to propel changes in *worlds? Words* and *worlds? JOLLIs* collided again and I expanded the theme to: *your word* to *our world.*

Then I considered what was unfair in my world. Instantly, I thought about aging in America. The immense focus on youth in our culture contributed to much of my *Not-OK Corral* mental state. I doubted I was alone in my struggles. Maybe this was another opportunity for me to help our world? ~ Thank you, Gloria!

By that point in my **artIT** year, I had turned about many old patterns, uncovered inner clues and unlocked puzzlements that had perplexed me for years. I'd also continued journaling and begun daydreaming of writing a book.

A quick photo with my **shero**.

Inspired by my involvement with many book projects, I'd created a few mock cover designs for a book with titles such as *ReVirement! The New Mentality* or *The T-to-V Switch, JOLLI Good!* I visualized myself bringing my *word reVirement* to the *world*, helping others *SEE* the **tiredword** from a fresh angle. Could I really write a book that could help others revamp the second half of their lives?

Old or *Bold?*

Thanks to my **shero**, I returned home from the luncheon and filled my *Streams* journal with a fresh flood of insights. Gloria had reignited my commitment to turn about all that I found unfair. A renewed verve opened my **reViramentality** and I launched into a search to banish any other *word* influencing my *world*.

That evening, I silently reprimanded myself in the bathroom mirror only to realize that my teeth-brushing mantra routinely affirmed an old-*word* status on my inner *world*. *"Geeze, Amy, look at those crow's feet; you are getting so old!"* Turning my head from side to side to consider all angles, I failed to brush away my critical thinking. *"Wow, girl, you are* reeeally *gettin'* old." Brain bandits blasted me with a three-letter word perhaps even more exhausting than the **tiredword:** old.

Even with new-found **verbalation** (ver•bal•a•tion; verbal elation) over discovering *JOLLIs*, I sheltered hidden layers of old thinking that effectively blocked my journey to the inside winning lane.

Turning from the outside track of cultural focus on youth, I pulled to the inside lane to focus on my own judgments about aging. I returned to the simple word *old* and realized a ripe *JOLLI* rested *right-in-front-of-me,* waiting for me to notice.

By adding a "b" to that *old*, I could now get good and *bold* about all of this! Combined with the *JOLLI word* into *world*, this new *JOLLI* advanced my thinking from the *old word* to a *bold world*.

"Sold!" I thought, smiling. "AHA, that's solid *gold!"* I was on a *roll*—maybe this was my life's new *role,* finding *JOLLIs* to inspire the transformation of *old words* into *bold worlds?!?*

I turned back to my writing and flipped open my laptop to type out an intriguing impulse. In a fit of playfulness, I typed a short paragraph entirely composed of the word *old*.

> "Amy, you are old, old, old, old, OLD! Old: old, old, old old, old, old, old, old. Old old; old, old, old old and old! So very old, old, old, old, old, old, old. Old, old? OLD! Old, old, old, old, and old. Old, old, old. Oooooooold, old, old. Old, Amy. Old? Yes, really OLD!"

Then I read it out loud as if the collective bundle of old words described all the thoughts in my mind. As I read the paragraph, my back slumped and feelings of dreary fatigue swept in.

"*Wow!*" The playful experiment hit me with resounding clarity. "*Amy, look how much power that three-letter* word *is having on your* world." I tested my *word-world* theory by typing out another paragraph.

"Amy, you are so bold, bold, bold, bold, BOLD! Bold, bold, bold, bold bold, bold. Bold, bold, boldy bold. Bold with bold, bold ... bold, bold, bold, bold, bold bold, bold. Bold? Yes, bold, bold, bold. Boldly bold, bold. Remember you are bold, Bold, BOLD!"

As I read the bold paragraph, an invisible steel beam shot up my spine. My face relaxed and a smile emerged. Everything in me shifted and responded to the change via *just-one-little-letter.* I wondered, "*What else do I hold onto that is old and needs a bold turnabout?*"

How *odd* that the word *old* held so much influence. What was happening to my body, mind and spirit as, over and over, I quietly reaffirmed how old I was? How could I *SEE, DO* or *BE* anything *bold* if I constantly reminded and directed myself with the opposite word, *old?*

Once again, it seemed so simple and so *right-in-front-of-me.* Why hadn't I seen it before? How could I forge a *bold reVirement* turnabout if *old* thoughts directed my *SEEING, DOING* and *BEING?*

Another word was banished from my inner kingdom. No more *old* ... just *bold!* Instantly, this simple decision to ban one *word* had commenced to revamp my *world.*

Unexpected realizations arrived with painless **reverbalations** (re•ver•bal•a•tions; revelations of a verbal nature). My commitment to change more hidden words was launching me towards linking the thinking that filled my mind.

Such a simple choice. Would I continue spinning my mental wheels on verbal tracks leading nowhere, or upset their negative race by pulling into the inside lane, where they could turn my world around? Another decision to commit was deployed: *"Amy, you've got to spot all those silent words you're linking together in your thoughts. What are you thinking about? How many other old thoughts need a bold turnabout?"*

I considered the thoughts running 24-7 on my inside lane with the outsides of my everyday living. How could I sustain a revolution from *your word* to *our world* if I didn't get down 'n' dirty about my own *Not-OK* thinking? I remembered my eye-peelin' knack and reminded myself, *"Amy, keep your mind's eye peeled on your own thinkin'!"*

Thanks to Gloria's inspiration, I embraced the bold adage of *walking* my *talking* as I strove to move permanently into my inside lane, where my **reVirementality** was expanding. There I could *SEE* that my sinking, shrinking thinking had been the *fuel* to my inner *duel* all along.

And, just as I made the decision to pay more attention to the words I spoke and thought, a series of serendipitous events occurred, leading me to even greater understanding.

SUMMARY> Power of Words

◆ *Ms.* changed the world with *just-one-little-letter.*

◆ *JOLLIs* could inspire *your word* to change *our world.*

◆ *Old* or *bold?* Banning more words from the inner kingdom

CHAPTER 7

Think about Thinking

- *Think Thing* Typo
- Ger's Think Test
- The Blame Game

Renewed determination led me to *SEE* the real power in the words I used; more importantly, I now understood the impact of the silent words racing around my mental racetrack. It became apparent that, hidden from obvious view, an excess of *old* sinking, shrinking thinking required some resurfacing if I were ever to smooth out my inner path towards a *bold reVirement* turnabout.

Thinking. I rarely took time to think about thinking, a phenomenon so *right-in-front-of-me* that it ran in the background of my every waking moment. Due to my lack of attention, the millions of neurons firing at nanosecond speeds within my brain had etched deep neurological ruts where my thoughts became stuck.

Some neural reruns repeated so often they switched into cruise control, disappearing from conscious awareness. By slipping into the passenger side of life all too often, I'd allowed *old* thoughts to take *hold* of the steering wheel that was driving my thinking. Slowing down to consider a turnabout only occurred when I hit a mental speed bump and landed in another internal *Not-OK Corral*. This had to stop.

My *reVirement* fascination with the power of words was no coincidence. For decades I'd thrived on thought-provoking books such as *Change Your Thoughts, Change Your Life* by Dr. WAYne Dyer. (Spelling Dr. WAYne Dyer's name with cap letters accentuates his wisdom that inspires so many to find new WAYs of thinking.)

For years, I attended Mile Hi Church, more of a spiritual center than a church, in the Denver area. One of the Mile Hi tenets is *Change your thinking, change your life*. With over a decade of classes under my belt, I'd learned a fair amount about the power of words and their influence on outcomes. In fact, I'd already manifested many of my *IT* dreams such as moving to New York City and taking a year off to do my **artIT**.

I couldn't deny the revitalizing power just one word, *reVirement*, had introduced to my entry into midlife. *ReVirement* thoughts propelled me forward, encouraging me to change directions in order to arrive at altered destinations. But, as my *reVirement* pace quickened, it became painfully clear I couldn't maintain a *bold* state of turn-aboutness. In fact, the more *bold* outcomes I desired, the more *old* thoughts showed up. An immeasurable reservoir of *fuel* for any internal *duel* seemed to prolong ongoing battles instigated by my Brain Bandits.

Those *infernal internal* words continued to link together, creating hard-wired neurological paths. If I professed to *walk* my *talk*, I really needed to actively think about my thinking.

Once again, this realization materialized in the last place I would think to look. And the think about thinking … (**O.P.T.** – I meant to write "the thing about thinking ….").

But wait a minute …. *Think. Thing.* There it was again, a *just-one-little-letter* shift and, *voilá,* what I *think* becomes a *thing*.

So the thing about thinking is that thoughts fly by at a speed of 10-100 a second. The number of thoughts in a day is somewhere between 12,000 and 50,000. That's a whole lotta' thinking to think about, let alone get good at turning about!

Most thoughts are innocent enough, the ones that get me through the day: *"It's Wednesday; remember to put out the trash"* or *"I'm hungry; time to eat lunch."* Key to my *reVirement* turning-about required revealing the identities of those camouflaged Brain Bandits that were leading to my shrinking bouts of doubts.

However, while my Brain Bandits were firing off thoughts at blinding speeds, I began experimenting with a burning question: *"How does thinking about my thinking work in real time?"* With the help of my friend, Ger, I further investigated thinking about my thinking.

Ger's Think Test

As an architectural consultant, Ger designs his renovations on multiple Mac computers. A corner cubicle in his office with a spare Mac temporarily became Amy's writing space. Living and working at home alone, I'd developed a case of cabin fever. Ger offered this solution to help me focus on my literary goal of writing a *reVirement* book.

One morning, I awoke with a nonstop flood of ideas. I packed up my enthusiasm and left for Ger's office, fifteen minutes away.

Nothing unusual happened on the drive over, but after arriving and talking with Ger for a few moments, I suddenly felt terrible. Was I tired? Did I need coffee? What was going on?

Convinced my negative feelings couldn't have come from me, I wondered what was going on with Ger. Had he and Kathy fought that morning? Maybe Ger didn't really want me writing at his office. What was wrong here?!?

Ger and I continued to chat until I ventured to my back corner. Confused and thrown by my upset feelings, I started writing in my journal about the previous fifteen minutes. I started linking my sinking thinking and, sure enough, discovered my *think* had become a *thing*.

I wondered, *"Does everyone think about their thinking, or is this one of those old ideas that's taken me five decades to figure out?"*

Was I alone in my inability to understand my thinking? A "think test" might reveal some answers, so I left the cubicle and asked my friend, "Ger, do you ever think about your thinking?"

Ger peered up from his monitor. "Sure," he said, "I've been thinking about eating that apple since eight a.m."

I gave him more details. "No, Ger, that's a thought: 'I want an apple.' What I'm referring to is thinking about HOW you're thinking? What's playing in the background of your thoughts?"

He looked confused. "What do you mean? I told you; I'm hungry. I think I want to eat that apple."

My *think-thing* theory wasn't translating. I recounted my morning insight. "Remember how I walked in the door this morning all discombobulated?"

"Yeah, I figured you were exhausted and in dire need of a morning cup of coffee." Ger grinned.

"No, Ger, I thought YOU were cranky and needed coffee."

He laughed, shaking his head. "But nothing was wrong with ME; you were Ms. Discombobulated!"

"Before making up a story about YOUR crankiness, I stopped to think about my thinking. I wondered, 'Did I get enough sleep last night? Do I need a cup of coffee? Maybe I'm not supposed to write today. Maybe I'm not even supposed to write a book!'"

Ger nodded as he followed my story.

"My thinking didn't match the anticipation I'd felt packing up to drive here. What happened in that fifteen-minute drive? As I retraced my morning thoughts, I recalled that during the drive I'd imagined the brilliant women of my book club reading my book.

"In less than a minute, a stream of negative thoughts took me hostage. Within seconds, I convinced myself a *JOLLI* story was ridiculous. My *think* had become a *thing* of hopelessness. It happened so fast, I didn't even notice the thinking—only the frustration. And then it was much easier to blame YOU than to think about my thinking.

"Then I remembered the power of words. I retraced my thinking to *SEE* what was going on. That's when I uncovered the deeper doubts lurking below my surface thoughts."

I grabbed my journal and read out loud to Ger just ten of the sinking thoughts on my list:

1. Amy, who do you think you are? You can't write a book!
2. You don't even know where to start!
3. You're delusional. Your book group is going to think you're silly!
4. Come on now, get real, what are you thinking?!?
5. You can't even spell and your grammar is terrible!
6. There are a gazillion books in the world; do you really have something worth saying?
7. Are you going to be an artist or a writer? You should just get a job; you're spending all of your savings on your **artIT** escapade!
8. Everyone is going to think you're silly! *Just-one-little-letter* can't possibly change everything!
9. WHAT ARE YOU DOING?!?!?!?!?
10. Get *reeeal*, Amy! When are you going to finally get *IT* together?!?

I summarized my list with some startling statistics. "Ger, I just read that we think about 10-100 thoughts a second. If all these ten thoughts happened in less than a second, is it any wonder I was discombobulated? That's some serious sinking, shrinking thinking!"

Ger's expression changed to a smile. "Wow, Amy, you sure are mean to yourself. And yes, there was nothing wrong with me."

"Fascinating, isn't it, Ger? By not wanting to feel my own pain – birthed from my misdirected thinking – it was much easier to blame you. How great to know that I can shift gears and pull into my inside lane, retrace my thinking and link my sinking feelings."

Ger smiled again, "Ahhh, I see. I guess I don't really think about thinking. I bet there are times when I do blame outside stuff."

Ger and me at my **artIT** *opening.*

"You got it, Ger, that's exactly what I meant by thinking about your thinking!" ~ Thanks, Ger!

The Blame Game

One consideration with thinking about thinking is that it does take a little extra time. Would I get lost now in endless cycles of **amylyzing** (amy•ly•zing; Amy over-analyzing) my thoughts? Now that I knew what was going on, maybe it wouldn't take much more than paying attention and being willing to *SEE* where I spent time on my mental racetrack.

I returned to my writing and considered how many times I'd gotten myself into a *game* of *lame blame*. Could it be avoided with some simple thinking about my thinking? How lame was it that I had blamed other people, places and things for invisible causes because I didn't want to feel my own insecurities or pain?

My *chance* to *change* had arrived. Now, I could do a turnabout. Instead of focusing on everything on the outside track, I could pull into my own inside lane, a place where I could direct my own steering at all times. If I were going to create my *reVirement* revolution from the inside out, I needed to get really good at changing mental lanes and staying in the winning inside track. And that began when I paid attention to my sinking feelings and *lame-blame* games.

"What if?" questions flooded my thinking: What if I could teach myself to *pause* and consider the *cause* of my sinking thinking? What if this was the key to igniting my **reVirementality**? What if this was the route towards changing *your old word* to *our bold world?* What if everyone started to link up their sinking thinking and *lame-blame* games—what kind of world would that create?

Was my own thinking the cause of ALL my *Not-OK Corrals?*

Someone who always encourages me to think about my thinking is Melm (my nickname for her combines her first initial and last name:

Michelle Elm), a wise, sage-like long-time friend and mentor. She taught me a great phrase: *The punishment does not fit the crime*. Loosely translated, this meant that the mental punishment I was dishing out on myself or others didn't match up with what was really going on. Instead it was the result of misdirected and unskilled thinking.

The larger ramification of my *think thing* made me wonder, *"Amy, what if EVERYTHING you dislike or criticize in your* world *shifts with changing your* word?"

This was the *SEEING* turnabout I needed to revolutionize the "punishment and crimes" I'd mentally dished out for years. How often had my thinking raced around on the outside track, when I really needed to switch lanes and get to my inside track in order to *SEE* my thinking?

Thinking about thinking proved to be a critical skill I needed to master. It wouldn't shift overnight. I needed to practice this throughout the rest of my second-half, but at least *now* I could *know* what was going on. Now I had the thinking *chance* to *change*.

What if my midlife revolution was all about something as simple as changing the direction of my thoughts? What if I started to replace my *old* thinking with *bold* thinking? What if shifting my consciousness could be directed towards *linking* my thinking rather than blaming the *sinking?*

It was certainly something to think about!

I'd entered a whole new race, one on my own inside track, a race of victory won by grabbing hold of my mental steering wheel and heading in the direction I wanted to go.

I made another decision and committed myself to it: *"I need to get really good at turning about my thinking."* And that's when Providence showed up once again—and led me to another life lesson on thinking.

My friend Melm helped me take sinking thinking to a whole new level. She opened my eyes to an even better game to replace my old *lame blame* one. And so I learned the Opposites Game.

SUMMARY> Think about Thinking

◆ I moved to the inside track, where thinking races all around.

◆ An uneasy trip to Ger's instigated a mental think test.

◆ Blame games disappeared when thinking about thinking.

CHAPTER 8

Stalk My Talk

- **Easterescapade** Gone Wrong
- The Opposites Game
- Inner Guerilla Warfare

Melm and I first met just before I'd landed in the *middle* of my midlife *muddle*. She became instrumental in unlocking many of my *old words* and opening them into *bold worlds*. Many a Starbucks coffee was shared with Melm as **I nagivated** a dark mental conflict that landed me in another *Not-OK Corral*.

Melm's top two thought-turning-about questions were *"Amy, what's the thinking?"* and *"What are you telling yourself?"* My willingness to answer these two simple questions became powerful lane-changers in my *ability* and *agility* to move from the outside track and pull into the inside lane, where significant changes happened.

If I could start *SEEING* the self-talk that sent me into my mental *Not-OK Corral*, then turning it about in a new direction would become much easier. The tricky part was how very fast and clever my sinking thinking had become after fifty-plus years of practice.

Most of my **nagivations** seemed to occur at times when strong *emotions* made their *motions* known. The Opposites Game, introduced later in this chapter, helped slow down my thinking so I could turn it around; it became easy when I could *SEE* it.

This created a real personal puzzlement—a mystery to the story that had become my life. There were times when I'd find myself back in some mind-dueling *Not-OK Corral*, held hostage by a grizzly set of

Brain Bandits shooting thoughts of destruction my way. It wasn't just me; others had them too. At times, we were our own worst enemies.

I knew the key lay hidden in sinking thinking. But the challenge remained: *"How do I slow my rapid-fire thoughts long enough to turn them in another direction?!"* Another question followed: *"How did I get here?"* This required looking at my history. I recalled two different Easters, one that set me up for success and one that sent me into a disturbing and very *Not-OK Corral*.

The Thorntons loved Easter, and my parents tried to top the previous Easter celebration with some fun **Easterescapade** (eas•ter•es•ca•pade; escapade around Easter). One year, Dad was enthused by *The Egg Tree,* a Pennsylvania Dutch story wherein two children discover hand-painted eggs hanging from their grandmother's cherry tree.

How appropriate that my Grandma Beulah had Pennsylvania Dutch ancestry, and the cherry trees were in full bloom that Easter. Dad convinced us we should reenact the entire tale in full **thorntonesque** (thorn•ton•esque; with the flair of a Thornton) fashion. The scheme involved surprising the congregates of King of Glory Church with a surprise Egg Tree just outside the church entrance on Easter morning.

We needed to paint and decorate eggs and adorn the church's cherry blossom tree by four a.m. in order to leave plenty of time before the Easter Sunrise service began. And, in typical **Dad-elation** (dad•e•la•tion; Dad's unbridled elation), he thought of the brilliant escapade the Saturday afternoon before Easter Sunday. We stayed up past midnight poking holes in raw eggs, draining the sticky yellow yokes, hollowing out the eggs and lining them up to dry.

Then we huddled around the kitchen table to hand paint the eggs, making our own custom designs. While Julie and I painted tear-dropped peace signs and round-petalled flowers, Mom daubed purple brush-strokes for a Columbine—her favorite and Colorado's state flower. Dad painted a compelling portrait of Jesus on one of his eggs and a mother duck with her ducklings waddling around the middle of another.

When our egg masterpieces dried, we slipped silver ribbon loops from the yoke-holes—perfect for attaching to tree limbs. When we finished, we drove the ten blocks to church where, by the headlight-dim of Beetlebug (our 1965 red Volkswagen), we hung all the eggs. Whispering like cat burglars, we hung the hand-painted eggs among the fragrant cherry blossoms.

We raced home giggling and exclaiming about which eggs had turned out artistically superb. The best part was our sworn-to-secrecy

Examining Easter eggs with Dad.

Thornton pact. A few hours later, we arrived in our Easter regalia for the eight a.m. service.

A crowd had gathered around the Easter egg tree. We joined in with the ooohing and ahhhing, pretending to wonder WHO could have done it?! Although we were all highly suspect, I don't think anyone ever found out it was the Thornton family's caper. In following years, we pulled out the dozen eggs we'd kept for our own cherry tree in the backyard.

Decades later, when I was going through Dad's belongings after his passing, I found three of those eggs, poignant reminders that help keep my family memories alive.

The influence of my family's **Easterescapades** on my life turned out to be greater than I could have imagined. Into my fifth decade, I was still creating my own holiday escapades with the same exuberance as Dad.

Then one **Easterescapade** went terribly wrong. It opened my eyes to *SEE* how low my sinking thinking could get and provided the impetus for me to learn the Opposites Game.

On a Saturday before Easter Sunday, I drove around Denver in my white Subaru, Blanca (*blanca* is the Spanish word for white), delivering baskets filled with chocolate Easter bunnies and eggs. I pulled up in my friends' driveways and left the car door open. Engine running, I rushed up, rang the doorbell, left the basket by the door and raced back to Blanca to make a secret, fast getaway.

That particular Easter, I raced home after my **Easterescapade** to fix a candlelight dinner for Mr. Hotartist, a painter I'd met three weeks earlier and with whom I was completely smitten. I'd saved the most artistic basket for him, thinking I'd impress him with my Easter creativity.

Later as Mr. Hotartist napkined the last dinner juices from his lips, I presented him with the multi-colored Easter basket. Poking through plastic green grass, a silver-wrapped, smiling chocolate bunny leaned against speckled malted eggs.

"Hmmm. Chocolate!" he exclaimed while unwrapping Mr. Bunny and ceremoniously biting off his head. Suddenly he spit out the head of Mr. Bunny, spurting out of those previously mesmerizing lips something like: "Where did you get this chocolate ... at a gas station?!?"

I sat there as if he'd slapped me. A flood of crimson washed over my face as I tried to cover up for my obviously poor chocolate shopping. Filled with shame, I became completely disoriented and unable to fake my way through the torrent of emotions racing through me. All this from Mr. Bunny losing his chocolate head!

The fact that one line from a guy I'd known for three weeks would lead me into such a bout of sinking thinking made me go **thornallistic** (thorn•al•lis•tic; when a Thornton goes ballistic) inside my head. A *motion* of *emotion* drove me to a new all-time low, and none of it made sense to me. I quickly ended the dinner, confused by my embarrassment over Mr. Bunny's poor pedigree.

I rushed Mr. Hotartist – who by now had a very odd look on his face – out the door, fully aware my punishment of him didn't fit his crime. After all, he'd just made a silly comment about not liking my chocolate choice. Why hadn't I been able to turn it about? Why did I feel so completely undone?

I was well on my way into a downward spiral of shrinking and sinking. Unable to link any of my thinking, I tossed and turned all night. Even pages of writing in *Streams* failed to offer insights. I landed in yet another *Not-OK Corral*.

Desperate by morning, I hoped my friend Melm could steer me straight. I used our *JOLLI* password for needing *Help!* and sent the simple text— *"Helm!"*

The Opposites Game

Melm agreed to meet me at Starbucks to help me with my sinking thinking, which had amplified, convincing me I was losing my mind. Ironically, that's just what had to happen; lose the *mind* I was in—in order to excavate and *mine* a new one.

As I drove to meet Melm, I thought, *"Amy, what's going on here? You are a successful artist. You're an adult woman, not a love-struck teenager! You're buying a house, driving a paid-off car ... you're a responsible 'grown-up.'* WHAT *is wrong with you?!? I thought you were getting* IT *together! This is* NOT *what your* reVirement *is supposed to feel like! There is nothing* bold *going on here. This is* old, Old, OLD!"

I pulled into the parking lot and stared at my reflection in the rearview mirror. The grey, runny mix of mascara and tears leaving tracks down my cheeks said it all. I was emotionally undone because Mr. Hotartist had spit out Mr. Bunny's head. Engrossed in a mental *lame-blame* game, I couldn't turn my thinking around on my own.

I met Melm at the coffee shop door and she encouraged me to relax with one of her famous lines, "Amy, if you're hysterical, it's historical." Instantly I felt a bit of relief, realizing that Mr. Hotartist must have pushed some deep internal buttons.

Melm ordered our steaming cups and we cozied into the brown velvet chairs in a corner. I delineated my lively *lame-blame* game over Mr. Hotartist and his inability to fully appreciate my Easter genius.

Following my **Amyrant** (amy•rant; when Amy goes on a rant), Melm asked me her classic two questions, "What's the thinking, Amy? What are you telling yourself?"

I looked at her, thinking she must be deaf. "What do you mean?" I demanded. "I've just gone into great detail about Mr. Hotartist and my shrinking thinking!"

"But what's the thinking, Amy?" Melm possessed a spectacular **knackability** (knack•abil•ity; a knack for expanded ability) for keeping a grid-locked focus when asking a question.

"I'm sinking! That's what I'm thinking! And he's a stinkin' jerk and I should tell him where to go ...," I paused for emphasis, " ... to buy his chocolate bunnies."

"AAAmy, think again." She urged me to stop playing my *lame-blame* game and to *pause* my *cause*. But by now I felt almost clueless.

I asked Melm to break it down in six-year-old billboard style. This is a favorite graphic guideline I've told design clients for years:

> *If a six-year-old passes your billboard on the highway at 65 mph and can't grasp the message, then it's too complicated!*

Melm explained again, "Amy, what are you TELLING yourself *about* Mr. Hotartist? What is the thinking behind your upset? What are you making up *about* yourself? Eliminate him entirely from the equation. What are you telling YOU about YOU?"

Now this meant I had to quit spinning in that outside track and *tame* the *lame-blame* game I'd been entertaining myself with for the past twenty-four hours. I attempted a strategic pull into my inside lane.

"OK, Melm. I can do this. I'm thinking, why didn't I go to the Godiva store in the Cherry Creek Mall and buy better chocolate for all those surprise Easter baskets?"

Melm chuckled at my inability to get what she was asking me and my frustration increased until she broke it down more.

"Let's just start with the self-talk going on in your thinking. I know it's the next day, but what EXACTLY might your thinking have been in the same Amy-language your thinking uses? Here, write down the top ten thoughts." As she shoved a tan napkin towards me, I grabbed my purse and dug for a black Sharpie pen.

"Okay, I'll give it a go, but this isn't going to work!"

Oddly enough, there was no delay in my ability to identify the stream of negative thoughts that had been running on my internal mental racetrack. I listed ten of the sinking thoughts I'd been telling myself:

1. Amy, you're so stupid!
2. You should never have asked Mr. Hotartist over.
3. You're so lame for not speaking up and blaming him for not liking your chocolate.
4. You'll never find a guy who will like you.
5. You are such a failure at dating.
6. You can never get this right!
7. You always take things too personally.
8. When are you going to get *IT* together?
9. There's something really wrong with you.
10. You are one lousy shopper of chocolate!

I looked up in shock. It was humbling to reveal to Melm these awful thoughts. No matter how successful I was in my outside life, thoughts like these still raced around my head. And they had the capacity to capsize my best efforts for a bold turnabout.

Familiar with her own negative thinking, Melm put a hand on my shoulder. With a compassionate smile, she assured me she was about to offer me something new to turn my thinking about. Melm then taught me a strategy we called the Opposites Game. It was so simplistic that, at first glance, I didn't think it would work. But it did, and eventually it would allow me to lock up most of my Brain Bandits for good.

Shoving a fresh napkin my way, she said. "You're doing great, Amy;

have faith. Now, on this napkin, find the operative words to create the exact OPPOSITE meaning of each thought. List them out."

"What do you mean? Like that *Seinfeld* episode where George says or does the exact opposite thing and everything turns out for him?"

"Well, sort of. Create the opposite thought and write it down. You don't have to believe it, Amy, just do it and see what happens. What have you got to lose?"

My **perfectionoughta** (per•fec•tion•ought•a; ought to be perfect) persona jumped at the chance to get an A on her Opposites Game. I searched for the word or two to turn each thought into its opposite.

1. Amy, you're so <u>smart</u>!
2. You <u>should have</u> asked Mr. Hotartist over.
3. You're so <u>sane</u> for not speaking up and <u>not</u> blaming him for not liking your chocolate.
4. You <u>will</u> find a guy who will like you.
5. You <u>are</u> such a success at dating.
6. You can <u>always</u> get this right!
7. You <u>never</u> take things too personally.
8. <u>You are getting</u> *IT* together!
9. There's something really <u>right</u> with you.
10. You are one <u>great</u> shopper of chocolate!

Hmmm. As I wrote out each sequential, opposite thought, a notch in my spine clicked back into place and I sat up straighter. Instead of hunching down, peering over my steaming invisible caldron of *lame blame,* I was filled with an inner strength. Whether I believed what I'd written or not, I felt 99.9% better.

Melm's game showed me a revolutionary approach to thinking about my negative self-talk. In the past, I'd always given my sinking thinking so much power. This simple Opposites Game quickly and effectively tamed the beasts in my brain with just one or two opposite words.

I had switched lanes long enough to *pause* and consider the *cause* of my **Amyrant** such that I could now *SEE* where my **Easterescapade** had gone wrong. I saw the link between my thinking and sinking feelings. My spiral of self-degradation had been more connected to historical pain and shame than to that day's reality. The key to changing directions was all about understanding what I told myself.

Once again I realized the driving power of my thoughts—power strong enough to help me change directions with just a switch of one or two words. Did it matter if I believed the opposite thought or not? Do my thoughts really care? After all, my thoughts dutifully followed whatever invisible directions I think them to think. At least playing the Opposites Game would give me the *chance* to *change*.

My favorite photo of Melm.

Right there in Starbucks, Melm had given me the ammunition I needed to face down my *Not-OK Corral* Brain Bandits. I would be ready the next time a group of them threatened to derail me as I made my way down the *reVirement* path to a bold new life. ~ Thanks, Melm; I could never have seen this without your patience— and the Opposites Game!

Inner Guerilla Warfare

Driving home, I felt like a completely different woman. Even a glance in my rearview mirror to check out my cried-off makeup yielded the revised thought: *"Hmmm, Amy, you're lookin' kinda cute today!"*

Returning home to fix an early dinner, I decided to chill out in front of the TV; all that internal turning-about had been exhausting.

I flipped on the television to a news channel and made dinner. The news in the background highlighted the nation's economic **turbulations** (turb•u•la•tions; a turbulent flow of tribulations). Storms were on the rise in the Midwest. Then, the broadcast turned ugly. A group of guerilla terrorists had set off bombs, killing innocent bystanders in a Middle Eastern restaurant. The anchor reported on the type of ammunition and the clever ploys the terrorists had used in order to detonate the explosion.

Disturbed by the news, I stopped in my tracks, muted the television and plopped down on the couch. As images of rubble and destruction filled my periphery, it dawned on me that I experienced my own mental-thought bombing by guerilla terrorists who secretly plotted inside my head.

These inner guerrilla terrorists were more serious than my *Not-OK Corral* Brain Bandits. They were more camouflaged and plotted the annihilation of Amy. They hung out in my deep neural dugouts behind my inner enemy lines, where they had waged mental warfare for decades.

During the most surprising moments of my life, these inner terrorists often caught me off guard. I couldn't deny it. Somewhere in my brain, a secret band of thought-bombers lurked behind barriers, ready to bomb an innocent day or event and destroy my peace of mind.

At times I fell so victim to their negativity that, in the destruction, I wondered about my sanity. A couple of times in my early twenties their mental devastation was so invasive I feared for my innocent life.

These inner terrorists had carefully collected **Amy-intel** (amy•in•tel; highly classified Amy intelligence) since the beginning of my time. They knew all my vulnerabilities and weak spots. And they secretly crouched at all these vulnerable points of entry, silently motioning to each other *"Ready – Aim – Think!"*

In an AHA flash, I realized Melm had given me some strategic mental militia and allied-thought ammo to start blocking the ability of such terrible thoughts to take me down—just what I needed for the inner *reVirement* revolution I was building.

I wondered if there might be a connection between combating real-life terrorism and stomping out my own inner warfare. If my **Amynation** (amy•na•tion; the nation living within Amy) couldn't control her own inner guerilla terrorists with all their subtle espionage tactics and thought bombings, how could any real-world nations find change?

I reflected back to my earlier *JOLLI*, *"Amy, in order to change* our worlds, your words *need to change. You won't get to the* evolution *your* revolution *promises with your own inner guerilla terrorists on the loose!"*

Even if more optimism or positive thinking could turn things around, that would be too simple; it's been *right-in-front-of-us* for centuries. There was something deeper to this game of inverting negative thoughts into positive ones without any paralysis of analysis.

Lurking just below the surface, my inner thought enemies had fired off thoughts so fast they'd dodged conscious containment for years. They convinced me to play the *lame-blame* game instead of *SEEING* them. For decades, they thwarted my efforts to discover their real identity as they moved from the outside track to the inside, blocking my way forward.

For me to truly change directions and create a new second-half filled with the authenticity I craved, I became convinced I needed to expose all my inner enemies and their thought bombs; at times it seemed they truly had the power to stop me in my tracks.

The Opposites Game worked. It really did. By using the same self-talk I'd already used for years, I made just a few tweaks and began turning in the opposite direction. I launched an internal boot camp to retrain my inner thought-troops so they could recognize those inner guerilla-terrorists before they could sneak up on me and fire off more sinking thinking.

This may sound like a lot of work, but there was not a lot to figure out. With the Opposites Game, all I did was pause long enough to list the negative thought-bombs and then change one or two words. The more I called my inner terrorists on their stuff, the less power they had over me.

The great thing about awareness is that it's like a big pothole in the middle of your street. Once you're aware and *SEE* it, you can start to go around it, eventually driving an entirely different route. Within months of learning to *stalk* my *talk*, my thinking world changed dramatically. There was freedom to be had in the Opposites Game, and I wanted more.

Swat that Thought!

After about a year of stalking my thoughts, I discovered a quickie maneuver to use when shrinking thinking needed some quick sinking.

While folding my skinny jeans in my tiny laundry room, I thought, *"Amy, can you really call these skinny jeans? The last time you wore these, they seemed way too tight; you're really getting* fat!"

AHA! Fat. Another three-letter word—almost as bad as "old". That three-letter "fat" word packed such a powerful punch it dampened many a day or innocent moment. My inner terrorists used this word over and over again as one of the most powerful thought bombs in their arsenal.

I felt terrible. Just then, a big, black fly buzzed around my head, and I reached for a blue plastic fly swatter, waiting for him to land. I tried to remember to *stalk* my self-*talk* and ask myself Melm's two key questions: "Amy, what's the thinking; what are you telling yourself?"

While I worked on linking my sinking "fat" thinking, the big black bug buzzed past my nose again. I grabbed the blue fly swatter but, instead of swatting the fly, I slapped myself on the forehead, blurting out loud, *"Amy, swat that thought!"*

I burst into a smile. Recognizing the unwanted "fat" thought flying around in my head, I'd turned it around. With that one swat, I realized how far I'd come from my **Easterescapade** fiasco to my inner revolution. A renewed peace filled me with an increasingly new *kind* of *mind*.

Although deeper turnabouts would lie ahead along my *reVirement* expedition, I found renewed vitality, often in unexpected ways—even with a blue fly swatter.

Old thoughts were finding *bold* ones and the *gab* (**O.P.T.** – I meant "*gap*") between my *IT* searching and *IT* thinking closed.

SUMMARY> *Stalk My Talk*

◆ Mr. Hotartist triggered despair and got my attention.

◆ Melm taught me the Opposites Game that changed everything.

◆ My worst enemies – inner terrorists – came out of hiding.

CHAPTER 9

OverITs and NexITs

- *Pain* for *Gain*
- A DIA Decision
- V's Pivoting Path

As my *reVirement* expedition progressed, a distinct pattern emerged. With predictable regularity, the opportunity to change evolved from some pain or frustration I didn't want to deal with. But I embraced a new quest to find the *best* and leave the *rest,* no matter how painful it might be.

I maneuvered to the inside lane of many of my first-half *IT* searches, and the route proved to be anything but comfortable. Any idea, pattern or action that was *old* had to go if I was to transform into something *bold*. The common adage no *gain* without *pain* seemed more than a *JOLLI phrase;* it embodied the very *phase* of the life/death cycle of *old* to *bold*.

An invisible fluctuating route wavered its up/down, push/pull cycle as I ventured through a winding course into uncharted internal territory. An unspoken agreement suggested that, at any moment, I might have to stop everything, correct course and change directions.

Like a snake that sheds its skin many times over, I had to shed all that no longer fit. I'd love to say it was uncommon courage or unbridled passion that welcomed in the willingness to make changes from the inside out, but it was not. Sometimes it was a long goodbye.

Changing the *bit* that no longer *fit* required two necessary *IT* components. I called them **overITs** (over•it; the state of being completely over an *IT)* and **nexITs** (nex•it; the need to exit before any next *IT* can begin). Here's how they work.

I'd be involved with some new part of my *reVirement* adventure and discover that the way I thought about something was worn out and in dire need of a turnabout. Prior to reaching any turnabout decision, however, I first had to land in a state of mind called **overIT**.

I needed to get so massively good and over some *IT* before *IT* would transform and point me in a new direction. I had to *SEE IT* – whatever *IT* was – before I could leave *IT*, move *IT* or turn *IT* about. And, until I reached the point of no return where I was totally **overIT**, nothing seemed to change.

At the same time, I couldn't exit and move on to any next-*IT* or **nexIT** unless I felt completely **overIT** – whatever *IT* that was. Reaching an **overIT** seemed essential before any **nexIT** could arrive.

Although I would eventually leave the whole *IT* rat-race altogether, I likened my **overITs** and **nexITs** to the same metaphor of a racetrack. If I started spinning my wheels to no avail, I took this as a sign that I was on my way to an **overIT**. The more spinning of my mental wheels, the greater the intensity of the **overIT** and the need to exit that mind-track.

The good news about landing in a state of **overIT** was that this occurred when the waving flags signaled an opening and the lanes could be changed. My **overITs** helped me get to the inside track to find out what was *really* going on so I could then turn *IT* about.

Some call this sweet surrender. For me, it is a state of doing something over and over so many times that I become simply and completely over *IT*. And **overITs** are pivoting points for my **nexITs**.

A prime example was my June 6th **vepiphany** when four dreary options led me to one massive state of **overIT**. The **tiredword** ignited such an **overIT** momentum that it opened a way for finding my **nexIT**.

Something pioneering occurred on this *reVirement* journey as I began to actually welcome my **overITs**. As uncomfortable as they were, they were exactly what was needed for me to pivot in another direction. My **artIT** year off provides a poignant example.

Knee-deep into working as a full-time artist, I found myself living the dream I'd nurtured throughout the first half of my life. Convinced that this was my true professional *IT*, my **artIT** year culminated in a one-woman show to open on Denver's First Friday Art Walk.

With enthusiastic conviction, I hoped my rewired second-half would lead to grander art successes. While at other times between jobs I'd done my artwork on a full-time basis, I'd never gone for *IT* with both feet. This was *IT*. My **artIT** was *reVirement*-ripe.

Since Dad first taught me how to hold a brush, I was *supposed* to be a fine artist. But my Brain Bandits reminded me over and over that I *should* already have mastered my **artIT** – or so I kept thinking.

Stalking my *talking* taught me to pay attention to my *shoulds* and *supposed-tos*. They presented cautionary yield signs most often leading to an **overIT** or **nexIT**. I could pretty much guarantee that, if there was any *should* or *supposed-to* in what I was thinking, it wasn't authentic to me; it usually proved to be someone else's great idea.

During my **artIT** year, I struggled with uncertainty in believing I could succeed as a professional artist, even though I had tangible evidence otherwise. The lethal combo of *shoulds*, *supposed-tos* and insecurities concerning my **artIT** slowly gave way to a humdinger state of **overIT**.

Mornings were filled with painting while afternoons found me developing new art-marketing strategies. I worked in the evenings finishing graphic projects to keep the cash flowing until my art made *IT* big. I kept the **artIT** flame burning, night and day.

Then, something went terribly wrong. Nine months into my **artIT** year, I started to wonder where the joy of *IT* had gone. Why hadn't *IT* come? I was doing everything I *should* do to live out my **artIT** dreams.

I kept at *IT*, reassuring myself that all new endeavors require some internal **obstackles** (ob•stack•le; obstacle to be tackled). I felt an empty *hole* where I should have been feeling *whole*. I hungered for the day my **artIT** would fill in the invisible gap within.

During the four months prior to my art show, I pulled out all the stops. I launched into creating a new series of paintings that promised to top all previous creative accomplishments. In full **thorntonesque** style, I set out to reach that ever-elusive pinnacle of artistic *IT*.

Concurrently, I started to *stalk* the *talk* that played repeatedly in my daily thoughts. The phrase, *"I'm* **overIT***!"* became a low hum in my background thinking. As my savings account dwindled and the pressure to have an **amyazing** art show increased, the louder and more frequent my **overIT** mantra became.

Inner conversations sounded something like this: *"Amy! What's going on with you? This just can't be happening! You're becoming a complete contradiction to the dream you've built for decades around becoming an exhibiting artist. People dream of such an opportunity. Look how many decades you have invested in this. You're in your* reVirement *now. It's not possible you could be* **overIT***!"*

Friends and collectors commented on how lucky and fun it must be to live as an artist. But, on that inside track, a silent roar raced away: *"But I'm* **overIT***!"* I did my best to ignore *IT*, turning to my practiced patterns of running the rapids of that inner river of **de'Nile**.

As the crescendo of activity built to the opening night of my show, I worked around the clock to get *IT* all set up. I needed to frame all of *IT*, advertise *IT*, hang *IT*, celebrate *IT* – all while the stress of secretly feeling completely **overIT** only increased. I did my best to put on a great smile and pour all the love I could into my paintings and show.

The show opened with great triumph but inside of me, dissatisfied embers of frustration smoldered. A growing despair of secret thoughts around reaching an art **overIT** could not be stalked or swatted into silence. I couldn't figure *IT* out alone, so I called on Melm.

The night of my Collectors Party, after the exhibit lights had dimmed, we went to share a nacho plate next door to the gallery. Melm dipped her chips in salsa as I strived to explain my art **overIT**.

Did Melm have any clues to the despair I felt over my art **overIT**? I was terrified to admit this because I hadn't planned any other *IT* options. I could go back to graphic design, but I wasn't sure that was *IT* either.

I told my patient friend, *"Melm, I have no idea what to* do *next ... my* **artIT** *is sooo not* IT *and I'm dueling IT out in yet another* Not-OK Corral. *All I do know is that I'm* **overIT** *and that I need a* **nexIT** *...fast!"*

Melm encouraged me to keep on linking my thinking, suggesting that my **overIT** might guide me to my **nexIT**. She emphasized her two questions, reminding me to keep asking, "Amy, what's the thinking? What are you telling yourself?"

As a reward for completing my exhibition, I flew to New York to celebrate a girlfriend's engagement. My friend, Ms. Had*IT*all, had been my first new friend in the eighties after I'd arrived in New York City to pursue a dream of living and working there.

Ms. Had*IT*all excelled at life. A successful art director in the world of magazine publishing, she glowed in my mind as the shining *IT*-of-all-*ITs*. She was engaged to the man of her dreams, lived in an incredible home just outside of Manhattan – and she was a great success at all of *IT*. In the opposite sense of the phrase, she was full of *IT!* At least full of the *ITs* I thought were *IT*.

As I arrived at New York's LaGuardia Airport, memories of my Manhattan years flooded back. In the wake of my art **overIT**, my thoughts were filled with so much sinking, shrinking thinking that no amount of playing the Opposites Game could turn them around. Not a great way to start a trip.

At every engagement event I attended my compare despair fueled more sinking thinking. At Ms. Had*IT*all's spectacular bridesmaid luncheon, I sat smiling as she opened gifts, surrounded by her successful friends. My Brain Bandits attempted to convince me that everyone there had found their *ITs*, and my **artIT** hadn't been *IT*.

As I walked away from the brunch wearing the Dolce & Gabbana imitation sunglasses I'd bought on the street, I could no longer hide the *tears* of *fears* inside. I trudged down Madison Avenue to cross E. 82nd Street to the entrance of the MET (Metropolitan Museum of Art). I felt like a complete fraud as I reached a new, all-time **overIT** low.

My thinking raced ahead: *"How could this be? You've turned your life around, you've gone for* IT *and once again* IT *wasn't there. You don't have a clue about* IT. *You've spent a lifetime of moving toward an* **artIT** *that wasn't* IT! *You're getting* OLD *and you better find* IT!"

I barely noticed that my three-letter *OLD* word had slinked back in. As I walked through the MET viewing the works of all my favorite artists, I silently thanked them for a lifetime of inspiration and, at the same time, secretly apologized that I would never be an artist who had *IT*. I stopped at the museum shop and bought a new *Streams* journal and started **nagivating** my way through a torrent of mental rapids.

The remaining days in the city were a struggle as I wrote and walked while visiting art galleries and museums. I thought that, somehow, if I could get enough inspiration and immerse myself in enough artwork, I could shift whatever *IT* had gotten me to such a state of artistic **overIT**.

A DIA Decision

By the time I adjusted my seat on the flight back to Denver, I knew I had to *DO* something – anything – to get over my **overIT**! I grabbed the black Sharpie from my purse and adjusted the air in the overhead dial to help disperse the strong marker smell.

I scribbled away on a salty napkin, recalling and listing all the *ITs* I was now completely OVER:

"I'm OVER feeling like I HAVE to be a great, successful artist.

I'm OVER feeling like I'll never have enough money.

I'm OVER comparing and despairing over everyone else's *ITs*.

I'm OVER feeling like I'll never find *IT,* know *IT,* meet *IT,*
see *IT,* do *IT,* or be *IT!"*

And then came the culminating *coup de grâce:*

"I'm <u>*sooo*</u> OVER being **overIT**!!!"

Napkin number two was filled up by the time the pilot announced
our approach to DIA (Denver International Airport). I reached as far back
into my mind as I could and completed my **overIT** list. Then I closed my
eyes and leaned back, letting my head sink into the headrest.

I was ready to be completely and utterly **overIT** all. I inhaled a slow
long breath and made a deep inner vow: *"When the wheels of this plane
touch down, I surrender* ALL *of these* **overITs.** *I don't know what to* DO
ab*out any of* IT. *I don't know what my* **nexIT** *will bring. All I* DO *know is
that I am* **overIT**!"

When the plane landed with a soft kurplunk and slowed, turning
towards the gate, I sat holding my **overIT** napkins as if they contained the
greasy remnants of all that I was OVER.

As I joined the exit line, I started tearing the napkins in half, then in
quarters. Over and over again, I tore the napkins until the shreds became
a fist-filled emotional wad of **overITs.** I made my way through the exit
tunnel, eyeing the nearest trash bin.

I gathered my courage and decided to commit without hesitation.
I ceremoniously tossed the ball away, declaring *"I am now officially*
overIT!" Then I spun on my heels and headed towards the concourse.

Immediately something shifted.

My mind found freedom, as though I'd been lifted onto a magic,
mental carpet. After a ten-hour flight with two delays, I suddenly found a
revitalized energy, the turnabout vigor I'd hoped to find on the streets
of New York.

Something felt different. What happened? Had I found the sweet
spot of complete surrender? Was this the point of absolute no return
where a pivoting decision met utter **overITness** (o•ver•it•ness; noun for
state of **overIT**)?

This provided insight into the missing piece before I could move on to any **nexIT**. It seemed so simple; why had it been so difficult? I encouraged myself to #1: Get completely *OVER* any *IT* and then ...

> #2: Make a very deep decision to put both feet into my exit and allow whatever would be the **nexIT** to come, without conceiving a predetermined outcome. Then wait to see what happened next.

V's Pivoting Path

As I walked through DIA, W. H. Murray's quote of commitment and boldness came to mind. For months I'd carried a copy of his encouraging words in my wallet. I stopped to pull it out and read it. Was my **overIT** the necessary ingredient for Providence to know I was serious so that all manner of unforeseen things could finally sweep in to turn me about?

Did I really have to know where or what my **nexIT** was? Or did I just have to gather up a deep internal decision to commit? All of me – body, mind and spirit – had to arrive at that focal point of decision.

On the shuttle to the airport parking lot, I studied the quote as a new V-insight emerged. The *T-to-V* turnabout *à la reVirement* followed an often predictable path—a path not unlike the structural typography of the letter V. My mental graphic artist sketched out a new V-theory.

I located Blanca in the lot, tossed in my baggage and climbed into the driver's seat. Before starting the engine, however, I grabbed my Sharpie to sketch out my V-idea.

Beneath Murray's quote, I sketched my pivoting V-path, realizing that reaching the downward state of **overIT** was like reaching the turning point of the V. After my **overIT**, the only way out was up! As I reread the quote, I silently challenged Providence to step in at this turning point and steer me in a new direction.

I drove home with an uncanny clarity of focus towards an unknown destination. I'll never forget the feeling of freedom that **overIT** brought.

When I arrived home, I emptied my suitcase on the living room floor as an exciting energy filled me to my core.

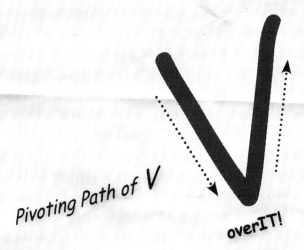

"Until one is committed, there is hesitancy, the chance to draw back. Concerning all acts of initiative (and creation), there is one elementary truth, the ignorance of which kills countless ideas and splendid plans: that the moment one definitely commits oneself, then Providence moves, too. All sorts of things occur to help one that would never otherwise have occurred. A whole stream of events issues from the decision, raising in one's favor all manner of unforeseen incidents and meetings and material assistance, which no man could have dreamed would have come his way. Whatever you can do, or dream you can do, begin it. **Boldness has genius, power, and magic in it. Begin it now.**"

– Attributed to both William Hutchinson Murray (1913 - 1996) and Johann Wolfgang von Goethe (1749 -1832)

Pivoting Path of V

overIT!

Climbing the ladder in my garage to store the suitcase, I harnessed another inner conviction:

"There goes all of that **overIT** *baggage. Time to* **nexIT***!"*

As I walked around my home putting away things from the trip, I reviewed my life with new eyes. I felt as though I had disappeared for years and stepped back into someone else's life. Did all this stuff really belong to me? The me who'd left a week earlier had shifted with my **overIT** decision.

I saw my year-long **artIT** struggle from a new angle, one comprised of gratitude and insight. It had taken everything – the energy, expense and focus – to arrive at my **nexIT**.

The mess of distress I'd battled in New York was, in fact, a huge blessing. I couldn't have arrived at my resolute decision if I hadn't gone through my own artistic fires. I grabbed my *Streams* journal, and a flow of revived ideas led to novel directions for my next steps. Murray's quote became more of a reality.

All sorts of things arrived that would never otherwise have occurred. A whole stream of events issued from my **overIT** decision, raising all manner of unforeseen assistance in my favor, which no prior Amy could have dreamed would come her way.

I'll explain further in Part Two: *DOING*.

However, I want to share one last chapter about how my **overITs** and **nexITs** paved the way for yet another turnabout tactic I call **quantumesque** living.

It started with an insightful hike with another of my friends, Ted.

SUMMARY> **OverITs and NexITs**

◆ Dreams of an **artIT** derailed and I landed in an **overIT**.

◆ A decision to commit launched more internal reversals.

◆ The V mapped out a pivoting path for my **nexIT**

·Chapter 10·

A Quantumesque Life

- Ted's *Walk 'n' Talk*
- Goodbye, Mr. Farmile
- The Inner Frontier

Ted and I met up on the outskirts of Golden, just west of Denver, where the town hugs the base of the Rocky Mountains. Winding dusty paths lead the Apex trail to a breathtaking overview of downtown Denver's skyline and its surrounding areas.

Ted and I often engaged in some heated discussion that would, characteristically, culminate in some profound insight as we reached the overview. From its vantage point, we could peer over the entire metropolis, which included the suburb of Arvada, where I'd spent the first seventeen years of my life.

Something always seemed to happen from that vista, and our insights would usually collide into some great AHAs. The perspective of hazy challenges somehow cleared and I could *SEE* anew from that panoramic view.

Ted is a business coach, author and teacher. He helped me with some great marketing ideas during the year of my **artIT**, and I wasn't sure how to break the news that I'd reached an art **overIT**.

I planned my art **overIT** speech. I would explain to Ted that, although I loved to paint, my vision of making a living as a poor, starving artist in my studio had to change directions. Beyond the change of heart, I had no idea what or where my **nexIT** led. Excited to share my *Pivoting Path of V* theory, I began my Apex-trail *walk 'n' talk* with Ted.

Still enthusiastic about my DIA napkin-shredding ceremony, I launched into my art **overIT** story. Halfway to the top of the Apex overlook, I waited for Ted's thoughts on what my **nexIT** might be.

Instead, Ted changed the subject. He proceeded to describe research he was studying about quantum physics. He was developing some innovative approaches for his clients in building their businesses.

Quantum physics was a topic I'd heard about for a few years but didn't fully comprehend. Ted kept using the phrase "quantum leap" to describe the ability to make instant decisions and change directions—midstream. I asked him to break it down in *six-year old billboard style* so I could really get the hang of it.

Ted reached down and grabbed a fallen pine cone. "Well, Amy, picture a bunch of atoms vibrating over here, doing their thing in this spot when suddenly – out of seemingly nowhere – they leap and start vibrating over here." For added emphasis, Ted tossed the pine cone from hand to hand to demonstrate his point.

"What makes them decide to leap from one place to the other?" I asked, pointing to the leaping pine cone.

"There is a certain quantity of frequency at which those atoms are vibrating that instantly propels them over to the next spot. It's an exciting frontier—uncovering just what it takes for the leap to happen; but that's why quantum physics is such a fascinating field of scientific study."

Then Ted applied his quantum leap theory to my New York state of mind: art **overIT**.

"Amy, what if your yearlong **artIT** provided all the necessary momentum and heightened state of frequency that you needed in order to leap on to your **nexIT**?"

We were approaching the overlook's expansive vista, right on time for reaching a broader insight into Ted's quantum leap idea. "Amy!" Ted continued. "What if your whole first half of life was comprised of exactly the right collection of atoms that provided the perfect amount of frequency needed for you to take a quantum leap into your second-half and *reVirement?* Why not just think about all of your *ITs* as the necessary frequency you needed to start vibrating from a new space over here?" Ted snapped his fingers in the air on his left side for emphasis. "Amy, what if your DIA decision was the quantum leap you needed to start living from a new place over here?" Ted then snapped on his right side.

"Hmmm. It's a great theory, Ted, but I've spent the whole first half of my life getting to where I am right now. Do you really think change could be as simple as that?" I snapped my fingers in response.

"Amy, look at all you've done just since turning fifty. Do you *SEE* all that your *T-to-V* switch has shown you? Of course you can do it! If you hadn't taken that year off and done your lifelong dream, how would you have ever known the change of direction you now desire? Do you *SEE* how even this *IT* could appear like a negative when, in fact, *IT* was the perfect *IT* you needed to move from over *there* to *here?*"

Ted playfully tapped his index finger from the right side of my head to the left before continuing. "Amy, why not think of your *reVirement* as the new environment that you've leapt into—complete with turnabouts that are as easy as quantum leaps!"

I nodded back. "Hmmm," I said. "Yes, I could call it **quantumesque** (quan•tum•esque; with the quality of quantum leaps) living. And I would let the frequencies of my *old* **overITs** be the pivoting points for *bold* **nexIT** turnabouts."

We breathed in the crisp Colorado air from over 8,000 feet above sea level. It all sounded very doable from the Apex overlook. We turned to head back down the path and our conversation leapt from one inventive idea to another. Once again, my ever-expanding *reVirement* revolution would not stop evolving.

When we got back to Ted's place, he scrambled into his office to grab one of the scientific books he was reading on quantum physics. He began flipping through the pages when an illustration caught my eye.

I screeched, "Look, Ted! There's the V again—the sure sign we're onto something. It's a diagram of two V's showing the quantum leap frequency from V-to-V!"

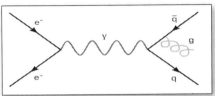

We leaned closer to study Feynman's diagram, and Ted attempted to explain the radiation of a gluon as depicted in the uncomplicated illustration. I failed to truly grasp the intricacies, but for me the diagram provided more **vevidance** of how the V continued to show up—as if it were prodding me onward towards more *reVirement* turnabouts.

V's connect in Feynman's diagram; Ted and I enjoy some of my art.

Like clockwork, I soon got a real-life opportunity to try out my novel **quantumesque** living theory.

Goodbye, Mr. Farmile

My friend Audrey invited me to join her at a talk by Dr. Deepak Chopra at Mile Hi Church. I leapt at the chance to hear Dr. Chopra speak live because I'd read many of his books. I loved his ideas on energy and our ability to influence our manifesting destinies. Surely he'd have more great insights to add to my evolving **quanumtesque** living theory.

Audrey had two preview tickets for us to join about fifty guests lined up to meet Dr. Chopra in person prior to the lecture. We hurried into the long line and, suddenly, out of the corner of my eye, I caught a glimpse of Mr. Farmile, whose name has been changed to protect his innocence.

Mr. Farmile was, perhaps, the deepest love of my life. We'd spent a couple of years together and were shopping for wedding rings when he displayed his own quantum turnabout and leapt from the relationship.

The grief I'd felt over our breakup had been worse than some of the family deaths I experienced. I'd thought he was *Mr. IT.*

What's important here is that, in the years following our breakup, every time our paths crossed I launched into some heavy-duty thought bombing, landing in a massive *lame-blame* game, either pointing a finger at him or myself in efforts to ease my ache.

Although time had relieved some of the pain, there was an added punch of shame I felt around our breakup that I could not turn around. Somehow I must not have been enough for him. I must have done something wrong. My *lame-blame* game around Mr. Farmile was more like a lame shame-game. I always had to pay close attention to my sinking, shrinking thinking whenever I saw him.

The good news is that, with my new mental militia on board, I learned to recognize my *lame-blame* games for what they were—tactics used to avoid feeling my own feelings of shame and pain.

Fast forward to standing in line with Audrey to meet Dr. Chopra. Suddenly, Mr. Farmile moved into the line with a beautiful brunette *right-in-front-of-me.* A blaze of rapid thinking started within seconds: *"Oh, gosh, there's* Mr. Farmile. *What are the odds he would be here? I hope he doesn't see me. How can he be with someone so much younger than me? Oh Amy, you are sooo* OLD! *Even* Mr. Farmile *found someone younger than you. No man is going to find you attractive now that you are on the other side of fifty. He was the Mr. IT of your life and now he is with someone else!"*

I reached for some quick, mental **Amyammo** (amy•am•mo; Amy's mental ammunition). With lightning speed, I dispensed my Opposites Game tactics: *"See, Amy, you are so <u>YOUNG</u>! So what if* Mr. Farmile *has found someone <u>younger</u> than you. <u>Every</u> man is going to find you attractive now that you are on the other side of fifty. He was <u>not</u> the Mr. IT of your life, and now he is with someone else. Hurray!"*

I instantly felt great. My **Amyammo** worked! By switching the operative, opposite words in my thoughts, I felt better in a flash. I monitored my thinking long enough to snap a photo with Dr. Chopra and ask him to sign his book for me. Then Audrey and I moved along to find our seats for the lecture.

Audrey and I thank Dr. Chopra.

I sat down thinking I had successfully stalked my self-talk out of another shame-*lame-blame* game around the entire Mr. Farmile topic. Then came round two.

After Audrey and I sank into our seats, Mr. Farmile appeared out of the corner of my eye, just two rows behind us. As he gently guided Ms. Beautifulbrunette to their seats just catty-corner from ours, I braced myself for another wave of shrinking, sinking thinking that might be sure to follow.

But then, something happened. I remembered my hike with Ted and my idea about living a **quantumesque** life. I reminded myself of the energy and time I'd spent rehashing the Mr. Farmile failed romance. If ever there were an **overIT** filled with the momentum and the frequency to make an inner quantum leap, it was now.

I prompted myself, *"Amy! Here's your opportunity to do a major turnabout. Think about the huge amount of internal data you have with your entire sad* Mr. Farmile *story. Aren't you ready for a massive turnabout leap?!?"*

I closed my eyes. I arrived at another mental fork in the road. I had the clarity of a bird's-eye view. What was my decision going to be? Would I commit to living my theory? Was I going to *walk* my *talk?*

If I continued down the familiar mental hike along the Mr. Farmile path, I'd end up playing another *lame-blame* game, possibly entertaining myself for the whole lecture, missing everything Dr. Chopra had to say.

Or .... I paused, wondering, could I really take the leap?

Yes! Inwardly, I confirmed with no doubt that I'd collected enough mental mileage on Mr. Farmile to be good and **overIT**. I had more than enough of the necessary fuel-frequency needed for an **overIT** decision worthy of one big quantum inner leap. I'd reached the end of my V point and it was time to decide and commit.

I mentally passed through our past while gathering up my body, mind and spirit, silently proclaiming throughout my inner Amy kingdom, *"Attention all ye of* **Amynation***! We hereby decree that we are so* **overIT***, it's ridiculous! We will never know why* Mr. Farmile *left, why it didn't work out, blah-de-dah-dah! We are sooo* **overIT** *it is time to* **nexIT** *and travel down a completely new relationship path!"*

I anchored both feet into the swirling carpet design below me as if its pattern were an invisible swirling whirlpool, and I energetically deposited all my **overIT** frustrations deep down into the earth.

Inhaling deeply, I collected my Amy atoms together, preparing for an inner quantum leap. I held my breath, thinking one last parting thought: *"Thank you,* Mr. Farmile, *for the wonderful times we spent together; whatever happened with you, I will never know. I wish you the highest good of all. I am now ready to move on with my life and discover my* **nexIT** *relationship."*

I slowly exhaled, releasing everything about my Mr. Farmile story. I pictured a *bold* breath flooding through all those *old* mental grooves with a cleansing wave of *gold* current. No more bouts of doubt.

I allowed my exhale to *seal* the *deal* on my **quantumesque** leap and mentally declared: *"Mr. Farmile, I'm* **overIT** *...* **nexIT***!"*

Upon opening my eyes, I was sitting up straighter. The lights on the stage seemed to reach out to me like V-rayed spotlights – more **vevidance** – applauding my **quantumesque** decision. I turned to Audrey and smiled. Little did she know I'd made an inner quantum leap while she'd been reading the evening program.

Dr. Chopra's lecture inspired us all. His words were bright and their meaning rich with depth as he held my complete focus. Any thought of Mr. Farmile had completely disappeared. What a pivoting victory!

Later that night in bed, I realized I hadn't even looked back or noticed the couple filing out of the auditorium. This was profound considering the amount of shame and pain that was connected to my previously sad Mr. Farmile story.

Dr. Chopra spoke to us about energy and our ever-present ability to direct the passion of our thoughts towards the manifestation of our desires. In some **quantumesque** way, he was talking about the very thing I was doing. By gathering up my **overIT** energy, I surrendered to some unknown passionate commitment to **nexIT**. I catapulted onto an entirely new mental route towards a future free of the past.

I began to successfully turn about the past stories of my life without spending valuable time *trying, prying* and *crying* to figure them all out. I could harness enough of my own Amy atoms to successfully leap into a new *kind* of *mind*. I exited onto a completely new **innerstate** (in•ner•state; interstate of my inner mind) of *BEING*.

In the next few months following the lecture I would continue to see Mr. Farmile occasionally, and my **quantumesque** living continued to work. I had found a whole new mental frame to place around one of the most painful and puzzling pictures of my past.

An Inner Frontier

How could my *Just-One-Little-Letter-Insights* continue to *lead* my *leap* into an inspired second-half? With unexpected enthusiasm, my voyage into midlife was becoming an exciting expedition of anticipation. Where would living from the inside lane lead me? Could I really get off that outside track forever?

I was changing directions and finding free ways of living from the inside out, sometimes by doing the opposite of what I'd always done in the past. My revitalized **innerstate** propelled me towards a new inner frontier, one to be explored and traveled deeply on the inside.

My *IT* itch eased as I realized that I no longer had to figure *IT* all out or know the *IT* outcome ahead of time. If I stayed pointed in the direction of my decisions and commitments, all manner of assistance would show up to lead a new way.

The V fueled this newfound inner revolution towards a riveting point of attention. The V became one massive **varrow** directly pointing to whatever *old spot* needed a *bold shot*. I might be headed in one direction and need to turnabout quickly. I'd encourage myself: *"Amy, pay attention! Look, this is the hidden secret; do you SEE it? This is a truth that will set you free. Don't miss IT! Keep your eyes peeled for the V!"*

I adored the Colorado Rockies, and my childhood was filled with mountain adventures. In my family's green-and-white four-wheel-drive Scoutie-outie (nickname for our green Scout), we traversed the Rockies along rarely explored routes to cross mountain passes and visit abandoned ghost towns where early miners once dug for gold.

These mountain travel adventures were similar to the inner *reVirement* frontier I now scouted. While wrestling with my own grizzly Brain Bandits, I visited the ghosts of my past, seeking all that had to go. While mining the *mine* of my *mind* in order to strike my own *gold,* I crossed an invisible inner passage from *old* to *bold* towards a new high way.

My eye-peelin' talents had given me the insights to *SEE* my life from the inside out and, from there, I could start *DOING* something about *IT.*

And so the road to bold continued.

SUMMARY> A Quantumesque Life

◆ Ted suggested a *chance* to *change* in quantum leaps.

◆ I tested my **quantumesque** living on Mr. Farmile.

◆ Finding an inner frontier, I traversed from the outside in.

PART TWO

DOING

Chapter 11

Vhorizon of Perspective

- *Gap* in *Map*
- V's were eVerywhere!
- **Innerstate** High Ways

When I latched onto living a **quantumesque** life, I stumbled upon what would become a resurrecting approach to living out my second-half. Key to living this new life would be the practice of paying attention to the mental **innerstate** I was barreling down.

Over time I gained increasing skill at changing directions and turning about, sometimes doing so with the speed and velocity worthy of a quantum leap instant. Like a pilot flying to undetermined destinations, I started living my life as a constant journey of course correction.

A few days after Dr. Chopra's talk, I headed to the mountains for a weekend ski trip and planned to stay with my friends Annie and Rich, a pair of inspiring Boomers who incorporated renewable, green energy into everyday living. They are two vivid examples of *reVirement* renovation and innovation.

Rich is passionate about designing and building homes from reusable components. The beautiful home he built with Annie has walls and a foundation made of more than 160 bales of non-recyclable materials and non-biodegradable plastics; that is, trash in various forms cinched together with metal strips into huge blocks.

Rich installed a "truth window" that opens to reveal a peek at the compressed bales that support the 36-inch walls of their stucco home. The trash bales, an efficient and brilliant use of repurposed material, illustrated the reinvention and repurposing I was exploring.

How many times had I considered some of my life's stuff as trash only to find that it could bind together as the foundational impetus I needed for repurposing

A visit with Annie and Rich and the secret, truth window.

myself? I was about to discover a whole new relationship around my stuff and renewed riches within it. ~ Thanks, Annie and Rich, for the inspiration!

Annie and I shared decades of professional camaraderie as book designers, artists and nature lovers. She and Rich also shared my love for skiing and are incredible ski pros who know the ins and outs of the Winter Park ski resort.

I looked forward to telling them about my ideas around *reVirement* and my growing hope of writing a book. We spent the last evening of my visit in a vital dinner discussion about my emerging ideas.

They were enthusiastic and supportive of my creative efforts. As I spewed forth many of my *JOLLI* thoughts, Rich and Annie tossed in a few of their own. Everything we talked about seemed to have a unique renewable and repurposed spin to it.

We finished our lively conversation with an update on the *"not-to-be-missed"* slopes I should ski the next day. Annie marked up a trail map for me with a thick magic marker.

The next morning, I loaded VIDA (my new Subaru Outback, whose name means "life" in Spanish). After hugging Rich and Annie goodbye, I headed to Winter Park. Driving along Highway 40 from Fraser to the ski resort on a wintery-fresh Colorado morning, I let my thoughts wander back over the lively *reVirement* discussion from the previous night.

The flashing yellow dashes of the highway dividers sped by just below VIDA's front windshield at the bottom of my peripheral vision. The blur of yellow hypnotized me deeper into my thoughts. Without warning, I doubted the enthusiasm from the night before. My mood took a turn south in a sudden downward spiral.

BAM! – some Brain Bandits jumped at the opening: *"Amy, you reeeally DO need to figure out what you are going to DO next! What's your next IT move? You can't possibly write a book! You don't know how to DO that! For gosh-sakes, you can't even spell! You need to DO something and DO IT NOW!"*

My mental deliberations focused on what *IT* I planned to *DO* next. After what I'd experienced since turning fifty, I often slipped back into yearning for some new *IT* to *DO* that would make my life count. The thought bombs continued trying to convince me I'd made no progress whatsoever since my *reVirement* discovery. Was I doomed to repeat the same-old same-*IT* while searching for yet more *ITs?*

The flashing yellow highway lines caught my attention again with a shift of insight. A vibrant inner voice encouraged me, *"Amy, look up, pay attention! Where are these thoughts leading you?"*

Highway 40 stretched out ahead in a gigantic V to the horizon, pointing towards the peaks on the mountain range up ahead. As VIDA sped along at sixty miles per hour, I'd almost missed *SEEING* the huge V ahead of me due to the chattering doubts that were filling my head.

A gentle strength from deep within reminded me: *"Amy, pay attention to your* **innerstate**. *Keep your perspective on your highway. Your thoughts are your map leading the way to your next steps. Is this the thinking you want, or are these thoughts creating a* gap *in your mental* map? *Is this the direction you want to go?"* A turned-about perspective hit my Brain Bandits right between the eyes; they vanished.

I returned to a more positive frame of mind and adjusted my thinking. Fascinated by the highway-V stretching ahead of me, I recalled years of art studies around the principles of perspective. I considered these fundamentals from a new angle. *"Hmmm, look how the highway's perspective has a double meaning: the perspective of my thoughts focusing on where I want to go and the principles of artistic perspective."*

Highway perspectives point straight ahead to a V.

From years of training, I'd mastered the art of representing a "real" world on a two-dimensional flat surface. The principles of perspective allowed me to do this. I'd rarely thought about the parallels of the different meanings of this one word – perspective – though it was ingrained in my psyche from years of artistic study.

In drawing and painting, the principles of perspective combine the use of angles (V's, I might add) to direct the composition to a horizon line. The relationship between all of those V's along the horizon line is what creates the impression of ity. This allows artists to represent a three-dimensional world on a two-dimensional surface (visual aids to follow). The other meaning for perspective relates to a viewpoint or attitude one has about something, as in the phrase, *"...from my perspective, I see it like this ...."*

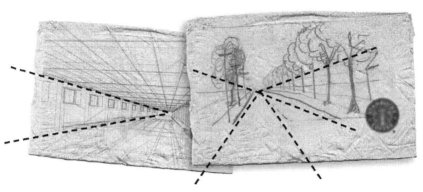

V's are a non-negotiable in the principles of perspective.

Another AHA sank in, *"I wonder if the V is trying to show me something again? Maybe it's about keeping my eyes peeled on the path up ahead and keeping my focus on the point of my destination. If I don't, I'll be lost in the* gap *of my* map!"

A cold morning shiver coincided with my mental redirect, and I saw a Starbucks coffee shop ahead. I pulled into the parking lot, grabbed my backpack and headed inside for a warm-up and regroup.

What was going on with the V and the principles of perspective? A V-inspired **Thornism** came to mind: Is it a new **vhorizon** (vho•ri•zon; V-inspired horizon) of perspective pointing me to focus on where I'm going? I sent out a silent challenge to the letter V to show me a sign.

As if on cue, a whole series of V's commenced to appear, delivering undeniable **vevidance** to encourage me to not give up and pay attention to my **innerstate** highway. It would seem as if eVerywhere I looked that day, V's presented themselves. The capital "V" inserted into the word accentuated this essence of the V ... which seemed to be ... eVerywhere.

V's were eVerywhere!

I picked up my decaf and set up camp in a back empty corner. I pulled a pencil out of my backpack. To refresh my memory,

I made a couple quick sketches on tan Starbucks napkins. In a flash, my studies of perspective came back, but from a revised V perspective.

It was undeniable. In order to create a successful reality, the use of the V was key. A set of radiating V's pointed to the horizon line, just like in the I-40 highway image. Was this **vhorizon** reminding me to stay focused ahead, in the direction of my dreams?

I shook my head in awe. *"The V just continues to show up!"* A familiar vitality slid over me as more **vevidance** burst forth.

A blinding light flooded through the windows, and I had to shield my eyes to look up. The sun stretched out with a vast amount of V-rays over the V-mountain peaks on the other side of the road. Rows of dark green evergreens lined up in a row of upside-down V shapes.

A sweet glow of renewed perspective swept into me as the sun's V-rays warmed my little coffee spot. I reflected on what had led me to that moment, all my **overITs** and **nexITs** that hadn't been *IT*. Yet now, a brilliant light of perspective shimmered across the miles of trials I'd traveled, as though trying to help me figure my *ITs* out.

With the **vhorizon** of perspective reminding me to stay focused, I wondered if the V had been simply pointing me to the current moment—a point of being present; a place where no outside *IT* was needed. What a refreshing idea.

A small grove of bare aspens nestled ahead of the evergreen trees. The contrast of their light, cream-colored bark against the dark forest

Aspen limbs and evergreen trees celebrate the V.

greens delineated an abundance of V-shaped limbs reaching up towards the sun's rays.

I closed my eyes to breathe in the visual **velights** (ve•lights; delights of the V) and wondered, *"Okay, V, I have no idea what you are trying to tell me, but you have my attention! I must be going* **vrazy** *(v•raz•y; V-crazy), but I'm willing to pay attention. I SEE you ... but what am I* supposed *to DO now?"*

I looked around to see if anyone had noticed I was having a conversation with an imaginary V. The clock on the far wall pointed to quarter to eight. *"Oh my!"* I thought, *"even the hands on that clock are shaped in a V!"* Time to head to the ski slopes.

I reached into my backpack and pulled out Annie's ski map. A day of skiing promised reVitalization. When unfolding the upside-down trail map, I noticed that Annie's bold highlights sketched out even more V's. Without recognizing it Annie had sketched mountain **velights** for me to ski .... Indeed, V's were eVerywhere!

Was this a V-coincidence or was I hypnotized by the V, making it

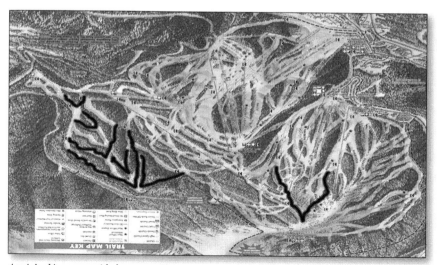

Annie's ski map provided more vevidance.

all I could see? When I headed out of the coffee shop, I noted a playful vitality in my step and a renewed perspective ... via the V.

The rest of the day, I swooshed down ski slopes, guided by Annie's highlighted V-routes. While sitting on the swinging chairlifts, passing over rows of evergreen trees below, I stretched out my skis to create V's to frame the skiers gliding under the lift twenty feet below.

I passed over the "bunny slope" – the beginners' hill – where a long row of children followed the instructor down the mountain. Their little legs were in the shapes of pointed V's as they learned the snowplow, one of the first positions skiers learn.

A few times during the day, in honor of the V and my new-found **vhorizon** of perspective, I pushed my ski edges out and bent down into the classic snowplow position. I was flying down mountain terrain on my own ski-created V path. Perhaps I'd been destined for my V course all along and didn't know it!

Skiiers assuming the V-snowplow position.

Memories of my family and of learning to ski filled me with appreciation that day. In the late sixties, Julie and I had been thrilled at the prospect of learning to ski. Concerned about the financial investment, Mom had insisted we trek to downtown Denver's main Salvation Army store. We bought cheap wooden skis with cable bindings and lace-up boots. I paid $10 of my print-shop money to buy my entire ski setup. The following weekend, we headed to Lake Eldora's bunny slope for a brief lesson by Dad on how to snow plow.

Concerned that "us girls" might not like skiing, Mom declined to buy us the $8 lift ticket for that first visit to the slopes. With skis on our shoulders and clunky tied-up ski boots on our feet, we spent the day hiking up the bunny slope and sliding down the mountain in snowplow position.

Walking up the steep slope for such a short joy-ride down wore us out. Julie and I complained. I felt poor and embarrassed that we couldn't buy a lift ticket, but my parents' enthusiasm convinced us that we were building good ski-character ... and muscles, to boot.

Dad and I swooshing up the T-bar ski lift.

At the end of the day, my sister and I convinced Mom and Dad that we loved skiing and they promised that next time we could skip the walk up the mountain. We would take the lift like everyone else.

Perhaps lessons like that helped me gain some of my determination to overcome challenges and persevere for the reward at the end. In a way, my whole life seemed to be about working hard, *DOING IT* right and then arriving at some *IT* reward. But gradually, from the perspective of retrospect, I could *SEE* that all my *IT* escapades and exertions were essential. The V continued to pivot my life about.

Innerstate High Ways

At the end of my Winter Park ski day, I packed my memories along with my skis and headed home to Denver. The thrill of the slopes and a plethora of V's filled me with a courage to continue my course onward and pay attention to my perspectives and where they were leading me.

I kept my eyes on the **vhorizon** ahead and considered my two new mental metaphors: **innerstate** and high way (just one little space inserted into highway created a two-word idea for finding a "higher way").

Several "what if" insights chimed in.

"Amy, what if your reVirement *is all about creating a* **quantumesque**

life of turning about whatever **innerstate** *is not leading you to the high way of your vision? What if it's all about paying attention to your thinking and the direction in which it's leading you? What if it's all about filling the gaps in your mental maps? Maybe this is what your* **nexIT** *is going to be about?"*

I wasn't sure what all of it meant or where the **vhorizon** of V-inspired perspectives would lead, but I couldn't wait to find out.

Pulling into my driveway, I decided to unload VIDA before making dinner. Juggling my backpack and ski bags through the front door, I stopped and glanced around.

Standing at the entrance to my small house, looking for a spot to drop my ski stuff, I felt a sweeping sensation come over me, suggesting that I'd arrived in my past; yet I wasn't the same. It was that same feeling I'd had when returning from New York a few months earlier. Was I on the verge of yet another turnabout due to a new **overIT**?

Unpacking from the trip, I grabbed my three-foot-long, nylon ski bag, hoping to figure out how to cram a few more things into the side pocket. When my favorite black ski gloves wouldn't fit, I emptied the pocket. Six colorful pairs of ski mittens popped out.

They were all perfectly good ski mitts I'd collected over the past twenty-five years from hand-me-downs and multiple thrift stores, but I suddenly stopped, as if *SEEING* them for the first time. *"Why am I holding on to all of these? I don't use half of them."* Every time I went skiing, I grabbed my favorite black pair. Why was I holding on to all the others ... out of habit?

"No!" I immediately mentally protested. *"You keep these mittens in case you need them. And, look at these orange ones ... they remind you of that great trip you had with Mr. Farmile."*

"Mr. Farmile?" I stopped in my thought-tracks. *"You're* **overIT**!*"*

I opened more pockets in the duffle bag, spreading stuff onto the living room rug. Suddenly I was *SEEING* all my things from a new angle. Why did I have so much ski stuff? The irony of holding on to so many pairs of unused ski gloves made me realize that my stuff might hold the clues to the next steps along my **innerstate** journey.

A new **Thornism** came to mind that said it all: **MyStuff** (my•stuff; my vast collections of stuff, worthy of its own word).

The insight from the morning about the *gaps* in my mental *maps* made me wonder *"Is all* **MyStuff** *slowing the progress to my vital* reVirement *high way? How is* **MyStuff** *affecting my* **innerstate** *travels?*

"What if all of **MyStuff** *is hiding my* **nexIT** *so much I can't SEE my way through IT in order to DO anything about IT?!? What's all* **MyStuff** *about, anyway? I think I need a serious* **MyStuff** *turnabout!"*

Suddenly I knew what to *DO*. I made a **nexIT** decision to get good 'n' clear about **MyStuff**. Brilliant! *"Amy, you have one more week off from work. If you can't set your hands on everything you own in a week, there is way too much of* **YourStuff***!"*

My stomach growled. I tucked the mitts into the open ski bag and piled the ski stuff in the corner of the living room. I would reconsider **MyStuff** from a higher vantage point in the morning. Then I would consider my **nexIT** challenge of putting my hands on all **MyStuff** in the upcoming week. I went into the kitchen to heat some soup.

The challenge began in earnest. Little did I know what would ignite. All manner of unknown insights and discoveries evolved when I navigated through the land of **MyStuff**. And in the process, I discovered a few revolutionary ways of *DOING* something about all of *IT!*

SUMMARY > Vhorizon of Perspective

◆ Thinking, like maps, directed life's destinations.

◆ V-signs encouraged me along the path of *reVirement*.

◆ Was my *old* **innerstate** driving me along a *bold* high way?

Clear the Magnet

• *SEEING* All **MyStuff**

• Magnate or Magnet?

• A *ReVirement* Rendezvous

The next morning brought a revitalized frame of mind as the intention to get clear about **MyStuff** blazed in my thoughts. While puttering around, I wondered where the heck to start.

I opened the kitchen cupboard to make a bowl of cereal. Looming before me was a cupboard stuffed with stacks of dishes. I reached for the blue ceramic bowl on the middle shelf and, as I filled it with soy milk and oatmeal, flashed on the bowl's history.

The bowl was a gift from my good friend Amytoo (my nickname for her since we share the same name). A wedding gift from my 1984 wedding, the bowl had followed me to New York City after my divorce and then back to Denver.

The bowl's mother-of-pearl glaze swirled around its chipped rim. As the bowl filled with invisible ingredients from over two decades of memories, I remembered many lonely nights when it had held warm soup or cold ice cream in efforts to bring me comfort.

That morning, however, I looked at the bowl from a revised perspective. Why was I holding on to it? I sat on the counter, eating my cereal, eyeing the other stacks of bowls, mugs and plates. There was such a range of dishes, most of them linked to some event or occasion that had been packed with meaning during my first half of life.

My thoughts stirred, *"Amy, why are you holding on to all these dishes? How can you continue on your* bold *turning-about journey if*

YourStuff *is stuffing up any new direction you want to go? Gosh, you*
really need to get clear about **YourStuff***!"*

I reminded myself that perhaps sitting and breathing would help
me calm down and consider my next steps. For decades, I'd been an
avid meditator—mostly in efforts to calm my massive **amyzonian**
(amy•zon•i•an; Amy gets the size of the Amazon) *IT* searches.

While living in New York, I'd started a tradition of having a
little altar area in my home that would physically remind me to sit and
meditate. Inspired by the blue bowl's story, I sat at the corner altar in my
living room and breathed a bit.

I looked at the clock and decided to breathe for a few minutes.
I assumed my favorite lotus position – cross-legged on pillows – and
breathed out a long slow exhale. Hoping to calm my thoughts, which were
currently overflowing about **MyStuff**, I reviewed the past couple of years.

Sweeping a broad brush of perspective across the canvas of my
mind's eye, I recalled the excitement and insights I'd gained by taking
a year off to do my **artIT** and making my DIA decision to launch a new
journey into the unknown.

I wanted to write a book about *reVirement* but wasn't sure where to
start. My dream of changing *old* to *bold* and supporting other Boomers in
the process came to mind. I could *SEE* clearly that my life of over*DOING*
IT had not delivered the *IT* life I'd hoped for. Still, I had no idea what to
DO about *IT*.

"Calm your mind, Amy. You don't need to DO anything right
now, just BE with all of your ITs," a simple voice encouraged me from
somewhere on the sidelines. I breathed a bit more.

My mind refused to listen as it continued to *pass* over the *past* years
since I'd turned fifty and another stream of "what if" queries flooded in.

"What if I really could write a book about reVirement? *What if I*
could share my turnabout ideas with others to help change the direction
of their thinking about aging?" I thought of Rich and his repurposed

trash bales at the foundation of his house and wondered if **MyStuff** from the first half of my life could be used as the structural foundation of my reinvented second-half.

What if a *right-in-front-of-me* insight was hidden from my view because there was too much of **MyStuff** in the way, blocking my ability to *SEE IT* or *DO* anything about *IT?!?*

Magnate or Magnet?

Out of the blue, an image flashed. I felt an intuitive urge to go out to my garage and get one of the heavy-duty magnets from among the many tools I'd inherited from Dad and Grandpa Byron.

"Random – weird," I thought. *"Why go outside in the cold to get a magnet from the garage?"* When I couldn't silence the idea, I dashed to the back door, secured my robe and went out to the cold garage.

A chilly dawn blasted me as I left my cozy house, but soon I was in the garage in front of its long wooden tool bench. I knew exactly where the magnets were hanging as they clung to the big metal ruler my dad had used in art school more than fifty years earlier.

I let out a groan as I made a mental note. *"Amy, you have to get clear about* **YourStuff** *AND you've got your* **FamilyStuff** *too!"* Over the previous ten years, I'd inherited about three households of **FamilyStuff**.

I reached up to grab a magnet off the ruler but lost my grip, causing the magnet to fall into a plastic tub below. Stuffed with mismatched odd-ball nails, screws and fasteners, the tub collected hardware that never made it back to original containers. I dug in and pulled out the magnet. In the tub, it had been transformed into a steel conglomerate that looked like an outer-space spider robot.

Eyeing this new creation from all sides, I thought, *"Very cool! Look how this magnetic energy works!"* A shiver reminded me I was standing in the garage in my robe on a very cold morning. I gripped the space-spider magnet and shuffled back inside, where I set the magnet on a kitchen counter and turned the stove on for tea.

Waiting for the water to boil, I played with the magnet, pulling the screws and nails on and off, letting them snap back into place. It was fascinating to see the invisible powers of magnetization in action. The kettle whistled; time for chai.

Opening the kitchen cupboard, I saw a stacked tower of collected mugs that reminded me of the leaning tower of Pisa. Reaching for my favorite black mug, I groaned at the reminder: *"Ugh, more* **MyStuff** *to get clear about!"*

The spider-magnet held my attention while the steaming tea cooled. I hated to admit it but, from a metaphorical perspective, I felt like I was also a glommed-up magnet. Then my AHA hit, *right-in-front-of me.* *"Wow, Amy, you're a magnet so glommed up with* **YourStuff** *there's no room for you to find your* **nexIT**!

"Are you going to be a magnat *of* **YourStuff** *from the past, or are you going to clear your* magnet *and magnetize a new* reVirement *life?"*

Could "magnet" and "magnat" be a new *JOLLI?* I opened my laptop's dictionary. Nope, I'd forgotten the "e" and misspelled magnate.

magnate a wealthy and influential person, esp. in business: a media magnate.

magnet a piece of iron or material that has its component atoms so ordered that the material exhibits properties of magnetism, such as attracting other iron-containing objects or aligning itself in another magnetic field.
• Figurative: a person or thing that has a powerful attraction: the stretch of white sand is a magnet for sun worshipers.

A stream of questions followed. How could I be a wealthy or influential magnate if my magnet was too full of **MyStuff**? How could I live a **quantumesque** life if lots of *old* **MyStuff** prevented anything *bold* or *gold* from leaping onto it?

My previous decision to get clear about **MyStuff** was gaining momentum. The spider-magnet had led me to know exactly what to *DO* next. *"Amy, think of* **YourStuff** *as though it's a glommed-up magnet. During this next week off you've got to ... clear your magnet!"*

I finished my tea and went to change into more appropriate unstuffing-expedition attire. I knew things might get messy, so I pulled on old grey sweatpants from a jam-packed bottom drawer. The best place to start was right there – my bedroom dresser drawers.

With a renewed determination to trade in my magnet mentality for a magnate one, I reached for my *Streams* to start a game plan of listing the types of **MyStuff** in the bedroom.

Starting with clothes, I immediately understood they fit into specific categories and multiple subcategories. For example, I didn't just have "tops", I had tops for summer, winter, fall and spring. And within those categories were tops that were long-sleeved, short-sleeved, sleeveless, dressy, professional, formal and ragged enough to get paint on. Within minutes, my clothing list filled more than two pages.

I opened drawers and closet doors, realizing I rarely wore more than half of the clothes I owned. I'd collected clothes for different *seasons* and *reasons* for years. Some *infernal, internal* dialogue started to shout, *"Amy, when did you become such a clothes monger?!?"*

In addition to subcategories of clothes, I'd also collected approximately three sizes of clothes in each category. I had skinny, normal and fat clothes as a result of decades of yo-yo battles with eating and weight.

Even though my *reVirement* revolution and decades in recovery had helped me find a normal-size body and lose my middle-age middle, I'd still saved the clothes as if to remind me of my weight battles. Memories of those struggles flooded my thoughts in the mere seconds it took to list my winter wardrobe.

My outfits had become an "outer fit" of **MyStuff** frustration!

I sensed that creating a bold life required getting to the other side of **MyStuff**. I dashed into my home office and grabbed some paper and a Sharpie to make signage to help me map out my plan.

Back in the kitchen, I boldly taped my turnabout intention on the fridge door:

Ah, that felt better! Writing my desire as if it had already been achieved gave me a lift. Like a highway sign leading to a desired destination, this sign pointed me in the right direction. Hopefully, I wouldn't get lost in the land of **MyStuff**. I made a mental note: *"Okay, Amy, all signs now lead to a new* **innerstate** *destination. Do you SEE IT? Now DO IT!"*

I AM NOW CLEAR ABOUT MyStuff!

A *ReVirement* Rendezvous

Before lunchtime, I listed another half dozen **MyStuff** categories: kitchen, laundry, cleaning, garage, gardening, tools, art ... a veritable plethora of **MyStuff** was everywhere. One would think I lived as a millionaire instead of a poor starving artist. I was certainly a successful magnate of thrift-store bargains, but I possessed much more than I needed. Not only was I a master collector of **MyStuff**, I was full of *IT* (in the most ironic sense of the phrase).

As I prepared lunch, I examined the kitchen. Cupboards and drawers were filled with organized rows and categories of **MyStuff**. The vast collections emerged as I became fully aware of them for the first time.

For years I'd done such a good job organizing and categorizing that it looked like I owned just the normal amount of **LifeStuff**. Just what was a normal quota of **LifeStuff**? How could I rendezvous with my *reVirement* vision and let go of all the rest? How could I embrace a new *bold* self with all the *old* **LifeStuff** in the way?

It was mind-boggling. As with my clothes, there were subcategories within all **MyStuff**. A plate wasn't just a plate it was a favorite; a super-nice plate; an ancestor's antique plate; or a hold-on-to-in-case-I-break-one plate. I leaned against the counter and ate my lunch, considering the additional kitchen cupboards that required more lists with even more extensive subcategories.

Mental rapids of overwhelm started to flood in. I reached for my *Streams*. I needed to row my way out. *"Why do I have so much of* **MyStuff**? *Am I holding on to the past? What does it all mean? Am I going to be a magnate of* **MyStuff**, *or can I clear my magnet for an inspired second-half?"*

And lastly, emerging as the most important question of all ...*"What's truly underneath all* **MyStuff**?"

SUMMARY> Clear the Magnet

◆ I opened my vision and started *SEEING* all **MyStuff**.

◆ Would I be a cluttered magnet, or a greater magnate?

◆ Understanding **MyStuff** started a *reVirement* rendezvous.

CHAPTER 13

Tough on Stuff

- *Cargo* that *Cango*
- *LiveIT, LoveIT, LoseIT!*
- **InCASEitis** and **S.M.D.**

I munched on my lunch, immersed in questions about **MyStuff**. I simply couldn't get my head around what to *DO* about all of *IT*. I eyed the banner taped to the fridge with growing trepidation. Where to begin?

Reviewing my long list of categories, I decided I needed to get tough on **MyStuff** if my turnabout was going to move from *talk* to *walk*. My inner eyes needed to be peeled to make my way through the fog of mental clutter created by **MyStuff** madness.

One thing was clear—it might take more than a mere week to put my hands on all of **MyStuff**. I wrote out my *fears*; soon *tears* of apprehension rained down upon my *Streams* pages.

Embedded in **MyStuff** was the physical remnants of a life spent searching and collecting a whole lotta stuff. My endless searching for the right *IT* stared back at me in the physical remains of all that now surrounded me. Would all of *IT* become the clues to eventually lead me to a new kind of home, a home inside of me that was free of outside clutter?

The *fears* 'n' *tears* subsided with this new awareness. I started to *stalk* my *talk*, realizing that linking my thinking about **MyStuff** could become another gateway towards clarity. I reminded myself: I AM NOW CLEAR ABOUT **MyStuff**. I took a few deep breaths and listened. I silently asked for the next right move.

Out of nowhere, a mental movie flashed on a recent visit I'd had at the home of another architect friend of mine, Bruce House. (His last name really is House.)

Bruce told stories about **HisStuff**. He showed me the Western paintings and historic photographs that he cherished. He displayed **HisStuff** with pride and joy, even as he admitted he needed to lighten the load of **HisStuff**. He also admitted he wasn't quite sure where to start.

At one point during my tour, Bruce chuckled and pointed to a book on his coffee table. A longtime favorite read was displayed with pride: *Guns, Germs, and Steel*. Bruce paraphrased a choice quote from the author, who'd written about the takeover of Native Americans by Europeans. The original indigenous people noted the volume of **WhiteStuff** as it was unloaded from the Europeans' ships. The tribes wanted to know *"Why does the white man have so much cargo?"*

This short phrase from my visit with Bruce leapt into my thoughts as I finished lunch. I was **amyazed** at the amount of cargo I'd collected from the first half of my life. A mystified smile came as I made up my own playful version of Bruce's quote, *"Why does this white woman have so much* cargo? *I need to figure out where it all* cango!*"*

I laughed at my *JOLLI*, realizing I would either capsize from all my cargo or make my way through it. Instead of racing around the mental track on the problem of **MyStuff**, I needed to pull onto the winning lane to get clear about it. My eyes wandered back to the sign on the fridge door and, in a flash, I knew what to do next.

"Amy, think in a new way. What if the journey through **YourStuff** *became an expedition into your second-half? What if you were a pioneer woman blazing the trail for her bold new frontier? You would need to pack up and move."*

Eureka! Simple. Whenever I moved, I needed a sizable number of empty boxes. I dashed to my car, VIDA, to make a box run to a local store. I filled her cargo area to the brim with tiers of stacked cardboard boxes.

When I stopped at a traffic light on the way home, a homeless woman rested curbside, leaning against a shopping cart. The cart was piled about three feet high with her precious cargo. I surveyed her collection, fascinated by all **HerStuff**. Her layers of coats were torn into tatters that resembled the fringe on an ancient ceremonial dress.

I flashed on the historic photos of Edward Curtis I'd studied in art school. Curtis captured epic images of tribes in their natural environments. I remembered one sepia photo of an indigenous couple traveling across the plains. Their teepee-turned-travois carried all of their belongings with efficiency, a baffling concept to this white woman.

Photo by Edgar Curtis of a 19th-century Blackfoot couple crossing the Plains with their tepee-turned-travois.

I rolled down the window and handed Ms. Shoppingcart a dollar while feeling a surprising envy. If only I could simplify my cargo into a shopping-cart travois. I turned towards home and, right on cue, the next steps came clearly to mind.

"What if something drastic happened and you HAD to live on the streets like that woman? What if you only HAD one shopping cart in which to fit all of your most loved and needed possessions? Maybe this is your strategy to get through the land of **YourStuff***?"* Another simple idea had emerged on how to *hone* my *home*.

Like water filling a glass, **MyStuff** always filled the container in which I lived. Whether I lived in a tiny studio apartment or a two-bedroom house with a garage, **MyStuff** could only fill the space allowed.

What if I only had one closet for all my clothes and only one desk for all my office supplies? What if I could define the final location of **MyStuff** first? The size of its new home would help me *refine* and *define* the amount of **MyStuff** to keep and what *cargo cango*.

I flashed on another image, that of homing pigeons who, year after year, intuitively know the route back to the same landing perch. What if **MyStuff** returned to its own homing destination time after time? Not only could I decide what to keep and what to release, but I could also locate **MyStuff** whenever needed.

This simple idea gave me a renovated mental map for launching the next steps along my expedition through **MyStuff**.

Recalling Ms. Shoppingcart, I decided it was probably fair to say she knew exactly where everything lived in her traveling travois. She could probably locate her flashlight or roadside cardboard sign at a moment's notice.

If I knew the new homes for any category of **MyStuff** first, I could pare it down to fit the designated spot. It would be like the "NOW" in my affirmation on the fridge. Conceiving the desired destination of an item first would guide my steps to subsequently fulfilling its destiny.

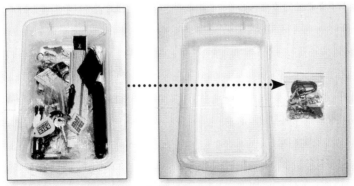

A collection of stuff shrinks to fit in its new home—a small pouch.

The direction of my **MyStuff** sorting expedition changed as I considered my new honing ideas. I embarked on a strategic treasure hunt, keen on finding only what could fit into a new smaller location. Although it seemed a bit backwards to create the new space for **MyStuff** first, it didn't matter. As in the Opposites Game, how I got to a new destination wasn't as important as getting there. Once again, innovation reigned supreme for my latest *reVirement* renovation.

LiveITs, LoveITs, LoseITs

The next steps appeared as a play on words. I could reduce **MyStuff** to three categories: my *LiveITs*, *LoveITs* and *LoseITs*.

LiveITs: The stuff used to live my life, like toothbrushes and socks.

LoveITs: The stuff I loved, like the turquoise belt buckle my dad had adored and passed on to me.

LoseITs: Everything else.

A rush of goose bumps raced down my arms with a verve of enthusiasm. Even my next un-stuffing clues were playful *JOLLIs:* *Live-Love-Lose*.

This was it, the needed simplification to continue my *reVirement* rendezvous. If the item was not a *LiveIT* or *LoveIT*, it was a *LoseIT*. How clear about **MyStuff** was that? My refrigerator map worked! I'd instantly become pretty darn clear about **MyStuff**.

LiveIT! LoveIT! LoseIT!

I unloaded VIDA, filling my living room with empty boxes. Next, I grabbed three boxes and headed into the kitchen. Paper signs taped to empty boxes were labeled *LiveIT!*, *LoveIT!* and *LoseIT!* Immediately, items began to find their places. All questionables landed in an additional empty box for further contemplation.

After a while, I felt a surge of renewed hope for getting through the land-o-**MyStuff**. My eyes landed on the top ledge of my stove and the white kitchen timer resting there. Cranking the dial to one hour, I commandeered myself, *"Okay, Amy, let's see what you can get through in an hour—you have three categories. Ready? Set ... Go!"*

As the tick-tick-tick of the timer propelled me onward, I pulled onto an entirely different **innerstate**. In full *reVirement* style, my decision and commitment to get clear about **MyStuff** had delivered some unexpected techniques to tackle it.

This **MyStuff** expedition quickly developed into a mission-finding exploration with the sole focus of seeking out my *LiveITs* and *LoveITs*, eliminating all else. Each item I picked up had to pass the test:

"Do I LiveIT *or* LoveIT? *Do I want to take this with me into life's second half? Yes? ... No? ... (Wow ... you're such an* **overIT***) ...* LoseIT!"

Within minutes I'd quickly differentiated the *LoveITs*, *LiveITs* and all the glaring *LoseITs* from my kitchen cupboards. But then I realized that the box of questionables that didn't fit any category was overflowing. I labeled it with a big question mark sign.

It became clear that not all **MyStuff** would fit neatly into just three simple categories. For example, what to do with perfectly good dishes and kitchen gadgets that had followed my relocations from Colorado to New York and back again? What about the hand-painted dishes that Grandma Beulah displayed in the cabin, or the blue juice glasses she'd treasured?

With the tick-tick-tick of the timer in the background, I started to think about my thinking in regards to **MyStuff**. More examples became apparent. It seemed I never threw out a single fork. My silverware drawer held twenty forks, and bags filled with extra silverware were stored in two other locations. Was there any chance I would ever run out of forks or host a party in need of hundreds of forks? Probably not.

I applied my new *hone*-my-*home* theory to my collection of forks. All *LiveIT* and *LoveIT* forks would now live in one silverware holder. All extras would be banned from the silverware kingdom.

As I made my way through **MyStuff**, my thinking filled with hundreds of likely reasons why I might need various and sundry stuff for future various and sundry events. My question-marked box grew to three boxes. A new level of clarity around **MyStuff** begged for answers.

InCASEitis and S.M.D.

Two simple words permeated my thinking around much of my questionable **MyStuff**. Whenever something wasn't a *LiveIT* or *LoveIT*, I justified why I needed to hold on to it. In my reasoning were two simple words, a verbal duo, that urged me to hang on to **MyStuff** for years. The words? *in CASE*: *in CASE* I needed it, *in CASE* I wanted it, or *in CASE* I might _eventually_ want to use it.

It didn't matter if years or decades had passed since I'd used it or even loved it—over and over again in my mind, my thoughts justified: *"I better hold on to this* in CASE _____ *(fill in the blank)."*

It was painful to realize I'd spent much of the whole first-half-of-life in preparation for a series of possible *in CASE* scenarios that might not ever occur.

Endless kitchen items embodied the *in CASE* factor. One drawer was stuffed with about a dozen sets of fancy napkin rings with matching cloth napkins. My thinking went something like this, *"Well, Amy, you might need these* in CASE *you start making romantic dinners for your future husband or* in CASE *you learn about French cuisine and serve a* soirée *of friends elaborate dinners."*

Another item, a plastic bag filled with cookie cutters, came with the corresponding thought, *"Well, I may need these* in CASE *I make artsy cookies, like during that great visit with Julie's family a decade ago. Or, I may need these* in CASE *I want to decorate holiday cookies with a friend's children some day."*

The *in CASE* stories completely ignored the realities of my present life situation. Like a metronome in sync with the kitchen timer, my thoughts named each *in CASE* scenario, justifying every questionable item's existence.

One kitchen drawer held a Tupperware bowl of about 100 flat plastic square thingies used to close bread bags. When I was a kid, those thingies had served as guitar or ukulele picks when my sister and I couldn't find official ones. But, really, when was the last time I'd needed one of those square thingies? I couldn't remember the last time I'd played my guitar, much less a ukulele.

Was I preparing for some major lock down? Did I really need to be fully equipped so I'd never have to shop for anything ever again?

I grabbed another sheet of paper and listed each *in CASE* situation that urged me to hold on to **MyStuff**. A large bag of paper plates and cups held the corresponding thoughts: *"I may need these* in CASE *I have a party for fifty people and they all need cups or I may need these* in CASE *there is a huge blizzard like in 1984 and I'm stuck without water for days and can't wash dishes."*

And then there was the culminating, *in CASE* justification of all:
"I may need this ... just – in CASE *– I need it!"*

My thoughts were spinning by the time the timer went off. Only one cupboard and two drawers had been emptied. I felt dizzy and sat down to regroup. I grabbed the *in CASE* list and scrawled out in a big, two-inch letter headline: *in CASE!*

I could see half of my kitchen from the couch, and even though I had three boxes of *LiveITs*, *LoveITs* and *LoseITs*, those question-marked boxes overwhelmed me. I felt woozy, lost in a haze of mental *in CASE* explanations that clouded my newfound clarity around **MyStuff**.

I wondered if I might be coming down with the flu and needed to stop this **MyStuff** madness. I shook my head, realizing that I would do just about anything, including getting sick, to avoid facing and getting clear about **MyStuff**.

As I recognized my mental diversion tactics, I breathed deeply and tried to think straight. With a short mental leap, two new **Thornisms** came to mind. *"Perhaps I'm coming down with an invisible dis-ease around* **MyStuff**. *Maybe I'm sick with a bad case of* **stuffonia** *with concurring symptoms of chronic ...* **inCASEitis**.*"

stuffonia (stuff•o•nia: disease of too much stuff; sounds like pneumonia). A dizzying condition of congestion caused by an overabundance of stuff; an inflammatory condition causing the head to spin with associated symptoms of **inCASEitis**.

inCASEitis (in•case•i•tis; justifying symptom of **stuffonia**). Infectious justifications for holding on to excess stuff, just *in CASE* it is needed in some imaginary unknown instance.

My serious investigations shifted. This creative word play opened the haze of being stuffed up about **MyStuff**. Nothing like humor to save the day. I felt lighter and clearer about **MyStuff**.

I wondered where I'd caught this dis-ease of **stuffonia** with symptoms of **inCASEitis**?

Instantly, a vision came to mind of my Grandma Beulah's dark, chilly cellar in Dad's childhood home. Boxes and containers of every size and shape had lined the walls of that mildewed, damp lower level of their small, white stucco home in southern Colorado. Memories of my sister and me exploring the damp cellar flooded back.

Julie and I would make our way down the cool, dark stairwell with its thick plaster walls of bubbly-bumps that scratched the skin of our palms. The light switch was at the bottom of the stairs, so we would pretend to be blind as we wound our way down the dark stairwell leading to the densely packed cave of **GrandmaStuff**. It appeared as if another household sat waiting underground, just *in CASE* something was needed.

Family heirlooms, boxes of receipts, photos, memorabilia, hats, clothes, jars of canned fruits and boxes and boxes of all shapes and sizes filled the cellar. Our favorite item, however, was the gigantic rubber-band ball the size of a basketball that balanced on the stack of Grandma's beauty shop records. She saved every rubber band that ever crossed her path *in CASE* she ever needed one.

Was this where I'd developed the predisposition to organize and categorize vast volumes of **MyStuff**? This propensity had been passed down through generations, probably from relatives struggling through the Great Depression, when everything was saved – just *in CASE*. As I faced down my carefully organized **MyStuff**, I feared that my **stuffonia** and **inCASEitis** might induce my own great depression.

I sat on my couch, entertaining myself with memories of exploring **GrandmaStuff**, not wanting to think about all the boxes of **FamilyStuff** I needed to face. Over the years, I'd become the family archivist. An ache hit my heart as I thought about going through my **FamilyStuff**, but I reassured myself that I would go there last.

I jumped up and stood facing the fridge, rereading my sign: I AM NOW CLEAR ABOUT **MyStuff**! I reminded myself, *"Amy, after tackling just a few kitchen cupboards, you're already much clearer about* **YourStuff***!"* As I stood among the piles of boxes, the next step instantly showed up.

"Amy, you need to expand your vision and get some holding tanks. There are six rooms in this house and a garage. Let's set up some temporary holding tanks to hone *your* home. *Pretend you're moving ... moving through* **YourStuff***!"*

I cranked the kitchen timer dial around to one hour again. With renewed energy, I transferred the *LoveITs* box to a far corner in my home office; this room would become the holding tank for *LoveITs*. The *LiveIT* pile returned to an empty kitchen cupboard.

The "**?**" boxes went to the garage and the *LoseIT* boxes were loaded into VIDA so they could be delivered to the local thrift store. When the timer dinged a second time, I acknowledged a huge jump in my progress. I'd made it through my entire kitchen.

While enjoying dinner accompanied by my steel-spider magnet, I ceremoniously plucked off a few bolts and nails, thinking *one room down, five more to go*.

That night, I recorded **MyStuff** findings in my *Streams* journal. I wondered if my **nexIT** move would show up when my spider magnet was empty. I fell asleep exhausted, but comforted; I was NOW clear about a whole lotta **MyStuff**.

It took longer than one week to put my hands on all **MyStuff**. By the end of two weeks, however, I had not only gotten over my bad bouts of **stuffonia** and **inCASEitis**, I decided I'd earned the equivalent of an **S.M.D.** (Stuff Management Degree).

I'd earned this honorary degree in **Stuffology** (stuff•ol•o•gy; study of stuff). As the hypnotic haze of my **stuffonia** lifted, I realized I could've written the curriculum for a four-year university **S.M.D.** degree that included a full range of studies on stuff management.

My courses would be called *Learn about Stuff 101, Get Stuff 102, Stuff Arrangement 103, Stuff Maintenance 201, Get Better Stuff 202, Get Rid of the Stuff 301* and *Moving Stuff across the Country 304*.

Higher levels of studies would include *Organizing Categories of Stuff 401, Stuff Justifications 404*. And, finally, the honor's course: *Getting Clear about* **MyStuff** *506!*

Maybe I'd even teach a few advanced workshops: *Stories about* **MyStuff** and *Comparing and Despairing over* **OthersStuff**. After getting through my **FamilyStuff**, I could definitely teach a class on *Getting through Generations of Stuff*.

Below are the official findings gained from getting through **MyStuff** and obtaining my **S.M.D.** doctorate in **Stuffology**.

First, the bad news. All **MyStuff** pointed to what had *ailed* and *failed* me during the first half of my life. The outer *IT* focus on **MyStuff** had kept my mental wheels spinning in the outside track.

I'd never pulled into my mental inside lane long enough to really find out what was underneath **MyStuff**. As long as I kept obtaining, rearranging and managing **MyStuff**, I remained hypnotized by my ever-changing and elusive *IT* search, hoping to find the **RightStuff**.

In the months following, I came to know what **MyStuff** hid. I dove below the surface of **MyStuff** in order to finally turn it about.

The good news was that my tough-on-**MyStuff** tactics had cleared my magnet. By identifying and only keeping my *LiveITs* and *LoveITs*, my home gleamed with an invigorating and revitalized freshness. Later I found a creative doodad to place atop my cleared magnet. Thoughts of what to *DO* next immediately filled my head, as if invited by the open space I'd created.

Concrete ideas for writing a book about *reVirement* took form. I collected ideas for creating *reVirement* workshops and a guidebook filled with more detailed turn-about tactics. Perhaps I could help other Boomers get through **TheirStuff**?

Within three weeks, I'd cleared my home and repainted the walls of my living room, dining room and home office in a warm white. By the time I closed the lid on the last can of paint, I felt as if my home had been transformed into a blank canvas ready to welcome my life's next great masterpiece.

I set the artful magnet on my altar, where it continued to remind me to keep my magnet clear. I was ready for the **nexIT** inspiration.

In celebration of completing my *reVirement* rendezvous, I prepared for a return trip to New York, this time to celebrate Ms. Had*IT*all's wedding. It hadn't been long since my DIA **overIT** ceremony had initiated a feast of *reVirement*-ripe ideas. Revamped and rewired, I would spend the plane ride cooking up plans for book chapters and possible workshop experiences.

In full **amyzonian** anticipation, I looked forward to dishing up a banquet of ideas to all my New York Boomer friends. I reminded myself of the enduring *chance* to *change* inspired by W. H. Murray's encouragement to decide and commit without hesitation.

Little did I know, the unfolding story of **MyStuff** had just begun.

Before and after photos of the garage free of **MyStuff**.

SUMMARY> **Tough on Stuff**

◆ Tough tactics cleared the way through the land-o-**MyStuff**.

◆ A plan for finding *LiveITs*, *LoveITs* and *LoseITs* arrived.

◆ Playful **Thornisms** helped the stuff-medicine go down.

CHAPTER 14

My Second Vepiphany

- *T-to-V* Number Two
- **Innerstate** Speed Bumps
- Needing an **Innervention**

I arrived in New York free of the compare-and-despair I'd experienced a few months earlier at Ms. Had*I*Tall's bridal shower. In fact, I felt thrilled for her and honored to celebrate in all of **HerStuff**.

I rode the Jitney bus out to the Hamptons and, over lunch, shared my emerging ideas with Ms. Had*I*Tall. She loved them. A powerhouse and successful publication manager, she encouraged me to write a business plan for my *reVirement* enterprises.

The next morning, I did a little research at the local library a few blocks away. It was a gorgeous **Hamptonesque** (hamp•ton•esque; a unique beauty unto the Hamptons) morning. The sway of overhead oak leaves rustled in the splendor of the crisp sea air.

Nestled in the heart of the village, the town library sat at the end of a row of antique shops next to a coffee bistro that infused the air with a lovely mix of bakery and coffee-bean scents. I sipped my decaf-to-go and sat on the library's front bench, waiting for the doors to open.

A brunette woman munching a bagel joined me. She squirmed on the bench, slightly annoyed as her internet had gone down and she needed to reply to a few urgent emails via the library's computers. We were sharing some friendly public-bench banter when I asked about her professional pursuits in Manhattan.

She casually mentioned she'd co-founded a small publishing branch of one of the big five publishers in New York. I'd been telling her some of my Manhattan experiences coupled with my emerging enthusiasm over writing a book. The library was about to open, so I quickly refocused our conversation and asked her what advice she might give an unpublished author with a powerful story to tell.

Without skipping a beat, Ms. NewYorkPublisher loudly exclaimed, "Amy, *WRITE THE BOOK!*"

I must have shrunk back a bit from the force of her response and looked slightly shocked, because she softened and encouraged me with an adamant summary.

"Amy, you can't imagine how many times authors delay writing their books only to discover that someone else has written a book based on their idea. If an idea is current and viable, then it's likely that someone else will write a book about it. So, if you are passionate about what you want to say, *WRITE THE BOOK!*"

I could hear the library door being unlocked as our eyes locked. Her gaze penetrated deep, as if tattooing the phrase *"WRITE THE BOOK!"* on the inside of my mind's eye. I shook her hand in thanks, and then we headed into the library to the computers. With renewed verve, I thought, *"Amy, if you don't write your* reVirement *book, someone else will!"*

As I waited for my emails to come up, I glanced down and made a mental note of the nice typography in the logo on the cloth book bag Ms. NewYorkPublisher carried. When she left, we nodded our goodbyes, and then I googled the name on her bag to learn her identity.

Ms. NewYorkPublisher was not only a successful publisher, but she was also the editor of one of the award-winning books my book club had just read. I couldn't wait to tell them about meeting her. Talk about serendipity. Surely, she knew best. I must … *WRITE THE BOOK!*

Before leaving, I explored the website of Ms. NewYorkPublisher's publishing house. I became so inspired by its mission statement that I printed it out to join company with my Murray quote. Throughout my writing efforts, her encouragement and her company's vision would continue to inspire me to *WRITE THE BOOK!* Below is a short excerpt:

Ms. NewYorkPublisher's Mission ... an Excerpt

"Whether we are publishing a novel or a memoir, a work of narrative journalism or bold invention that reframes our understanding of an issue, we aim to create books that share the potential to transform us and unite us in a common experience."

It still astounds me that three simple words – *WRITE THE BOOK!* – have carried my bold vision across miles, months and trials. ~ Thank you so much, Ms. NewYorkPublisher!

Almost immediately, I commenced writing the early chapters of a book about my *T-to-V reVirement* switch. When I told several more Boomer friends about my ideas, their enthusiasm encouraged me further to *WRITE THE BOOK!*

I experienced a very different plane ride back to DIA this time. I couldn't get enough of those salty airline napkins. I sketched out a few cover ideas and book-page layouts. Fortunately, as a professional art director and designer, I'd done the design and production on many published projects. I assured myself these experiences could guide me.

When I arrived home and walked through the front door of my house, I'd forgotten the weeks before my trip spent emptying my house of all my *LoseITs*. I hadn't yet made it through all the question-marked boxes in the garage, but I felt utterly free; I entered a whole new life.

MyStuff had shifted and so had I. Providence had guided the clearing of my life's magnet; I was free to write. In less than an hour, I unpacked and opened my laptop, letting loose a stream of book chapter concepts and interior designs. There was no hesitation whatsoever and no turning back ... I would *WRITE THE BOOK!*

Over the next few days I operated in full-steam-ahead mode. Pages emerged; research needed to be done. I checked out a dozen books from

My imaginary reVirement *headquarters and mock-up book covers celebrating the V.*

the library, including three on how to write a book proposal. I taped mock-up book covers to other books and set them strategically on the bookshelf above my Mac. My imagination went wild. I photoshopped a big V onto an imaginary building as my *reVirement* headquarters. I could *SEE* my desired destination as if it already existed.

I boldly set forth, intent on magnetizing the writing of my book onto my life's clear magnet. I became engulfed by an energetic *reVirement* flame. When I wasn't attending to clients' projects, I was hashing out early chapter drafts and research. I secretly envisioned a return Manhattan trip to meet with Ms. NewYorkPublisher to present my book proposal.

One day I needed to do some research for a graphics project, so I went to Denver's Tattered Cover Book Store. When finished with my research, I considered the competition for my *reVirement* book. I was curious to see what **tiredword** books were out there.

I asked two sales clerks where to find the **tiredword** section. I felt a little nervous, hoping another author hadn't embarked upon a close encounter of the V kind and written their own version of *reVirement*.

Oddly, both clerks shrugged their shoulders, uncertain where the **tiredword** books were. Apparently, there was very little out there—other than what investments would expand those nest eggs for those who had already found *IT*. Over the next couple of days, I visited a few more bookstores in Denver and found similar results.

I considered my findings disturbing. First off, there were few encouraging reads about the **tiredword** and, secondly, such books were sequestered to far back, dark and tired corners of bookstores.

A growing sense of gloom and unease dampened my enthusiasm. None of the **tiredword** books came close to the *bold* vision *reVirement* had ignited in me.

It wasn't long before remnants of my *Big 5-0* exhaustion around the **tiredword** returned. My thoughts raced with familiar phrases, *"Amy, why would you write a book that will just be doomed to the tired gloom of back shelves? Why are you returning to the* **tiredword** *after all that's happened? Haven't you banned that word from your inner kingdom?"*

My *verve* lost its luster, along with the *nerve* I needed to keep writing the book. Lulls of sinking thinking inspired more conversations with my friend Melm. Perhaps she could offer an insight toward a much-needed turnabout to get me back on track.

On a Saturday morning, Melm picked me up in her Ford Explorer so we could explore options as we ran errands. I was recovering from a sleepless night and had failed to combat some mental guerilla warfare that was trying to convince me that *reVirement* was delusional and I should chuck all my plans. I fastened my seat belt and launched into an **Amyrant**.

"Melm, why write a book that puts me smack-dab in the middle of the **tiredword** world? I want to move _away_ from the **tiredword**, not towards it. Nothing that's transpired since my *T-to-V* switch even relates to the **tiredword** anymore. My whole premise has changed directions. How can I keep associating with that old worn-out **tiredword**?!?"

In her usual manner, Melm replied, "What's the thinking, Amy?" I sighed, stretching against the seat back. My face scrunched as I realized I'd forgotten to think about my thinking. I turned my perspective around and brushed off my **tiredword** frustrations.

"You know, Melm, ever since clearing my magnet, I've been *SEEING* **MyStuff** from a whole new perspective. The direction I'm going in isn't even about the **tiredword** anymore."

I continued, "Everything that's happened since I turned fifty has been about changing directions—to turn about my life's second half. It's all about reinvention. I don't want to mention the **tiredword** ever again.

"But what do I *DO* now? It's as if the V is pointing me in an entirely new direction. I wonder if the *T-to-V* switch even matters anymore." I was on the verge of tears.

"Calm down, Chica!" Melm replied in her characteristic lightness. Then she lit up and blurted out a new idea. "Hey, Amy," she said, "maybe your book is about something bigger than *reVirement.*"

Without much thought, I considered this out loud. "Hmm," I mused, "too bad there isn't another *T-to-V* switch out there."

"Maybe there is, Amy. Think about what you're *DOING*." Melm's mental wheels were spinning now. *"Turn* about! *Vurn* about!"

I chuckled. "No ... *Vurn* sounds too much like *Burn* .... I think it needs to be a word that already exists."

I considered my *reVirement* rendezvous and pulled Murray's quote out of my wallet to search for a "*T*" letter that might switch to a "*V*" to describe my turnabout journey. While Melm drove and tossed out a word or two, I concentrated and reflected on my adventure to date. What message did I wish to share? My mind continued to pair words on my *T-to-V* switch hunt. What "*T*" could find its way into a "*V*"—and deliver a *JOLLI* new direction for my book's message?

"Amy," Melm said, "it's like your intentions are all about delivering a chance for reinvention." She paused and we looked at each other, hitting the same AHA simultaneously.

"InTentions!" we synchronized, *"...InVentions!"*

"That's it, Melm. All acts of initiative and creativity must begin with an *inTent* before one can *inVent*. There can be no *inVention* without an *inTention!* Yay, we just experienced another **vepiphany** (ve•pi•phan•y; V-inspired epiphany in a moment of sudden awareness)."

I couldn't stop gushing, "This is brilliant. It's exactly what my *reVirement* is all about!"

Melm pulled into my driveway and we high-fived each other. "That's awesome, Amy!" she exclaimed. "If you think about it, your book wouldn't be just for Boomers anymore. It's for anyone who wants to turn about and change directions."

A surge of excitement shivered up and down my arms, a sure sign I was on to something. I mentally reviewed the outlines and chapters I'd been writing. Sure enough, my *reVirement* journey so far confirmed that I was changing directions with an *inTent* to *inVent* personal revolution.

Even my **quantumesque** living theories held the collected momentum of an *inTent* to arrive at an **overIT** before any **nexIT** could turn towards a new *inVent*.

I leaned over and quickly hugged Melm goodbye. Then I blasted forward into revising chapters. This change of direction had delivered a flood of vitality, signaling that I was moving onto the right track.

Innerstate Speed Bumps

I moved steadfastly in the direction of my decision to expand my *reVirement* book and enhance its message via the *inTent* to *inVent*. Shifting once again into full-speed-ahead mode, I pulled onto my high way toward another revitalized **innerstate**.

But life has an interesting way of providing challenges just when the *old* arrives at a new *bold*. Two **innerstate** speed bumps tested my *inTent* to *inVent* my *reVirement* revolution.

Fifteen days after I discovered my second **vepiphany**, my Dad died of a heart attack.

Dad was the last of my immediate family; my sister had tragically died in 1999. Back then, Dad and I flew to Los Angeles to get **JuliesStuff**, which he stored in his basement and left untouched.

Every time we attempted to go through **JuliesStuff**, Dad's *fears* capsized all efforts in a puddle of *tears*. Dad had inherited his own knack of holding on to stuff from his mother, Beulah, our family's brilliant master stuff organizer.

Dad had rows of boxes from everyone else in our family—his **ParentsStuff** as well as a couple of boxes of my **MomsStuff** that he'd saved since her passing in 1973.

Upon Dad's sudden departure, I received <u>all</u> these boxes of **FamilyStuff**, some of which he'd held on to for more than half a century. Almost overnight I found myself promoted to an honorary magnate of my **AncestorsStuff**.

I had just spent weeks prior to Dad's death recovering from **stuffonia** and getting my **S.M.D.** degree as I developed sorting strategies for **MyStuff**. What were the uncanny odds that circumstances had delivered an immediate opportunity for me to practice my tactics on more challenging **FamilyStuff**?

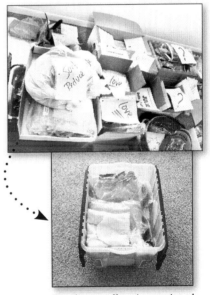

In some karmic way, it felt like my ancestors were supporting me from the other side, encouraging me to get even more clear about stuff. If I could make peace and get clear about **TheirStuff**, I would gain lifelong tenure in the field of **Stuffology**.

*Tough-on-stuff tactics continued to work on my **AncestorsStuff**.*

Unfortunately, losing the last member of my core family landed me in one of the worst *Not-OK Corrals* of all time. My emotional life's magnet had suddenly plunged into an invisible tub of **FamilyStuff** that had to be faced bit by bit. This task required the *inTention* of a hefty *inVention* if I were to forge onward in my *reVirement* commitment to *WRITE THE BOOK!*

As I tackled the task of sorting through my **FamilyStuff**, layers of stored and hidden grief resurfaced, practically paralyzing me. Living on my inside track became so overwhelming, I soon steered back onto the familiar outside track. I went after another *IT* ... and hit my second **innerstate** speed bump. I got a job.

During this painful adjustment in my life, a graphics dream *IT* job practically fell in my lap. Although I was juggling multiple freelance projects and hadn't been looking for a job, a colleague forwarded the description of the dream job I'd always wanted. I went for *IT*.

As the Creative Director for a government agency in charge of acres of colorful Colorado recreational lands, I combined my deep love of nature with my borderline psychotic passion for corporate branding.

I also hoped the regular schedule and paycheck would free up evenings and weekends for me to dive into my *reVirement* writing, which had taken a detour as I'd struggled to get clear about my **FamilyStuff**.

Alas, another layer of **JobStuff** would derail the completion of my book for the next three years. Besides the normal amount of **JobStuff** required for any new job, this particular job sent me into the depths of state government with its massive layers of **GovernmentStuff**. My life's magnet was soon brimming over once again.

A day did not go by without me thinking about the V and its path of turning about. The enthusiasm for my second *T-to-V* switch could not be quelled. With every challenge and bout of sinking thinking that cropped up I remembered; *"Amy, what's the thinking;* stalk *your* talk. *What is your* inTent? *This is what you will* inVent!"

I faced numerous **overITs** and **nexITs** during this time. There's nothing quite like the combo of grief and the government to throw one into the depths of challenge. I returned over and over to emotional *Not-OK Corrals* I thought I'd left behind.

I began to pioneer the last possible frontier available. I pulled within and dove full speed ahead into the **innerstate** of my innermost self.

I went to the core and faced key lessons at the very heart of my life, many of which I hadn't even known existed. I came face to face with what lurked below the surface of all **MyStuff**. On the other side, I received **soulace** the likes of which I'd never experienced before.

Needing an **Innervention**

It took the interruption of a self-imposed intervention to get to these core *issues* hidden within my *tissues*. I uncovered hidden gifts beneath **MyStuff** and my **FamilyStuff**. But, to find them, I needed an **innervention** (in•ner•ven•tion; intervening on the inside to get help). I needed it badly.

Once again, as soon as I decided to commit to my **innervention**, all manner of incidents occurred. Awareness and actions – multiple *SEEING* and *DOING* – came my way. Inspired teachers and guides arrived without consciously realizing I had asked for them.

Diving deep below the surface of **MyStuff** and my many *ITs,* I reached my own center point. I got to the *root* of all my *loot* and experienced another vital victory.

I went *in* to *win*.

Some of my oldest stories and patterns surrounding my first half of life completely changed directions during this **innervention**. I embarked on a *pass* through my *past* that led to an expanded understanding of my origins—and of the ill effects my lifelong *IT* search had always had on **MyStuff**, both inside and out.

Once again, my childhood offered metaphors that allowed me to undertake my needed **innervention**. Two childhood camping *tunes* helped *tune* me in and provided the right metaphor of encouragement I needed to refine my perspectives on my *in*-to-w*in* victory.

SUMMARY> My Second Vepiphany

◆ My *T-to-V* path expanded to include *inTent* to *inVent*.

◆ Dad-grief triggered speed bumps along the **nexIT**.

◆ Renovated answers arrived when going *in* to *win*

CHAPTER 15

Reviewing the RoughStuff

- Two Folk Tunes
- Melting the **Viceberg**
- Meeting *AsIF* Amy

Besides the creative, nonstop flurry of *DOING*, my early family life had brimmed over with travel adventures. My parents were avid nature buffs who were passionate about exploring and experiencing all that Colorado offered. Dad boasted his status as a second-generation native and told how he'd worked his way up the Boy Scout ranks: camping, fishing, hunting and hiking. His father, Byron, had done much of the same.

Mom had spent her childhood years growing up on a farm homesteaded by Scandinavian ancestors in northern Minnesota. She'd earned top rankings in 4-H, honing her substantial home-economic skills of home furnishing, sewing, cooking and canning. When Mom and Dad met at the downtown Denver YMCA in the late 1940s, their combined expertise and enthusiasm birthed an even stronger inclination for creativity and the great outdoors.

Among the *LoveIT* items saved from my **FamilyStuff** are handmade scrapbooks assembled by Mom with hand-painted covers by Dad. They hold priceless accounts of family explorations as well as clues for my midlife turning about.

Ahead of her time, Mom had excelled as a master scrapbooker and a quintessential family historian. I should also mention that, between her and Grandpa Byron's passion for photography, I am still going through about 4,000 color slides as part of my journey through my **FamilyStuff**!

Mom's scrapbooks with covers by Dad.

My parents infused Julie and me with their travel legacy; rustic road trips and colorful camping were integral to our childhoods. In 1963, when our Scoutie-outie was purchased, every weekend included some exploration into the Rocky Mountains. We traversed steep rocky passages, flew over dusty dips and picnicked in bright open meadows backed by thickets of dark evergreens.

One of the more joyful aspects of these travel adventures included my parents' love of music. A captivating repertoire of folk songs filled our evenings as we sang around campfires and roasted marshmallows. Singing 'round the campfire and having "Kumbaya" moments was much more than a cliché to the Thornton family. My parents' tunes became the uniting melodic threads that connected us when words failed. To this day, I can't hike a mountain trail or go on a road trip without humming many of their folksy stanzas.

As my **innervention** progressed around the mountains of my **InnerStuff**, two classic folk tunes came to epitomize the journey: "Goin' on a Bear Hunt"and "She'll be Comin' 'Round the Mountain".

The repeat-after-me song "Goin' on a Bear Hunt" went something like this: Julie and I assumed the "patty-cake" position, sitting across from each other, alternately clapping hands and tops-of-thighs. Then we reenacted a wildly imaginative invisible bear hunt.

The song took us through a long list of **obstackles** that had to be overcome with the encouraging banter, *"Can't go under IT, Can't go over IT ... Have to go through IT!"*

As a **metaphormorphosis** (met•a•phor•mor•pho•sis; a metaphor for a metamorphosis) this classic line repeatedly resurfaced as I faced the challenges of going beneath the surface to reveal my **InnerStuff**. As I forged through my **FamilyStuff** and **JobStuff**, I traveled my own invisible "bare-hunt," as I bared all that needed to be tackled.

In tandem with lively travel songs, our scouting trips on steep, mountain roads paralleled my own twists and turns along the trek through the dark sides of my interior uncharted lands.

As though traveling the circling topography of a mountain, 'round 'n' 'round I went to get to the other side, as illustrated by the classic folk tune "She'll Be Comin' 'Round the Mountain".

In this ballad, the lyrics repeat, "she'll be comin' round the mountain when she comes, when she comes ..." over and over again. On my internal roundabout adventure I trusted that I would eventually come full circle 'round my own mountains.

I had to dive beneath the surface, dismantling layers of myself to excavate the layers of my many *ITs*. As rough as this **InnerStuff** became, ultimately it also forced an undeniable truth to eventually emerge: No matter what *IT* I'd achieved during the first half of my life, I'd been unable to truly actualize an authentic sense of myself, a sensibility I call the *RealDeal* (noun combining *real* and *deal* for authenticity).

What I'd craved in all of my *ITs* was the unshakable self-love, appreciation and understanding of a *RealDeal* self, something I'd hoped to achieve in my never-ending *IT* searches. I'd craved an answer to the question *"Who am I really, and where can I find me?"*

Who existed as the genuine Amy-article apart from all the accumulated *ITs* I'd used to try to find and define me? In the same way I'd sorted through **MyStuff** to find my physical *LiveITs*, *LoveITs* and

LoseITs, I strove to sort through and identify my internal *LiveITs*, *LoveITs* and *LoseITs*.

One big *LoseIT* that had to go was an invisible mask I'd worn for years, hoping to convince myself and everyone else that I was always "sure" of myself.

This **sureface** (sure•face; the surface face of being sure) embodied the confident and successful image I wished to present to the world. My **sureface** hid the lurking unrest living below, in my depths.

When I looked under my **sureface**, I found a life spent *DOING* massive amounts of *ITs*, while I constantly hoped one day to be sure of all of *IT*. But instead, this effort had only separated myself from the *RealDeal* me. My misdirected and unskilled thinking was confusing the real me with my *ITs*. By age fifty, I didn't know who *I* was without all of my *DOING* or my *ITs*.

To cope with the loss of my *RealDeal* self, I turned to various vices over the years to ice over issues and cope with the inevitable pains of life. This led to the discovery of yet another mountain of **MyStuff**.

An upside-down, inner mountain of frozen **InnerStuff** lay within me. This invisible iceberg lurked just below the *surface* of my *sureface*. I named it my **viceberg** (vice•berg; an invisible iceberg of vices).

Melting the **Viceberg**

Through the years I'd turned to many vices in my attempts to ease my pain and shame. Such dependencies began innocently enough and worked for a while. As I continually turning to something out *there* to help make in *here* more okay, however, these *nice* things became a *vice*. After repetitive use, my vices became painfully addictive.

As my **viceberg** developed over the decades, it iced over the original pain at its core. Melting not only my **viceberg** but the frozen pain buried deep within layers would be rough. I couldn't go under *IT* or over *IT*.

I had to go through *IT* to finally discover who I really was.

Also daunting is the fact that what lies below the melting layers of an inner **viceberg** can often be triple the size of its visible surface. Many of my friends would be surprised to fully realize that I routinely showed the world just the tip of my frozen inner **viceberg**.

Although I'd spent decades in recovery to turn about my not-so-nice vices, at midlife I'd practiced plenty of other vices, such as overachieving and over-*DOING*. Thawing my **viceberg** ultimately revealed what was at the bottom of all my vices.

The path of the V offered a visual metaphor of a big floating V-iceberg that encouraged me to dive deep and get to what was underneath my **sureface** living. Only then could I discover transformational treasure beneath my **sureface** self.

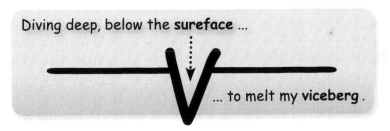

Diving deep, below the **sureface** ...

... to melt my **viceberg**.

I already knew I couldn't *DO* or *BE* anything *bold* before I could *SEE* the *old*. With the help of many friends, teachers and guides, I set out to traverse to the other side of this frozen mound of **InnerStuff**.

Although we'd never met in person, mentor Pia Melody helped me find the melting magic I would need for dismantling my **viceberg**. Her principles around the roots of addiction and its core symptoms provided the foundational impetus for me to go *in* to *win*. I put my own spin on her influential principles, but I would be remiss in not giving her substantial credit for her remarkable wisdom. One could say it was *via Pia* that I got to the core of my **viceberg**. I'm eternally **greatfull**. ~ Thanks, Pia!

To dive into the process of melting my **viceberg**, I passed through my past and considered my origins. Who was the mastermind behind my **sureface** and **viceberg**? I focused on my previous perspectives and considered them from a new **vhorizon**. Childhood dramas held the *clues* that would become *glues* in piecing together the *RealDeal* me. As Pia often says, "You have to get your history straight."

Meeting *AsIF* Amy

When and where had I veered from the original me to begin to create my **sureface**? This was the first question I needed to answer. Once again, Thornton family dynamics held more insights.

On the surface, our family resembled other typical Boomer families whose small brick homes lined our Denver suburb. I eventually came to know, however, that sizeable secrets lay hidden from view, festering beneath our family's confident **sureface** for many years.

Our family **dynomantics** (dy•no•man•tics; the dynamite antics of our family dynamics) had definitely started it all. And in order to cope with my family's **dynomantics**, I began to freeze layers of pain and shame, a habit that would contribute to years of inner unrest.

By getting to the *root* of my *loot,* I would gain a deeper understanding of the origins of **MyStuff** and my unique **viceberg**'s development. Attaining vital historical perspective was critical to my ability to piece together my history.

I eventually came to understand that my vices had evolved over the first half of my life in response to the **RoughStuff** I'd been so ill-equipped to navigate. Despite my best efforts I couldn't rise above the many struggles I faced. All too often, I found myself battling with deep inner self-doubt and dislike.

Looking back, I asked how my **sureface** mask had come to be in the first place. Almost as soon as I did, memories surfaced that helped me understand vital aspects of my **sureface** development.

Deep beneath my **sureface** self lived a part of me I call my *AsIF* (as•if; an alter ego of as-if acting) Amy. I'd grown up with a deep need to act *AsIF* I were sure of myself; *AsIF* I were sure of what I needed to *SEE, DO* and *BE*; *AsIF* I were allright (**O.P.T.** – alright with all).

My *AsIF* Amy emerged as the mastermind behind the departure from my *RealDeal* self, and she soon directed a host of decisions that determined my life's script. As I dug deep into my stories about growing up, I uncovered several turning points at which I'd moved away from my *RealDeal* self to give birth to *AsIF* Amy. My *AsIF* efforts had blinded me to the authentic self I had never fully embraced.

One of the instances that launched my *AsIF* life occurred in my fourth-grade reading class at Russell Elementary. As Mrs. Teacher handed out graded book reports, I sat waiting in anticipation of an A grade.

Prior to turning in my report, I'd spent hours at my Dad's wooden drafting table working on it. Enraptured by the process of creating a mini-book for my book report, I turned out quite a work of art for a nine-year-old, complete with a full-color cover and clipped photos. I'd been more passionate about making my report *look* like a *book* than writing a report on the novel, the real purpose of the assignment.

Mrs. Teacher soon handed me my multi-colored booklet. I lifted the cover to see an enormous red circle with a C- right in the middle of my first page. This was the first time in school that my artistic exuberance and creativity had been met with criticism, and this was also my first C grade. My young heart instantly sank, and a slow panic set in. I asked to go to the lavatory and hurried out of the classroom.

I will never forget how crushed I felt because of that C- grade. I shook and sobbed to such an extent, I remember feeling as if life as I knew it was over. This may seem overly dramatic, but from my nine-year-old perspective it made perfect sense. A bit of back story may help explain the pain and shame I felt in that moment.

The all-consuming goal in our home was to be right and good. I understood I was supposed to look good, do good and get everything right. From an early age, however, I also remember a lot of attention going to my sister when she started to get things wrong. Julie couldn't stay put and often refused to follow directions. Her bedroom resembled a tornado rescue site and once she snuck her pet, Mousie, into church, where she revealed it to our unnerved mom during the sermon.

In psychotherapy terms, Julie's role in the family was to be the rebel and scapegoat. This left for me the role of the perfect child, the good girl, the straight-A student. At some early point, I launched myself down a "good-right path" to make up for Julie's badness. Who knows if anything Julie did was really all that bad? I just remember her getting a lot of my parents' attention and attention implies a sense of importance.

The only way I knew how to get a share of such attention and to feel important was to become the opposite of Julie. By being as good as possible I, too, would be important. My entire value relied on being the opposite of bad.

Receiving a C grade meant I was average. It also cried out "unacceptable" in my child's mind. The minus meant I'd fallen below the middle — and was dangerously teetering on bad.

I still remember staring at my little face in the frosty, stainless-steel mirror of the girls' bathroom as tears poured down my face. My childhood sinking thinking sounded something like this: *"Oh no, Amy, what are you going to do now? Mom and Dad are going to be so* mad; *this is really* bad! *Julie gets the C's and D's; you are* supposed *to get A's. You can't ever get a C again; you have GOT to get A's. From now on, it's straight A's or else."*

I don't know what I thought my "or else" consequence might be, but the *emotion* behind it held the *motion* that defined my entire value as a human being. I never got a C in school again, and my frenzy to become "Straight-A Amy" fueled the **Amyzon** river I would ride through the first half of my life.

As I recalled this event, my heart filled with pain. In a matter of seconds, my nine-year-old self had made a lifelong decision that, at whatever cost, I _had_ to be a successful straight-A student, a **perfectionoughta** person who never caused my parents to worry, someone so sure of herself that it was clear to all that she had *IT* all figured out, *AsIF* she were okay.

This early decision, and others like it, would dictate a self-imposed script for the next forty years. It birthed my life's basic theme: Get an A in life ... get *IT* all right. And, if you don't ... at the very least, act *AsIF* you do and only let them see your **sureface**.

This guise of perfection set in motion my *IT* search. If I hadn't sought to "get" *IT* all right, I wouldn't have succumbed to the all-consuming need to "find" the right *IT* ... right?!?

Understanding the motivation behind my *AsIF* Amy became a key to **peacing** (peac•ing: the peace of piecing together) the pieces of my *IT* puzzle together. It also provided the basis for understanding the misguided sinking thinking that often separated me from my *RealDeal* self.

Some of my deeper *AsIF* repercussions occurred as I matured. During the spring of my sophomore year of high school, my mother started treatments for cancerous cells on her chest. In the mid-seventies, cancer was a scary word; the "C" word was off limits, at least in our family.

I spent school breaks, evenings and weekends helping Mom go to treatments and watching her slowly deteriorate. And yet, we all carried on the **sureface** act that she was getting better.

By the time we were singing Christmas carols at the end of that calendar year, Mom could barely breathe—and still we were convinced she was going to get better. It wasn't until I awoke from a dream two weeks before she died that I even suspected she might never recover.

Although my mom's death was a life-changing event that would shape my future, perhaps more impactful was the fact that I didn't have a clue how to deal with the feelings of grief, loss and confusion that followed. So I put on an even bigger and better **sureface** in order to make my missing mother proud.

When my mother died, my father collapsed, incoherent. My wild sister and I planned Mom's memorial and, within days, I took over making meals, doing laundry and supporting my father. I became his sturdy helpmate and confidant. At the time, I also worked two jobs and made straight A's, hoping to be voted prom queen and the most talented in my class. To cope with all my *AsIF* demands, I turned to hidden vices.

Dad went through his own identity crisis, leaving his job to take bartending classes and attend massage school. He remarried and created a thriving antique business. A year after his death, I learned that Dad had been gay, though he'd never openly acknowledged this fact. It deeply saddened me to think I could have celebrated with him his own midlife turnabout if he had only broken his own **sureface** code and embraced his authentic *RealDeal* self.

My sister left home at the age of 19 to become a hippie in the Haight-Ashbury neighborhood in San Francisco. Julie gave birth to a daughter and struggled for years with various vices that ended when she overdosed on methamphetamine at age 46, just four years prior to reaching her own *Big 5-0*. She was an exceptional woman who, I believe, never understood the depths of her own true beauty. ~ I love you, Julie!

Julie (left) with her daughter, Heather.

In looking back, I now understand that my family lived alternate identities and lives based on *DOING* without ever *BEING* real about whatever was really going on. None of us had the ability to embrace our *RealDeal* authenticity. There is no *lame blame* here; I'm simply telling the truth and getting my history straight, as Pia would say. My family's broken *RealDeal* code stretched back for generations, and I became determined to break it.

SUMMARY> Reviewing the RoughStuff

◆ Goin' 'round and 'round to melt my **InnerStuff**.

◆ Beneath my **sureface** lurked a frozen mountain of pain.

◆ I met *AsIF* Amy, the inventor of getting *IT* all right.

CHAPTER 16

Matter of Mattering

- I'm Not **MyStuff**
- Two Game Shows
- My Living Death

The act of storing my stories had become deeply embedded in everything I'd become. What was I *DOING* with them now that I knew they were old and had to go? These stories influenced my *inTent* to *inVent* and what I was to *BE* in my emerging new world. Were my stories really true? Were they really me? Who was I now that I'd met my *AsIF* Amy?

As I circled 'round 'n' 'round mountains of questions like these, I began to *SEE* the pretenses of my stories, including those that resided on the dark side of my **viceberg**. Searching through my history, I found a trail full of old patterns and habits that needed a turnabout in order for me to melt my frozen feelings. What were the real *issues* stored in my *tissues?*

A visit from Melm helped me get to the heart of the matter so I could begin to *SEE* the direct link between the physicality of **MyStuff** and the churning emotionality of my **InnerStuff**.

In the midst of tackling several more boxes of **FamilyStuff**, I hoped to consolidate my art studio. Boxes of my dad's **ArtStuff** needed to be sorted along with about three decades' worth of my own.

I began suffering from another case of **stuffonia** with some symptoms of art-**InCASEitis** while identifying my *LoveITs* and *LoseITs*. My art studio's wooden floors were buried under a profusion of plastic

tubs filled with many years' worth of art supplies. In one corner, a holding tank held dozens of pens, pencils and highlighters. I owned every color, size and style of writing utensil imaginable "in CASE" I needed it.

Melm arrived and sat with me on the floor among all the piles. Signs declaring *LiveIT! LoveIT!* and *LoseIT!* were strategically taped to three walls, but I couldn't seem to get my *piles* to the right *files*.

She thumbed through the deep bin of pens to pinpoint a diagnosis for my flare-up of art-**inCASEitis**. Suddenly, we locked gazes, and I could tell Melm was about to share a brilliant idea. She held up her hand with five fingers spread wide and suggested, "Keep only your five *LoveIT* pens from this bin."

I looked at her, aghast. You'd think Melm had asked me to pull the plug on a loved one's life support. I didn't know how completely attached I'd become to my art supplies until she asked me to part with them. In just this one category – drawing utensils – I had more subcategories than I *care* – no – *dare* to admit.

To compound my confusion, the unstuffing of my **ArtStuff** was occurring only months after I'd experienced my art **overIT**. I'd thought that eliminating **ArtStuff** would be a no-brainer.

Almost as soon as Melm asked for my five *LoveITs* from years of pen collecting, warm tears poured down my cheeks. An intensity of emotion fueled my justifications for why I needed hundreds of pens. I stared, transfixed, into the plastic tub of pens, confounded by the hurdle Melm's "command" required me to face.

Finally I burst into a fit of **overIT** frustration. "Melm," I cried, "don't ask me to do this! Why do I care so much about pens? Why can't I let these go? I can't imagine picking out just five!"

Melm's gaze remained steady. Softly but with clarity, she said, "AAAmy, it's OK. This is how you got your 'mattering'."

"Mattering? What do you mean? I've never heard that phrase before. What's the matter with me? I'm upset about this art-matter, Melm. I don't know what's the matter!"

"Amy, that's how you came to *matter* in your world—through your artistry and creativity. The more you had of *IT*, the more you mattered, right? Who *ARE YOU* without all of this?"

Melm spread her arms wide, as if casting a net over the room to sweep up all the piles of art supplies. "Amy, without your **ArtStuff**, who are you? That's what 'mattering' is all about!"

Her imagined flashlight of insight illuminated the dark room of my mental confusion. A deep awareness swept over me. "Gosh, you know, Melm, I don't really know. How can I be over fifty years into my life and not know that I matter without all of **MyStuff**?!?"

Melm looked deep into my eyes. With heart-piercing love and attention, she said, "Amy, you matter."

Tears came again, melting away some of my hidden frozen shame. She said it again, "Amy, you matter because you are here. You matter because you are YOU without any of **YourStuff**."

As emotion flowed, I mentally searched throughout my history. When had I ever heard this, felt this or known this from deep within? Never.

Without the template of **MyStuff** around me, I didn't know that I mattered ... and mattered deeply.

Where and when had I lost my authentic mattering? Had I lost it as an adult, when I'd entered the *IT* rat-race to get *IT* all right? Was it there before Mom died? Or before my fourth-grade decision to become Ms. **Perfectionoughta**? I went as far back as I could and couldn't ever remember feeling that I mattered just because I existed.

Melm's insight helped clear the *haze* around the *maze* of **ArtStuff** I found myself in. It seemed so simple now—so *right-in-front-of-me*. **MyStuff** was how I attempted to feel important, how I'd come to matter in my world. There it was at the bottom of **MyStuff**, the matter of mattering.

Had my need to matter fueled the searching scope of a false belief that some *IT* out-*there* would make my in-*here* matter? Was this where my *RealDeal* mattering had gotten lost in my *IT* shuffle?

After Melm left, I regrouped with my *Streams* journal, writing out how big a piece this understanding was to my perplexing *IT* puzzle. I could *SEE* what I'd been attempting to *DO* in order to *BE* important and matter.

Hoping to convince everyone else that I mattered, I'd sidestepped mattering to the one person who needed me most ... me.

Did I truly believe I could matter without **MyStuff**? Where and when had I gotten so caught up in running around my outside track, hoping to find my mattering? Masked in the rat-race of finding *IT*, had my whole *IT* search revolved around the matter of mattering?

In the past I'd thought that if only I could find *IT*, arrive at *IT*, achieve *IT*, grab hold of *IT*, study *IT*, access *IT*, get *IT* and – perhaps most importantly of all – figure *IT* out, my questions about what was missing would be solved. Suddenly, I was free to travel a new high way. If my **innerstate** could embrace that I mattered, I wouldn't have to spin around that *IT* rat-race trying to matter anymore.

Two Game Shows

As my **viceberg** slowly thawed, I realized this matter of mattering had put a whole new spin on my travels to the inside lane towards my *RealDeal* self. All along I'd been telling myself, *"Get real, Amy!"* With a great overarching clarity, the *reVirement deal* of turning about had gotten very, very *real*.

What did this statement really mean? *"Get real!"*

I'd heard that popular phrase so often growing up, I hardly took the time to *pause* to consider its *cause*. In a very direct way, it implored one to get to the truth. I asked myself if I were really telling my own truth. Was my *RealDeal* Amy hidden within the frozen layers of my **viceberg**?

'Round and 'round I went with this query, hearing the mantra: *"Will the REAL Amy please stand up?"*

Could it be a reprisal of *To Tell the Truth*, a popular game show from the 1960s? On this show, a celebrity panel attempted to select the authentic guest from the two actors in a lineup via a series of riveting questions. The imposters did their *AsIF* best to convince the panel that they were the genuine article.

My favorite line from the show came when the host asked, *"Will the REAL Jane Doe please stand up?"* I remember sitting on our family's couch with Julie as we tried to outguess the celebrity panel – and each other – in a race to identify the *RealDeal* person.

As I ventured through the inner layer of my **viceberg**, my *inTent* became to *inVent* genuine authenticity and stop all previous impersonations. I compelled myself to tell the truth, asking my *RealDeal* self to please stand up. No more imposters could be allowed if I were going to get real. No more *IT* deals were needed in order for me to matter.

Another classic television show that helped me *SEE* that I'd been looking for my *RealDeal* in the wrong places was the original *Let's Make a Deal*, where kooky contestants spun deals with host Monty Hall. The grand finale of the show always included the top two contestants choosing one of three big doors on stage. Prizes varied, but the question remained: Would the Cadillac convertible stuffed with prizes or a trip to Tahiti be behind door number one, two or three? When a loser chose the boobie-prize door, it opened to the clanging sound of bells and antics such as a donkey pulling hay on a cart that had the gigantic word "ZONK!" emblazoned on its side.

When my *AsIF* Amy took over running my Amy show, I "made a deal", so to speak, distancing myself from my original truth in exchange for less pain. For too long I hid my true self secretly behind some invisible *IT* door. Was *IT* behind number one-*IT*, two-*IT* or three-*IT*? Though I searched for an ultimate *IT* prize, no matter which *IT* door I chose – "ZONK!" – my *IT* mattering was never really there.

My Living Death

I had completely run out of *ITs*. Now that my *inTent* was to *inVent* a genuine *RealDeal* Amy, I had to stop making all *IT* deals and get real. But who would be left after the frozen layers of my **viceberg** melted? Who would I be without any *IT* to hold on to?

Soon I found my own breaking point; I ran out of options and ideas. I reached the end of my line of questioning and my imposters were exposed, along with all of the *IT* deals I'd made. I was scared. Where was the *RealDeal* me? Who was she? Where was she? How could I find her?

I'd hit the ultimate **overIT** of all *ITs*, the bull's eye in the center of my *IT* target without me in *IT*. I needed some *RealDeal* answers; answers I didn't have.

Although I walked around physically alive and well, I was dying on the inside. Who was I without **MyStuff** or any other *IT?* Emotionally, mentally and even spiritually, I'd always relied too much on having some outside *IT* to *hit*.

And so I reached another end of life as I knew it. Like a snake, I shed my last *IT* skin and prepared to go *in* to *win*. But to win what?

Although I have now blended all that's happened in recent years into a capsule for this story, it's important to note that it took over half a decade for me to thaw my **viceberg**. And I'm still finding a few hidden layers that I missed the first time around. I'd always been the queen of the quick-*fix*, but this was a bold new *mix*. In order to get through it, I had to travel through a very painful *sore* and get to my *core*.

I discovered courage previously unknown. In deep moments of ache, I felt devastatingly alone. At such times I reached out, holding my own hand, and fought to redirect old thinking by assuring myself, *"Amy, you can get through this, you can* DO *this. I'm here; I've always been here."*

I cried tears worthy of a big thaw and released an invisible mountain *range* of *rage*, reminding myself that the size of my **viceberg** was related to the depth of tears that needed to be shed.

And I wasn't alone. Others had gone before me. I'd reached out to Pia, Melm, a few therapists and other fearless travelers who'd trudged through their own inner frontiers to get to their healing truths. People encouraged and supported me with unparalleled hope in times of my deepest darkness.

There were times I awakened with stabbing pains in my chest strong enough to take my breath away. My newfound insights had helped me understand why I'd spent years running from *IT* to *IT* in a land filled with *ITs*. With the melting of my **viceberg**, however, I also learned that some of the layers of pain and shame it harbored weren't even mine.

During the first half of my life I'd soaked up others' torments, including generational distress passed on down the line. This "carried-shame and pain" explained some of the depths I now had to visit.

Paradoxically, not only was I melting frozen pain, but I was also going through real-time boxes of **FamilyStuff** given to me after my dad's death. I felt ancestors encouraging me to pass along the karmic-baton of pain and shame they'd never resolved. *Years* of *tears* and *fears* washed through me as I carried the baton over my new V-victory line.

More than a few times I tried to pull onto the outside *IT* track, reaching for anything and everything to help me avoid so many intense feelings. In *lame blame*, I looked to others – and to outside conditions – for causes and effects. Even though these played a part in the game, I understood that no one else carried my shame and pain. It was mine to feel and heal now. The *issues* I'd stored in my *tissues* had risen up into my *BEING*. All I could *DO* was to die off—die off the *old* with faith that I'd soon find a new *bold*.

The Opposites Game reminded me that I often had to do the opposite of what I'd done before. Rather than rely on my powerful *DOING* résumé to get through intense feelings, in the midst of my big meltdown I had to focus instead on *BEING* with all of it, on allowing it out to just *BE*.

Like a huge sponge that had soaked up years of pain, blame and shame, I felt wrung out from the inside out. I was dying to my previous *AsIF* self. There were times I wondered if I ever would get to the other side of this dark mountain of my own living death.

Then again, I had been there before.

SUMMARY > **Matter of Mattering**

◆ I mattered *as* I *was*, without all of **MyStuff**.

◆ Would the *RealDeal* Amy please stand up?

◆ It was a time to die while still alive

·CHAPTER 17·

Getting My Enoughness

- *Addiction* to *Addition*
- Breaking my **Theremometer**
- Falling in Love

In 1979, after graduating from college with my Bachelor of Fine Arts degree, I traveled throughout Europe to explore the art I'd studied for four years in art history classes. At least that was my *AsIF* **sureface** motive for my European escapade. Under that intention hid a desperate attempt to resolve my dark, secret vices that had begun to spiral out of control.

I visited almost every main European highlight, vowing to myself that in the **nexIT** country I encountered, I would get *IT* together and stop my uncontrollable and secret binges. After years of "easing the pain", my vices had turned on me and were not so nice anymore. I'd hoped to turn them around with only a backpack and a $15-a-day budget. Surely the simplicity of this plan would lead me to face my inner demons. Alas, I failed miserably.

At the end of my travels, I reached a life-changing moment of choosing whether to live or die. It was December 12, 1979 in London, England when I hit the biggest **overIT** of my twenty-three years of life. Around two o'clock in the morning, I stood shivering under the Albert Bridge in Chelsea.

My best thinking in that moment urged me to jump into the River Thames and end it all. I didn't know that my inability to *cope* with my *core* pain and shame was festering at the foundation of my addictions. Using a *vice* to make *nice* my pain, I'd contracted a serious dis-ease.

Did other outwardly *AsIF* people entertain secret compulsions like mine? I'd never met anyone who'd done the things I'd done. I considered myself unique and alone in my misery and probably insane. I'd exhausted all my resources while *crying* and *trying* to pry my way out.

Under the white, twinkling lights of that bridge, I made a desperate plea for help. I cried to be led from darkness to light, from death to life. I stumbled back to my freezing flat and prayed to an indefinable greater power to deliver me. The next day, my life changed forever. I embraced my surrender and all manner of coincidence led me to the recovery process. Eventually I would live free of my life-threatening addictions.

Smack-dab in midlife, however, I realized I'd survived a living death from which I daily continued to recover. I made a new admission of powerlessness. And I reached the end of my *IT*-focused life.

While my more harmful addictions had subsided during thirty-plus years in recovery, I never understood the need to also melt my **viceberg** in order to get to the root of those vices. Instead, I turned towards more socially acceptable *addictions* I call *additions*.

Over-achieving, over-succeeding and over-thinking – not to mention over-stuffing – are a few of these additions and they are symptoms of an over-*DOING* life. Instead of living life, I became the cliché of a human *DOING* rather than a *RealDeal* human *BEING*.

My **Amyzon** motto ran like this: *"There is no enough that is ever enough and no over that can be overdone."* Luckily, melting my **viceberg** and discovering my inherent mattering started a series of rebirths that forced me to rethink this approach. It also led me to find my missing sense of *BEING* enough just because I was.

The tenacious mental grasp of my *IT* on my psyche had been pried loose. By the time I stared into my empty *IT* target, I could *SEE* that my "overs" – however nice they'd appeared to the outside world – had created additional layers of vices inside me.

Recovery gave me a template and a visceral, time-tested approach I could trust. I knew if I kept moving towards my *inTent* to *inVent* a *RealDeal* self, answers would arrive. I filled my empty *IT* target with me in the middle, trusting my **innervention** would work. Then, more great news arrived.

With a series of transformative steps, my authentic self pivoted into place. The next three chapters explore some of these pivotal practices in more detail. Like recovery, my practice required an insight turned into action that was then done, over and over, until it became a forged river that ran through me. Today, I use these practices to *live* my *life* as the *RealDeal* Amy.

The first pivotal practice involved getting my enoughness. This meant not only finding but embodying the conviction that I was enough through and through, from the inside out, without any outer *IT* to enhance me. I discovered that I'd previously carved out what a therapist might call "outer-esteem" instead of self-esteem. For me this translated into *IT*-esteem – turning to some outside *IT* in order to make sure I felt good and "enough" on the inside.

Getting my enoughness didn't happen in one clear shot; in fact, I'm still working on it. But the first thing I had to *DO* was to understand how I measured myself.

Breaking My **Theremometer**

This *JOLLI* **Thornism** sounds like thermometer, but it contains an extra "e". Unlike a thermometer that takes the body's internal temperature, my **theremometer** (there•mom•eter; an inner gauge determining inner-esteem measured by something "out there") was unique. It regulated my inner esteem and value based on the constantly fluctuating influences of outside people, places and things.

In *IT* terms, the false premise of using any *IT* on the outside to make my insides matter became banned from my inner kingdom. By depending on a host of "thems" and "theres" throughout my life to fill my inner self-esteem tank, I'd never found a way to fill it with my own self-esteem. It constantly ran empty and, as a result, I never felt like I was enough.

Baffled by decades of debilitating bouts of doubt, I'd become so convinced by my wavering internal temperatures of "not enough" that I rarely felt a sense of being very *OK*.

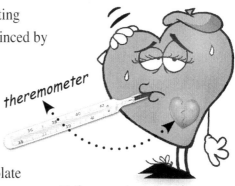

theremometer

My theremometer — *measuring my enoughness through people and things "out there".*

A keen example: When Mr. Hotartist made the comment about Mr. Bunny's quality of chocolate and I spiraled into a confusing and bewildering state of mind. The heat on my **theremometer** rose to an all-time high. The self-defeating story that I started to make up after that dinner incident shot straight to my inner core. Without a sense of my own enoughness, independent of anything on the outside, I landed in another *Not-OK Corral*. Never having experienced the anchor of my own enoughness from within, I had no ammunition that might help me dispute my dueling Brain Bandits.

In the past, I'd always lacked the unshakable conviction that I had value and worth, no matter what happens on the outside. Unable to trust myself, I was often thrown into a downward shame spiral of self-condemnation. Finally, I began to realize that no amount of thinking about thinking could fix this until I'd gone *in* to *win* and begun turning myself inside out.

Now I understood what my inner enemies had long been trying to hide: the pain and shame buried within my **viceberg**, and the need for a big defrost.

A lifelong issue of being dependent on outside people, places and things had made me question my sanity more than once. The very movable nature of everything outside of myself was just that ... movable. *All the time*. Everything on the outside was a moving target. This put my inner value in a vicarious state of teetering vulnerability. *All the time*.

In the race around my outside *IT* track, I'd lived in a perpetual state of changing and moving. Hence, there was no possible way I could ever arrive at the unshakable inner value and mattering that I didn't even know I craved.

Without realizing it, I'd created an internal underworld of spinning exhaustion as one after another *IT* (e.g., job-*IT*, boyfriend-*IT*, success-*IT*) failed to supply the much-desired enough-of-*IT* factor. Breaking my **theremometer** became essential to my ongoing abilities to know my value from the inside out.

How had I missed this for fifty years? Like my matter of mattering, just knowing about this was life changing. When I turned to people, places and things outside myself in order to feel that I mattered, I turned from my authentic essence of *BEING* enough all on my own, *AsIS* (as•is; being with whatever is, "as is").

Being okay in the *middle* of any *muddle* with myself as I was … *AsIS* … meant putting my *AsIF* Amy out of a job. My new *AsIS* Amy also had to let Ms. **Perfectionoughta** rest in peace. Only then could I recognize my enoughness for *BEING* who I was, as I was … *AsIS*.

This understanding granted me even more inner freedom. My living death cleared my inner magnet of stored *issues* in my *tissues* and my *inTent* continued to lead to the next pivotal steps I needed to take in order to *inVent* the *RealDeal* me.

Simply *SEEING* this was enough to start the pivoting shift towards *DOING* something about it. Once begun, a series of consequential **nexITs** fell into place. The timing of healing can be remarkable like that. When one insight for *RealDealness* shows up, there's room for the next one to fall into place.

Falling in Love

Recognizing my enoughness gave me new legs to stand on as I continued ahead into uncharted inner frontiers. I took baby steps at first but, in time, began to find the unshakable place of my own enoughness from deep inside my *AsIS* self. Ms. **Imperfectionoughta** (im•per•fec•tion•ought•a; ought to be imperfect) is imperfectly practicing to this day. I now consider this practice to be akin to an art form; feeling enough while *BEING* perfectly imperfect ... *AsIS*.

While trying out my new enoughness legs, I went for a walk around Denver's Washington Park with another one of my friends, Sara. I was anxious to tell her about my **theremometer** theories.

We started our walk with the usual casual conversation. Sara asked me how it was going with the guy I'd just met on Match.com. I made a joke that became the impetus for one of the biggest discoveries along my *reVirement* journey.

"You know, Sara," I said, "I'm not sure what's up with me. The last few guys I met were nice enough, but something lacked. I think it has to do with me. Maybe I need to start up my own internet dating site called MeMatch.com. Until my *RealDeal* self matches up with me, I don't think I'll find my love match."

Sara laughed. She'd been married for years and we'd shared a lot about relationship ups and downs. Then Sara made a suggestion that rocked my world. She said rather off-handedly, "Amy, until you fall madly in love with yourself, I doubt you're going to fall in love with anyone else." I smiled, nodding in agreement as I let her words sink in.

Suddenly I was *SEEING* this idea from a deeper perspective. Like most Boomers, I knew about self-love. I'd read about it and talked about it for years. I did "mirror-work," staring into my own eyes to tell myself "I love you, Amy." In my mind, I knew all about it. But after living through the death of my *IT*-focused life, I realized that previous efforts to love myself had relied on an *IT* factor. I possessed deeply ingrained *IT* requirements for loving and being worthy of love.

My *talk* of self-love hadn't matched my *walk* of it. I found myself asking *what does RealDeal love feel like? What is it and where do I get some of it?* Previously I'd looked outside to find it. In a process of *IT* elimination I now found no other option: I knew, once again, that I had to dive *in* to *win*.

The timing of Sara's comment seemed like divine order. It was one of those moments when someone says something in just the right way, with a new word or two that allows the insight to plummet straight to your soul. ~ Thanks, Sara!

The backdrop of my revised mattering template made it clear that the *AsIF* Amy had never truly loved herself just *AsIS*. With my **viceberg** now thawed, a new "heart magnet" seemed to open up for some self-love to finally stick to it. As my journey unfolded, the V led me to greater heights around love — both for myself and others. I set out to *DO* just what Sara had suggested: fall madly in love with myself.

This wasn't a narcissistic infatuation type of self-love. And, based on the newly acquired enoughness of my *AsIS* self, I no longer needed to look for love in the rise and fall of some outer **theremometer**. This wasn't about "getting" love from others. It was about discovering a newly generated love from the inside out.

This was a new kind of love, an *AsIS* kind of love. In the inside lane, my *AsIS* Amy was putting a reinvented spin on an age-old secret that had waited to be tapped. Unconditional *AsIS* love is the only *RealDeal* love there is.

The more I valued myself, the less dependent I became on my additions and *DOING*. And the more I outsmarted my Brain Bandits and diffused bouts of internal guerilla warfare, the more self-love swept in from deep within.

As I detached from the outside world as a place to shop for my inside mattering, I rendezvoused with a new me, a solid *gold* one that didn't have to be *sold* or *old* ... or even *bold*. I found an everlasting love deep within the *hearth* of my *heart,* one that celebrated exactly who I am — *AsIS*.

The gateway for a revitalized life swung open even wider from the inside out. And, with predictable timing, another pivotal step evolved.

◆ One last *IT* search uncovered the *root* of my *loot*.

· C H A P T E R 1 8 ·

ON NO Switcheroo

- Amytoo Lunch Story
- *Mystery* of **MyStory**
- Knowing My NOs

Inspired by my newfound trajectory towards getting my enoughness from within, I started to embrace my *AsIS* loving abilities. With the help of my long-time friend Amytoo, I arrived at the next step, which required a one-eighty turnabout.

I anticipated eating lunch at a favorite café with Amytoo. As a fellow member of the **Amyzon** club, she shared a few of my *AsIF* Amy characteristics. I looked forward to giving her a *reVirement* update with details about my *AsIS* discoveries.

Prior to lunch, we participated in a group discussion with a circle of friends. We sympathized as a friend named Sharon described a troubling situation at her job. She went into great detail about her boss and his knack for giving her more work than she could deliver.

"He's such a jerk. He won't let up on me. He doesn't care about us. He's a bad boss ...." A *lame-blame* game had kept Sharon busy for days. We nodded our heads in empathy. I was all too familiar with my own inability to set limits at jobs and say "no" to unrealistic work demands. I, too, had "blamed the boss" instead of looking within for self-direction.

Amytoo hadn't confirmed that she was still up for lunch. In hopes of not interrupting Sharon's sharing, I dug into my purse for a Sharpie and tore off a deposit slip from my checkbook. I wrote "Lunch?" on it, folded the note, tucked it under the pen's clip and passed it to Amytoo.

She jotted her reply and passed it back. Disappointment hit when I read Amytoo's *NO* in BIG capital letters. Staring at Amytoo's *NO* message, I dove into sinking thinking. Some quick-drawing Brain Bandits jumped at the opening and started to make up a story as to why Amytoo changed her mind about having lunch.

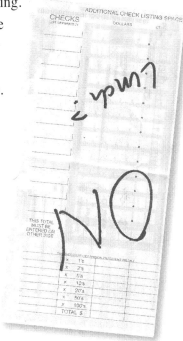

1. *Amytoo must be tired of me and my ideas.*

2. *She probably doesn't want to hear about my* reVirement *anymore.*

3. *She must need a break from me and doesn't want to have lunch with me!*

With no real evidence for any of these thoughts, my sinking thinking responded with an old default. Amytoo had always been one of my biggest cheerleaders. That's how clever sinking thinking can be. Because of my own insecurities, I'd immediately come up with a story based on myself not being enough.

How fascinating to *SEE* how quickly a *NO* had lowered my self-esteem temperature. As I realized I was using my **theremometer** to gauge my feelings on the inside based on what was happening outside, clarity started to arrive. Soon I sighed in relief as I redirected my thinking, reassuring myself.

"Amy ... Amytoo can say NO and change lunch plans. Pay attention; are you getting your **enoughness** *based on outside things and others? Remember, EVERYTHING outside of YOU is a moving target!"*

Calming myself with the Opposites Game, I started to *stalk* my *talk* and applied some quick mental militia to turn about my thinking.

1. *Amytoo must be <u>thrilled for</u> me and my ideas.*

2. *She probably <u>does</u> want to hear about my* reVirement.

3. *She must <u>not</u> need a break from me and <u>does</u> want to have lunch with me!*

This happened in a matter of seconds; no one in the room knew I'd just turned around a quick bout of sinking thinking. Even though I felt disappointed about not lunching with Amytoo, I felt the real emotion without adding any unnecessary **traumadrama** (trau•ma•dra•ma; additional trauma added to a drama). Amytoo's *NO* didn't have to be about me. It could just be a *NO*.

The group's discussion ended and we pulled on jackets to leave.

I did my best to also pull on my **sureface** "it's-OK face". I hoped to convince Amytoo I wasn't disappointed in her lunch cancelation. But then Amytoo came bounding over to me with a big smile. In her lovable way, she said, "Hey, Amers, do you wanna drive to lunch together?"

I scrunched up my nose and flashed her a curious glance. "What?" I said. "I thought you couldn't go." I reached for the note tucked into my pocket, pulling it out to show her the big *NO*.

Amytoo burst out laughing and grabbed the note from me. Stifling her giggles, she held the note up *right-in-front-of-my-nose* and, in slow motion, turned the note clockwise, revealing an upside-down, 180-degree **switcheroo** (switch•e•roo; switch in awareness, inspired by Amytoo).

"Amy!" she revealed, "I said we were *ON!*"

I grabbed the note and did another 180-degree turn. Undeniable. In full turnabout fashion, I'd turned her *ON* into a *NO*. We hugged, rushed out to VIDA and drove to our favorite restaurant, Café Sol.

Mystery of **MyStory**

I continued to laugh on the drive over, telling Amytoo how she'd turned me upside down with her *ON NO* **switcheroo.** It was fascinating how quickly I'd made up a story about her *NO*. In a flash, my thoughts had turned to feelings about not being enough. Once again, the power of what I told myself came into spotlight perspective.

How many of my old stories did I have upside down? How often had I made up incorrect stories that were followed by a whole repertoire of feelings based on those stories? How many times had I launched a *lame-blame* game based simply on a story I'd made up?

As we ordered our favorite, baked potatoes topped with avocado, we continued our lively discussion. It was **amyazing** to *SEE* what had transpired. I remembered a favorite phrase and shared it with Amytoo. "Gosh, I forgot to *check-out-the-data,*" I exclaimed. The *ON NO* **switcheroo** had reminded me to check if my story's data is true before I turn myself upside down through an upside-down story!

Another AHA hit. Because I failed to *check-out-the-data* and ask the truth about a simple situation, I'd entertained a host of negative feelings with the potential to send me spinning down a sinking thinking spiral.

How many of my life's stories spun like this? With striking clarity, I could *SEE* how often a sense of mystery filled many stories I'd made up. And, like **MyStuff**, I had so many stories they were worthy of their own word: **MyStory** (my•sto•ry; the story[ies] I'm making up).

The *mystery* around *MyStory* soon unfolded. Over and over again, I'd failed to confirm the truth in a story I was making up. This had created a *RealDeal* tactic that was brilliant: *check-out-the-data!* How helpful this would be in unfolding more of the *mysteries* of *MyStories*.

Amytoo and I expanded our conversation to consider another aspect of the *ON NO* **switcheroo**. There existed an interesting irony in the power of *NO*. When I received Amytoo's *NO*, it sent me *in* to *win* and turn my thinking around. In turn, I landed right side up by *stalking* my *talking* and allowing Amytoo to have her *NO*. In a way, this also led me to find my own sense of being *ON*.

Her *NO* forced me to find my own *ON* from within. We wondered if Sharon from the group would feel more *ON* within herself if she could tell her boss *NO*.

Our waitress plopped two steaming plates on the table of our cozy booth. However, instead of the dollops of avocado we'd ordered, mounds

Amytoo and I celebrating our January birthdays with our favorite lunch.

of sour cream were piled on top of our potatoes. Without hesitation, I blurted out, "Oh, *NO, NO*, please ... these need avocado on top, not sour cream." Without any lapse in time, I'd expressed my *NO* emphatically. I smiled, noting how much easier it was to express my *NO* to sour cream than to extra work.

Within minutes our lunch was returned to our table re-plopped with avocado and our taste buds were soon delectably happy. After downing her first bite, Amytoo grinned and exclaimed, "Right *ON,* Amy!"

When she said that, I did a double take. In light of our new **switcheroo** it was now clear that in order to be right *ON* I had to know my *NO.* This understanding provided yet another key to *BEING ON.* In the same way I'd separated my *LiveITs* and *LoveITs* from all of my *LoseITs,* the contrast of knowing my *NOs* would guide me to my *ONs.* I couldn't have seen this without you, my friend. ~ Thanks, Amytoo!

Knowing My *NOs*

After Amytoo and I parted ways, I reviewed how historically linked the word *NO* was to my enoughness and sense of mattering. I could *SEE* a direct link to why I sometimes had difficulty saying *NO.* Without my own sufficient level of enoughness, I'd not only feared others' reactions to my *NOs,* I'd made up untrue stories when faced with others' *NOs.*

I'd elevated people pleasing to an art form in order to avoid *NOs.* While consistently reaching outside of me in order to be okay, I couldn't possibly get to know my own *NOs,* let alone openly express them.

The repercussions of getting my enoughness grew. As long as my **theremometer** gauged my level of being okay based on my ability to never say *NO*, I would never truly feel *ON*. A *new now* was emerging from knowing my *NOs* as I came to understand how they linked to *BEING* right *ON!*

I felt fortitude rising within me as the old me was once again turning upside down. As I gained more enoughness, my confidence increased and my ability to say *NO* began to empower my *inTent* to *inVent* my *RealDeal* authenticity.

Sara would be happy to know these pivotal steps became vital to my ability to fall madly in love with myself. Not only were my *NOs* keeping me *ON* my path, but someone else's *NO* could no longer detour me.

Almost immediately, real life showed up with a test run. After my lunch with Amytoo, I ran a couple of errands around Denver.

I dashed into the Cherry Creek Mall in hopes of exchanging a pair of sunglass frames that didn't fit correctly. After I explained my reasons for returning the glasses, the salesclerk replied curtly, "I'm sorry, but *NO*, we can't do anything. It's our store policy."

I was not going to take *NO* for her answer and progressively offered up more reasons why I should be able to exchange the sunglasses for a more comfortable pair. The clerk delivered her same response over and over, "*NO*, I'm sorry, but we can't do anything. It's store policy." By the fourth or fifth store-policy reply, I figured she wouldn't budge.

I couldn't remember a time when someone was so unwavering in their *NO* as this salesclerk. I left the store, angry and frustrated. Immediately I launched into a mental *lame-blame* game towards that dang store policy and the clerk delivering it. I drove to my next errand, fuming. My *lame-blame* game and its ensuing **traumadrama** blocked any insights that could have come my way.

I scurried into the second store and scuffled into the long return line at the Customer Service desk. Irritated and still entertaining myself with a *lame-blame* game, I began to *pause* my *cause* and look around, taking in my surroundings.

Suddenly my eyes landed on a three-paneled sign above the return desk. The main sign's headline read STORE'S RETURN POLICY.

Clear bullet points detailed the exact requirements of returning items to the store. Clearly indented under "NOT ACCEPTABLE RETURNS" was a complete list of the store's *NOs*.

> • *NO* item can be returned after 30 days.
>
> • *NO* item can be returned if opened.
>
> • *NO* item can be returned without a receipt.
>
> • *NO* item can be returned if damaged and used.
>
> • *NO* item can be accepted if washed or faded.
>
> • *NO* item can be returned without original tags.
>
> • *NO* item can be returned for cash – credit only.

The *NO* list went *ON* and *ON*. In a flash, another AHA arrived: *"Amy, this store has better policies for returns than you have in store for your life! How could you be in your fifties and not* really *know your own policies? What are your personal policies of NOs that will keep you ON?!? Here you go: an opportunity to know your NOs!"*

I reviewed the previous errand, when the eyeglass sales clerk held her *NO* ground. Instantly, my *lame blame* disappeared. She'd given me a huge gift by demonstrating for me something I'd struggled to understand for much of the first half of my life—how to be okay with saying *NO*.

Never had I taken stock to come up with a clear idea of my own personal policies that would help me know my *NOs*. The antics of my *AsIF* Amy, acting in her role of Ms. **Perfectionoughta**, had required the agreeable script of a yes-gal. Without the essential foundation of getting my enoughness from within, I'd never clearly delineated my limits and needs for safeguarding the authentic value of my own self-love. But that was then. I reached for a *new now*.

During the next several weeks of *DOING*, I outlined some of my own personal policies. My list provided another set of guidelines to help me *SEE, DO* and *BE* my *LoveITs* and *LiveITs*—only now my *LoveITs* and *LiveITs* came from the inside out. How many **overITs** and **nexITs** might I have eliminated if I'd known my *NOs* with respect to *BEING ON?*

Here are a few examples from my growing personal policy list:

- *NO* **amyzonian** adventures without a 3-day hold.
- *NO* purchase over $100 without sleeping on it.
- *NO* new projects that take more than 2-3 hours without a day to consider implications.
- *NO* multitasking with the vegetable steamer cooking without using a timer.
- *NO* unattended candles left burning in remote rooms.
- *NO* new commitments without checking in with myself and considering how I truly feel.
- *NO* eating lousy things just to please someone else.
- *NO* having a bunch of feelings about untrue data!

The list continues to expand, *ON* and *ON*, with constant refinement as my *RealDeal* alignment unfolds.

This mystery was being zapped out of **MyStory** because I could now *SEE* the years of pain that might have been avoided if I'd only been clear about my personal policies and known my *NOs* from the beginning.

Voilá! Another pivotal practice essential to my reinvention would appear next. Complemented by my ability to know my *NOs* and my personal policies, I soon uncovered even more hidden truths.

◆ Upside-down thinking required *checking-out-the-data*.

◆ The *JOLLI mysteries* of **MyStories** unravelled.

◆ Right-*ON* personal policies helped me celebrate *NO*

CHAPTER 19

Selling or Telling?

- Rise 'n' Shine!
- *Delay* in *Relay*
- *Real-for-Me*

The previous practices combined to create a new freedom within me. An internal renovation and reinvention were bringing all the parts of myself into an **Amyalgamation** (am•y•al•ga•ma•tion; amalgamation of Amy, uniting of all parts). This one great word aptly described all that had come together ... and would lead me to my next pivotal breakthrough.

 amalgamation the action, process or result of combining or uniting a series of items.

This next shifting tactic seemed classically simple at first glance. But as I dove deeper into its meaning and considered it with regard to the sequential powers of my previous practices, a new reality was birthed from the inside out. A greater me united with my *AsIS* self from within, exactly what my *inTent* to *inVent* was all about.

With even more internal investigations, I uncovered the historical **Amy-intel** I needed to continue my bold journey. This next piece to my *RealDeal* puzzle fell into place when I got clear about what I was *selling* or *telling*, and uncovered a huge clue to my previous *ailings* and *failings*.

Living an *AsIF* life with my **sureface** mask fully in place, I'd been *telling* a story that wasn't always true and, because of this, *selling* myself short. I now wanted to get **MyStory** straight.

For decades I'd heard the classic phrase "To thine own self be true" but, honestly, I said the words *AsIF* I knew them to be true. After the thaw of the dense outer layers of my **viceberg**, I wondered how much of my truth had been determined by my *AsIF* and **sureface** selves? I continued to grow and ... slowly ... the *RealDeal* Amy eventually stood up.

As I deciphered the true from false, I re-mind-ed myself, *"Amy, you've got to MINE your MIND!"*

To find *"mine own true self"*, I turned back to the power of words and thought more about my thinking. Another *pass* through my *past* led to more revealing clues.

How had I learned the art of *selling* my truth vs. *telling* my truth? How had I arrived at my fifth decade and not really known my truth? When had I learned to disconnect from knowing what was true for me?

Somehow my true feelings had gotten lost in the shuffle of acting *AsIF* I were sure of myself. Because I was unsure of how I truly felt about many things, often simple decisions became very difficult. I had no clear idea what I really wanted.

A lineup of questions begged for answers, starting with discovering the contributing factors to my *selling* or *telling*. When was I taught not to tell the truth?

In the world according to Mom and Dad, weekends involved rising and shining before the crack of dawn to head up to the hills, otherwise known here in Colorado as the Rocky Mountains.

We'd scramble around, loading up Scoutie-outie, and soon head out in the dark. My parents loved arriving at the top of some mountain pass leading to an unexplored jeep trail or deserted mining town by sunrise.

Vivid memories include one of my parents shaking the foot of my bed and cheerfully commanding "Wake up, Sunshine, rise 'n' shine!"

I would balk, screeching, "I'm TIRED!"—a normal reaction for a kid who was sound asleep at four in the morning.

But quickly the parental reminder came: "Come on, Lazy Bones, the world's waiting! You're not tired; let's go!" Though I'd complain and invent creative excuses to stay in bed, such efforts were in vain.

The message inferred was unspoken yet clear. It was *Not-OK* to be tired at four a.m. Perhaps my parents were early risers with boundless enthusiasm for nature but, in my child's mind, I became convinced there must be something wrong with me if I couldn't rise 'n' shine on demand.

I will be eternally grateful to my parents for their scouting gumption and the passion they passed on to me for the rich beauty of Colorado. But a pang of regret festers at my inability as a child to truly share the wondrous joy of these adventures. I was always too dang tired to shine!

Exploring Colorado's mountain passes circa 1960.

This story epitomizes for me what happens when truth gets reinterpreted or denied many times over. I learned not to trust myself or tell my truth. Because I wanted to get everything "right" and please my parents, my childhood became laced with threads of disconnect. Over the years I not only learned to stop *telling* my truth, I learned to start *selling* my stories. This both justified to myself – and others – that I wasn't crazy and helped me excel as *AsIF* Amy.

The combo of the constant corrections my parents dished out and my role as the perfect child fueled my impetus for getting life perfect. But life is never perfect, so there was a big disconnect between my true feelings and my real life.

Along the way to growing up I surmised that somehow I'd gotten *IT* all wrong. This was a pretty big clue as to why my life eventually focused on finding the right *IT,* and why I felt I always had to get *IT* right.

This also explained why I turned to outside vices and things to *deal* with life because I wasn't sure what was truly *real*. Due to my nice-girl conditioning, I often mistranslated many normal reactions and responses to life. Simple human attributes such as being angry, tired or lazy were an unacceptable part of **MyStory**.

Another one of our family **dynomantics** centered on unspoken rules around feelings—having them or expressing them. In a nutshell, all feelings in the *mad, sad* or *bad* category had to be turned into glad.

My parents' good intentions to promote good grooming or instill an optimistic, fun-loving spirit into our household ultimately, in some respects, backfired. By focusing on a narrow set of "acceptable" good feelings, they left us with no room to express a whole range of other life-feelings.

Hence, early on, I'd faked *IT* in order to make *IT* and put on a sunshiny, happy **sureface**. I developed a wide range of tactics – including the use of vices – in order to deal with my "unacceptable" feelings. As I addressed these issues from my past, I finally understood my life-long struggle to know and communicate my authentic feelings and realities. Once again, I found it life-changing to simply *SEE* this and get my history straight.

Delay in *Relay*

I discovered what happens after practicing decades of disconnecting from one's inner-truth—I'd developed a severe case of *delay* in *relay*.

Simply put, my ability to *relay* my true feelings about something came at a great *delay*. For many years, I'd disconnected from what I was truly feeling and didn't trust myself. If I found myself in some *Not-OK Corral* with feelings I couldn't identify, I quickly made up a story about what was going on in order to avoid feeling completely crazy.

Certain *issues* in my *tissues* involved long delays in catching up to what was really going on within me. Because my *modus operandi* had been "Be glad, Amy! Don't be *mad* or *sad*," I became painfully aware I didn't have access to the full range of feelings I needed to live a truthful life.

Without this sense of mine-own-self-being-true, I battled with a baffling disconnection of the true from false. How pivotal it was to finally understand the serious repercussions of growing up in a world where I was consistently being *taught* that thinking or feeling what I *truly* thought or felt came to *naught*.

It's little wonder that, at midlife, I'd harbored a reduced sense of who I *really* was or what I *really* wanted out of life. Over half a decade later I now understood why a *RealDeal* self had been so desirable, yet so out of reach. What's more, I saw that my inability to know my own truth rested at the heart of my unending *IT* searches.

As this piece of the puzzle locked into place, almost immediately I began discerning when I was *telling* the truth or *selling* it. This is now a daily practice. *Telling* versus *selling* represents my *chance* to *change* from living an *AsIF* life to an *AsIS* one.

Real-for-Me

Another friend, M'or, taught me a simple phrase that effectively anchored my *telling* vs. *selling* the truth. M'or was facing some of his own darker truths about himself when our lives collided. Late-night phone conversations were thick with self-honesty and soul-searching as we forged a way into our *RealDeal* selves.

My nickname for M'or comes from the first three initials of his formal name: Michael O'Rourke. It was inspired by his knack for showing me <u>more</u> in any given situation. M'or became my truth-buddy who continues to help me *walk* the *talk* of telling my truth.

M'or taught me the phrase *what's-real-for-me*. During one of our in-depth conversations, M'or used this truth-serum sentence to alert me to his perspective, his reality and his truth within our discussion.

That one simple phrase changed things for me as I strove to embrace my own truth. By telling *what's-real-for-me*, I have permission to be *AsIS* Amy in any given moment. When I feel *sad*, *mad* or *bad* (or any other emotion on the vast human emotional scale), I stand up and show up as my *RealDeal* self and tell what's real for me.

"Re-examine all you have been told... Dismiss what insults your Soul."
—Walt Whitman

My new openness to the whole range of human emotions introduced me to the fascinating experience of being *RealDeal*. As a daily practice, this more fluid and real way of living would continue to help set me free. It became a solid cornerstone as I strove to carve out my ongoing *reVirement* life.

While editing this chapter, I sipped a cup of tea. The bag included a small tag with an inspirational quote. I happened to read this one in the midst of considering some of my *selling* or *telling* insights.

As I drank in the essence of his words, Walt Whitman confirmed my thoughts. *"Re-examine all you have been told ...,"* the quote read, *"Dismiss what insults your Soul."*

With my own *JOLLI* spin, I reconsidered Mr. Whitman's words; *"Re-examine all you've been* sold ... *that's* old. *You've* told *your Soul what's real for you ... now that's* bold!"

SUMMARY > *Selling* or *Telling?*

◆ A rise 'n' shine memory clarified default denial.

◆ Denying truth created *delays* in *relays*.

◆ M'or's *what's-real-for-me* truth allowed freedom

CHAPTER 20

A *RealDeal Heal*

- *Amyzon* or *Amyzone?*
- *LiveIT*, *LoveIT* Life
- **Mona Lisamy** Masterpiece

When I committed to an intention, things began to fall into place in what seemed like a sequential order to the process of reinvention. To magnetize a new *inVent* into form, all the stuff of the *inTent* showed up to go from *old* to *bold*. Simply put, everything unlike an *inTention* would show up for its revitalized *inVention*.

Hence, everything unreal about me rose up through my *reVirement*, exposing my imposters. The *RealDeal* Amy began to stand up without needing any *Let's Make a Deal* bargains.

I was slowly coming home to a **wholographic** me—a renovated *AsIS* Amy. Although it took a lot of turning in the opposite direction, living from inside out, going upside down and all around, the journey reaped untold rewards.

The *deal* with this *heal* was that I began truly living what was *real* for me. Old patterns and parts of me died off, demarcating a zone of new inner balance. I arrived in the **Amyzone** (amy•zone; the zone of Amy in balance), where my pivoting practices brought me to an underlying equilibrium greater than any I'd ever experienced.

Previously, I nicknamed my over-*DOING* tendencies as my **amyzonian** nature. I'd been a sprawling **Amyzon**, reaching my way through vast territories. Yet all of my achievements, travels, successes and *ITs* had failed to bring me the enoughness I wanted. My midlife

innervention and living death sent me to the last place I thought to look ... deep within.

Sidetracked by my *addiction* to *addition*, I had failed to *SEE* the high cost I'd paid for traveling the **Amyzon**. I'd lost the essential parts, the authenticity I searched for. Now as I practiced getting my enoughness, knowing my *NOs* and telling the truth, I found a renewed stability that was fueled from within. I didn't erase the past or *lame blame* it. I reinvented it with a twist, with the true desires and dreams at my core.

From the peaceful state of **Amyzone**, I now understood what Melm always said: "If it's hysterical, it probably is historical." Whenever my **Amyzon** overreacted in a way that was out of proportion to what was really happening, there was always some unresolved *part* of my *past* that needed a *pass*-through to reveal a *heal* towards *real*.

For decades, I'd lived in the dark about so many things. Now I could *SEE* just what to *DO* to *BE* a new me. My *chance* to *change* revealed an inner light that could now emerge bright and strong.

From the internal balance of my **Amyzone**, I hit a *bold IT* in the middle of my *old IT* target and *IT* was me.

I was now *IT*.

This one-letter *JOLLI* brought me great peace and profound understanding. *I* was the solution to my missing *IT*. And *IT* had found its proper place behind my *LoveITs* and *LiveITs*.

LiveIT, *LoveIT* Life

The deepest layers of my **viceberg** melted as I created a *LiveIT*, *LoveIT* life, as I rediscovered and recovered the essential and unique parts of me that I lived and loved. Previous aspects of me had united into an **amyalagmation** of living in the **Amyzone**.

In my mad rush to fix my uncomfortable insides from the outside, "I" had gotten lost. For example, when I took my year off to do art full time, I squeezed my art into an *IT*, making it an **artIT**. I realized now

I'd been operating from a plan based on an **Amyzon** past.

With a vengeance I'd rushed about, achieving what I thought I was *supposed* to do in a race to find my **artIT**. But with so many frozen layers of my **viceberg** weighing down the matter of my mattering, there was no way my **artIT** could have supplied me with a deeper satisfaction or **soulace**. As long as I lacked the solid knowing of my true self at my core, no amount of art success would have mattered.

From an emerging **Amyzone**, I realized that I'd missed one simple, yet critical thing. In my intense focus for my art to be an *IT*, I'd completely glossed over another *just-one-little-letter* – an "**S**".

I'd left out the "**S**" in the word **ArtISt**! Was this why my **artIT** led me to such an **overIT**?!?

When I put the "**S**" back into my **ArtISt**, I remembered how present and centered I felt while painting and creating. I painted from my *AsIS* self, lost in moments of creativity. At the core of my soul lived the essence of an **ArtISt**, *AsIS*, without the pressures of making *IT* big.

This one simple insight had been so *right-in-front-of-me* that I'd missed *SEEING* it during decades of creating my artistry.

As my pivoting path continued, I learned from the **ArtISt** within me and headed in a new direction. I came to embrace a loving attitude filled with a sense of direction for finding what I truly needed and wanted to be living, the perfect balance of a *LoveIT, LiveIT* life.

My race around the outside track slowed its pace, and I lived increasingly on the inside winning lane. Over and over I chose to take the high way, a freeway towards a transformed **innerstate**.

The more I left the speeding *IT* race, the more I saw that all of my past had occurred at the exact frequency I'd needed to find a new vision and purpose. In full **quantumesque** living mode, everything I'd ever lived had been necessary for me to go from *there* to *here*.

My *Streams* journals were now packed with **Amyalogies** (am•y•al•o•gies; analogies by Amy) leading to more expanded understandings. And, as a result, more self-love arrived. Was this the way to fall madly in love with oneself? An **Amyalogy** presented itself as a renewed "life-painting" filled with depth and brilliance.

Mona Lisamy Masterpiece

On my 1979 European art escapade, I visited the Louvre in Paris. I'll never forget the long halls leading to the "infamous" *Mona Lisa* painting by Leonardo DaVinci. After waiting in the long line to view the masterpiece, I leaned in to study DaVinci's iconic Renaissance style.

During the Renaissance, the world reached new heights, and DaVinci was one of the leading artists of the time. His paintings from this period in history reflected the revival of and renewed interest in the classical qualities of early Roman and Greek principles.

My *reVirement* rendezvous became a rebirthing through the reinvention of many parts of myself. It also became, in essence, a personal renaissance. I reached a revival and renewal of my own previous classics, a rebirth of myself comprised of richer perspectives and deeper realism that allowed a *RealDeal* Amy to be reborn.

As my emerging *LoveIT* and *LiveIT* ideals blended from past to present, I also uncovered my own unique topography. What a great word *topography* is—not to be confused with all the *typography* of my story!

 topography the arrangement of natural and artificial physical features of an area; as in the topography of an island.

The topography of my life's natural and artificial stories were merging together for a reuniting inner strength. This renaissance expedition followed a new terrain, transforming *old* into *bold*. In it, I found a striking parallel between the stories of my life and its art journey. As I reviewed my own art history, a fascinating **artobiography** (art•o•bi•og•ra•phy; life biography via art) emerged.

My early art studies in realism (art that portrays life in realistic terms) in many ways reinforced what I was taught about life and the so-called real world. In art, I learned how to draw and paint realistically.

Midway through my college art studies, I turned away from classical traditions. I wanted to find my own unique voice and vision as an artist, but I didn't know exactly how to do that. Much like I've done during my midlife turnabout, I leapt into uncharted territory.

All manner of assistance showed up to help me *inVent* my *inTent*. A few avant-garde college professors encouraged me to forge the beginnings of what would become my unique style in expressionistic art. After I'd spent decades exploring various forms of abstract art, my fascination with energy and movement expanded, revealing new depths. Was my life now doing the same?

Self Portrait, 1976

Autumn Unfolding, 2007

My artobiography *took me from the art of realism to my* RealDeal *expression.*

My graphics expertise in design and marketing also provided insights into my **artobiography**. Previously I'd worked in the field of advertising, where putting spins and visual deals on products are of paramount importance. A perfect profession for a **sureface** *AsIF* seller.

With a renewed dedication to truth and realness, I became unrelenting in my dedication to branding. An organization's brand reflects the importance of integrated core values and vision, and must be fully established before any *RealDeal* marketing can be effective. This renovated philosophy and approach to my work delivered a renewed **wholographic** approach to my graphic design résumé.

My **artobiography** now revealed a distinct alignment between life and art. I finally understood why I was so passionate about uniting with a greater cohesiveness from the inside out. Midlife had shown me how to piece all the parts of me together into full view in deeper and more realistic ways than I'd previously known. All the light and dark facets of my life's journey were being reflected back to me in vivid Technicolor.

During the Renaissance period, DaVinci created depth and realism in his paintings by using both the principles of perspective and the juxtaposition of dark shadow with bright highlights. These techniques gave his artistry its ity of volume and depth.

One of my favorite words resembles a **Thornism**, but it's not. Chiaroscuro (pronounced: Kiro-scurro) is the term used to describe the juxtaposition of light and dark in creating realism. Revisiting this favorite word triggered another *reVirement*-ripe concept.

 chiaroscuro the treatment of contrasting light and shadow in a painting to create volume and realistic shape.

From within myself, I'd found a contrast of the light and dark sides of me that were now juxtaposed to create a vibrant *RealDeal heal*. While my *AsIF* Amy had judged my inner, dark shadows as part of not being perfect or right enough, I'd missed out on the rich depths and vitality those shadows had actually created within me.

My *RealDeal heal* required that all aspects of myself blend together to create a new kind of *AsIS* realism. I became my own **Mona Lisamy** masterpiece (mo•na•lis•amy; Mona Lisa-inspired Amy), uniting all the colorful aspects of myself.

As I continued to fall madly in love with my own life's painting, a greater sense of me came to *BE*. I moved towards a life where everything I lived progressed towards a *LoveIT*. This encouraged the highest expression of myself—a point at which I continued to embrace my imperfections ... *AsIS*.

SEEING showed the linking of my thinking, which repaved the *DOING* of my mental maps. A series of revitalized actions then led my **innerstate** to a high way of inspired results. I bridged the *gaps* in my mental *maps* as my *inTentions* toward *inVentions* aligned with a grounded **Amyzone**. My whole relationship with *DOING* and *over-DOING* was then turned about. Less and *rest* became gateways to my *best* self. I emerged a bona fide human *BEING*, rising out of my human *DOING* past.

A verbal duo of two more letters provided one last insight for Part Two. Two letters that provided clues at the start of my **tiredword** revelations were the letters "r" and "e"—especially when they were at the beginning of words, turning them into repeat mode. This "re" factor got me thinking about a string of other words that I re-peated over and over.

I'd re-traced and re-covered many of the same themes I'd re-visited for decades. Now I was coming 'round to a deeper *RealDeal heal* within their layers. I wondered if this was why they called the healing of addictions *Re-covery*. I'd re-covered the same *issues* in my *tissues*— over and over.

I'd also re-found and re-fined aspects of myself to begin re-creating a *LoveIT* life. I re-charged my *reVirement* journey through an inner re-defining and re-aligning.

Re-novations of the neural connections linking my thinking and *stalking* my *talking* resulted in a greater mindset. My *new* mind was *now* re-mind-ing me to pay attention, for only my thinking could fuel my *inTentions* for what would become my *inVentions*.

And lastly, my *chance* to *change* was all about *re-inVenting*, over and over again. ~ Thanks "r" and "e"!

SUMMARY> **A RealDeal Heal**

◆ I forged a new balance from my *addiction* to *addition*.

◆ Discovered *LoveITs* and *LiveITs* helped eliminate all else.

◆ Life's dark and light aspects painted a rich masterpiece.

PART THREE

BEING

Chapter 21

My Third Vepiphany

- *Concepts* in *Concerts*
- *T-to-V* Number Three
- Light of Mine

The pivoting path of the V became a fascinating expedition into my life's second half. Sometimes slowly yet more often at warp speed, I uncovered the infrastructure for a *LiveIT, LoveIT* life. Everything I went through contributed to an emerging life-masterpiece created by my renovated **ArtISt**.

It felt like nothing short of a divine healing from the inside out. The combined orchestration of these *concepts* in harmonious *concerts* evolved into a living practice of paying attention to my *SEEING, DOING* and *BEING*, which did not always occur in that specific order.

The **vhorizons** of my perspectives cracked wide open, and my **amyzonian** tendencies eased into gentle inner spaces within my **Amyzone**. Most of the time I lived in a *Now-OK Corral*, with most of my Brain Bandits locked up for good. Occasionally they visited to shake things up a bit but, by and large, peace ruled over my internal kingdom.

The *revolving* treasure hunt around a few more layers of **MyStuff** was *evolving* one insight at a time. And my *inTent* to *inVent* a re-inspired second-half continued to surpass all previous expectations.

With absolute certainty, I came to *know now* that there was an undeniable divine order to it all. I'd found a truer destiny via the V and my *Just-One-Little-Letter-Insights*. I could now travel safely through my midlife meltdown, dissolving old ways within me.

A greater alignment into the oneness of my *BEING* occurred. Part Three offers a non-chronological collection of highlights from my transformation towards fully embracing my ability to *BE*.

An overarching impetus for Part Three's theme was an inspiring quote rediscovered from my past. In my thirties I read the book *Return to Love* by Marianne Williams, a brilliant author and lecturer who embodies her words. Everything about her quote reinspired bold encouragement to become the *ME* I truly came here to *BE*.

The liberation from my *AsIF* self brought a new light to the dark

"Our deepest fear is not that we are inadequate. Our deepest fear is that we are powerful beyond measure. It is our light, not our darkness, that most frightens us. We ask ourselves, 'Who am I to be brilliant, gorgeous, talented, fabulous?' Actually, who are you *NOT* to be? You are a child of God.

Your playing small does not serve the world. There is nothing enlightening about shrinking so that other people will not feel insecure around you. We are all meant to shine, as children do.

We are born to make manifest, on earth, the glory of God that is within us. It is not just in some of us. It is in everyone. And as we let our own light shine, we unconsciously give other people permission to do the same. As we are liberated from our own fear, our presence automatically liberates others."

— Marianne Williams, *Return to Love*

secrets of my *past* that allowed them to finally *pass* away. As this beautiful quote suggested, it was not my inadequacies that held me back, but my fears fueled by *old* thinking that kept me from embracing all the *gold* within me.

I'd never given myself permission to *BE* the *RealDeal* me. Now, however, I felt truly worthy of the brilliant life. I was endowed with a *right* to *light* just because I existed. This enhanced the matter of my mattering existentially.

With a new battery of enoughness installed to generate my *AsIS* self, I felt free to polish my inherent inner light. Before *reVirement* I'd reached through shadows, hoping to find brilliance in outside *ITs*. Now the *I* in *IT* ignited before me with a *right-in-front-of-me* frequency.

While writing about my second **vepiphany**, *inTent* to *inVent*, I wondered if there might be a third *T-to-V* switch that could translate all the illumination sparkling within me.

T-to-V Number Three

Throughout the writing of this book, my dedication to "three" prevailed. This kindled my desire to find one last switch that would **amyalagamate** my *reVirement* journey. When I continued to search without results, however, I began to doubt I'd ever find one.

Then I decided to tap into the power of commitment. If I were going to write a book proclaiming the powers of *inTention* I needed to use my theory to influence the *inVention* of a third *T-to-V* switch. I packed up for several hours of writing at my favorite window seat in a nearby Whole Foods café, planning to give my *inTent* to *inVent* talents a run for it.

I pulled out my laptop, Bhakti. (No surprise! My computers all have nicknames. It must put a good vibe into their circuitry as I rarely have computer issues. I've chosen Sanskrit names because Sanskrit words are prayers from ancient texts. Bhakti means to share in, to love, to worship with; all good omens for networking within myself and the world.)

I rolled up my mental verbal sleeves, ready to take a **quantumesque** leap towards my discovery. What was a third *T* that could become a *V* to describe all I was coming to *BE?* For added mojo, I pulled out the two quotes from Murray and Williams. Their brilliant words might be hiding a secret combo that embodied my *reVirement's* essence.

Breathing in a silent prayer of decision without hesitancy, I asked all manner of assistance to sweep in for a meeting of my *mind* to *find* the right *kind* of words to describe my midlife rite of passage. After inhaling and exhaling deeply to liberate myself from my doubts, I closed my eyes, challenging Providence to sweep in with a new thought.

Instantly I wondered, *"Hmmm, what if I didn't have to sweat this and figure it all out? What if I just <u>knew</u> that my* inTent *to* inVent *was already here NOW? What if I just start writing and see what happens?"*

This idea felt a little scary; I'd always practiced the approach of a master figure-outer. Could I really jump in and start writing without preparations or research, expecting a *JOLLI* miracle? Didn't I need to open a dictionary or thesaurus or Google my way to such an important discovery of word crafting?

"Amy, turn it about! Try something new; go for it!" I took another deep inhale and boldly typed out an affirmative mental map for my intent:

> I am now finding my third *JOLLI T-to-V* switch. It embodies all that I've come to know along my *reVirement* path. This all flows to me easily and effortlessly NOW!

Without thinking, I opened a new document and started brainstorming. "My *chance* for *change* has been the result of *TYING* together the puzzling pieces of my life, *VYING* towards a new order."

I typed up a few other versions of *TIE* and *VIE*. But they sounded too much like the word *DIE*—not quite what I was hoping to capture.

I typed out a couple other hopeful words that could have qualified for the switch and then, without thinking, typed out the phrase: "My *Just-One-Little-Letter-Insights* led me to find my *liTe to liVe.*"

I sat up straight, my back and shoulders locked into place as I looked at the two words again: *liTe* to *liVe*. Confirming its *T-to-V* classification, I wondered, *"Really? It couldn't be that easy. It's only been a few moments since I typed out my intent!"*

Then it sank in: These two words truly encapsulated all that had happened in the past five years. A welling up of tears confirmed my AHA, for these two words truly said it all—and flowed effortlessly.

A wave of tingles rushed through my right side, signaling I was on to something. I looked around the Whole Foods at the others diligently working. No one knew I'd just been swept away with my third *JOLLI* **vepiphany**. My *liTe to liVe* was an instant *LoveIT!*

I quickly googled the spelling and usage of the word *"liTe"* to verify that its definition suited my journey. Indeed *reVirement* had led to a much lighter version of myself. With a bit of creative license, *liTe* to *liVe* was my *T-to-V* number three!

> **lite** informal, simplified spelling of light, often used in advertising commercial products; denoting a simpler version of a thing or person.

I flashed back to the clearing of my magnet and the process of getting clear about all my **MyStuff** and thought, *"Amy, haven't you been on a significant* rite *of* lite, *simplifying yourself on the journey through all of* **YourStuff***? You're much lighter, having released so many* issues *in your* tissues." I now lived with a whole lot less. A "lite-r" version of myself undeniably was coming to *BE*.

Enraptured by my third **vepiphany**, I once again delighted in the power of the V to show up to turn things about.

Light of Mine

I reviewed some of the **roughStuff** tackled along my journey. How many times had I toned myself down and dampened my *RealDeal* sparkle? For how many years had I not expressed my *liTe* to *liVe?* For many *years* and through many *tears*. Certainly enough to provide the frequency needed to make a **quantumesque** leap into my inner light.

The manifesto of *reVirement* urged me to change this past pattern of dimming my light. A re-inspired second-half suggested it was now my time to turn it *on* and *own* it. After all, now *I* was my new *IT* to be *LIT* from within. It all flowed together in another *JOLLI* roll.

A childhood memory flashed of sitting with my family as we sang 'round the campfire. An all-time favorite tune chimed out as I recalled "This Little Light of Mine". I looked up the lyrics and, once again, the past emerged richer and more vibrant, holding deeper meaning. I selected my three favorite lines, which now flickered with a new glimmer:

This Little Light of Mine

This little light of mine, I'm gonna let it shine;
Everywhere I go, I'm gonna let it shine,
Let it shine, Let it shine, Let it shine!

I recalled ideas about a *life* I'd always hoped to *live,* one that was shining bright with the light I was born with, the light Marianne Williams encouraged all of us to shine. If I could truly shine, would I give others permission to do the same?

More of my history came into consideration. If we were all meant to shine, as children do, did my unique past and childhood hold more clues for finding my *liTe* to *liVe?*

SUMMARY > My Third Vepiphany

◆ A sense of *BEING* brought *concepts* into *concerts*.

◆ A third **vepiphany** lit up my *liTe* to *liVe*.

◆ Marianne's quote and a folk tune united with inspiration

CHAPTER 22

Bookending My Life

- *Song* to *Sing*
- My Life's Library
- *NewMe* meets *FirstMe*

Finding my third *T-to-V* switch lit me up. The message from the folk song, *This Little Light of Mine*, appeared almost too small to become my life's new motto in lieu of the rich, inner life I lived. Maybe I needed to upgrade the lyrics just a tad and make them *This <u>Inner</u> Light of Mine, I'm gonna let it shine?!?* An inner *"Yes!"* confirmed my upgrade.

Following Marianne's lead, I decided I was here to serve the world and make manifest my glory from within as children do. It was time to infuse my second-half with some of my original childlike glory.

I also felt deeply moved by a basic tenet that WAYne Dyer championed: "Don't die with your song still in you." Combined with my revised title, "This Inner Light of Mine", I considered my *liTe* to *liVe* as a *song* still in me, waiting to be *sung*.

One morning while getting tough on more of **MyStuff**, I sorted through bookshelves that held almost all the books I'd ever owned. Overdue for a *LoveIT-LoseIT* book-sorting session, I dove in.

First, I identified the new home for my final *LoveIT* books—a bookshelf that was streamlined and smaller. Before I tossed and sorted, I set the timer. *"Okay, Amy, one hour ... let's see which books are LoveITs!"*

By the time the timer rang, I'd made significant progress in organizing my books into categories. My **Stuffology** degree was paying off. I had become a master sorter-of-stuff no matter the category.

I took a break for a cup of tea and sat on the floor to consider my current *LoveIT* pile. A few art books, cookbooks, histories, novels and spiritual books had made the final cut.

I realized at this moment that my life was like a library of books that contained all my experiences and adventures. How many times had I exclaimed to a friend that I felt like I'd already lived out ten lives in this one short one—and I wasn't even half done yet!

As I considered the idea that my life was like a library, I became curious to discover what books already sat on its shelves, and what new books would be added during my second-half-of-life *reVirement* journey.

My Life's Library

After boxing up the *LoseIT* books to give away, I grabbed my current *Streams* to take a writing break with some wordplay. With the mental image of my life as a collection of books, I sketched some of the more poignant titles that would fill my life's library: *A Bite of the Big Apple* described my years in New York City and *Thornton Family Escapades* chronicled my childhood. A whole collection of titles flowed.

What a great metaphor this was for considering my life from a new angle! I brimmed with feelings of renewed respect and gratitude for how incredibly rich my life's journey had been—all of it.

Following this writing pause, I juggled the armful of *LoveIT* books and placed them on the new shelf I'd set up for them. Then another **Amyalogy** flashed.

As I considered my imaginary life's library, I imagined it on a bookshelf above me and realized bookends were needed.

Images of two aspects of myself emerged as symbols for each bookend. On the far left was the first version of myself, the *FirstMe*, who was born on a snowy Saturday morning in northern Colorado. The *FirstMe* had existed before I'd authored any of my future life's books. The *FirstMe* was the very beginning of me.

Then I considered the emerging me that could stand at the far right, the bookend holding up the current life-book I'm authoring. She represented the *NewMe* who now embraced my life's second half.

A bookshelf held my life's library, with my FirstME *and* NewME *as bookends.*

I wondered, *"What books do I want to write now, in my second-half? What chapters will I write in my reinvented life, filled with the inspiration of living my* liTe *to* liVe*?"*

A challenge rose up within me: *"Amy, what are the books to be written that will let you* sing *the* song *you came here to shine?"*

I was curious about the *FirstMe* who'd arrived on the Amy scene. What had she really come here for? I unconsciously asked that original part of me if she knew. Another stream of questions unfolded.

"Is there anything the FirstMe has not had a chance to SEE, DO or BE yet? Could the life-books I write from now on be closer to the original FirstMe's desires? Do I still have that original brand of Amy in me?"

One big AHA hit with significant clarity. No one else had been around my life as long as the *FirstMe*. She'd stood by me from my earliest beginnings. She knew me like no one else and lived with me all the time. She held the key to an inner vault of the **wholographic** aspects of me, a vast life library of information no one else on earth possessed.

Only a true expert on the life of Amy could discover what *song* remained for her to *sing*. As my personal librarian, she not only knew my **Stuffology** history better than anyone, but she held unlimited 24-hour research access to all my inner files. She could advise me on anything anytime—all at no charge!

An interesting sidebar came to mind. If I contained an inside personal expert such as this, why was she so often the last person I turned to for insight and information when the going got rough? This launched a query worthy of a further investigations.

What if my second-half journey needed to include the *FirstMe's* original genius and spark of light that was the glory I came here to manifest? What if this was the manifesto to herald in my true *liTe* to *liVe?* What if this was key to how I could now bookend my life's library?

I thought of the incredible joy and freshness of life that shines from the faces of infants and small children. Was this the *liTe* to *liVe* in us all? How could I retrieve some of that?

NewMe meets *FirstMe*

At the same time I considered the questions provoked by my bookend metaphor, I received the last several boxes of my **DadsStuff**. Two boxes were filled with four decades of full-color Kodachrome slides.

With my computer's slide scanner, I looked forward to digitizing some of my history to email images to my niece and cousins. Grandpa Byron and Mom had been avid documentarians of our family's life. I wondered what visual treasures I might uncover.

As I pulled out the scores of slides, I was stunned to discover full-color images from as far back as the mid-1940s, before my parents met and married. I was accustomed to seeing my family's past through the flatter dimension of black-and-white photos. I wasn't prepared for the Technicolor depth that now brought my history to life.

I found a small group of slides labeled "Amy 1957" and was

overjoyed. Prior to this discovery, I'd had only a few color images of myself as a little girl. They were highly retouched "perfect-little-girl-shots" from the fifties and sixties. A flat, black-and-white portrait of myself as a baby was etched in my mental library.

After scanning several of the slides, I brought them into full view on my 27-inch color monitor. Instantly, I stared eye-to-eye at bright, full-color smiling photos of myself from 1957. It was beyond remarkable. And best of all, in light of finding my *liTe* to *liVe*, I saw another *IT*.

There *IT* was, an *IT* that was all *LIT* up in me, the beautiful light I'd been looking for all this time. A spark of pure and utter joy, the original genesis that arrived here in the *FirstMe* was there in the mini-me on screen. Perhaps it's because I'm such a visual person, but it was as if I were meeting myself for the first time.

NewME *meets* FirstME *in color.*

I'm so **greatfull** to my mother and grandfather, who'd been so keen on their camera recordings. Through the gift of those images, I touched my original brilliance. I'd never experienced such access to my light like this. It kindled a flame of determination to find that spark again and live it all day, every day as best I could.

What had happened to that brilliance? How had my original light dimmed along the path of my life's first half? Had I really lost it? Could I still reclaim it? Could I anchor this illumination to *liVe* out my *liTe* for the rest of my *reVirement?*

I remembered another of WAYne Dyer's inspiring lectures when he asked the audience an intriguing question: "What have you 'unlearned' in the process of growing up?"

He told stories of childhood things he'd gotten in trouble for and the things he'd discovered on his own. Such experiences had contributed to his individualism and his ability to find his *song* to *sing* to the world.

This would take some time as I had to sort through what were my *AsIF* behaviors and what were truly my *AsIS* Amy's original ideas. But as I recalled the things I did on my own as a child they became just the details needed to fill in the brighter picture emerging.

As the drafts of this book unfolded into a reality, I found myself passionately writing day after day with a drive I'd never known before. A revitalized spark ignited—the idea of being a writer; not just a journal-hound, but a published author.

For years I'd traversed mountains of doubt regarding my writing abilities. Where had those doubts originated? The evidence of my love of words went back as far as I could remember. Yet I'd scripted a detailed internal Amy-novel with a convincing theme that proclaimed: "Amy will never be a very good writer."

Slowly, I unraveled this mystery by retracing the steps of my **writobiography** (write•o•bi•og•ra•phy; biography of writing). It clearly revealed how lost and separated I'd gotten from this one inner song.

In spite of my C- book report, I really had expressed myself in words and pictures quite well. When my fifth-grade social studies class visited a legislative session at the State Capitol, I wrote a shocking summary of what I considered apathetic lawmaking. My published editorial was the talk of our small town and made my parents proud.

In high school I wrote a winning essay for a citywide contest sponsored by the Lion's Club. The prize included a life-changing opportunity to live with a family in Brazil, representing Colorado as a good-will ambassador. In college I composed original music and performed with my college roomie. I named our folk duo *Explority* and wrote ballads that explored topics of early romance and rebellion.

I gained all my college English credits by writing my way through the credited exams, providing pretty good evidence I wasn't too shabby at writing. But no, **MyStory** insisted I was not a very good writer.

After college, I married my sweetheart, a stellar journalism major and city newspaper editor. Everything I wrote went under his eagle-editing eye. **Typoknackabilites** and **grammaring** did not amuse or enlighten him. His helpful corrections unfortunately got turned upside down when I made up a "not-enough" story confirming that I was so imperfect I must not be able to write. That's one **theremometer** I really wish I had broken! Instead, I became a closet writer for decades.

The V and my *JOLLIs* had certainly turned this old story about. I'd never felt more committed to re-finding my writers' voice. Ideas sizzled from an invisible source. Why? Because I'd uncovered that writing was a natural part of the *ME* I came here to *BE*. This opened a gateway to more insights around finding my *liTe* to *liVe*.

Were there other strong urgings that held *clues* to the *glues* I needed to secure my unique Amy puzzle together? What more had the *AsIF* Amy "un-learned" along the path of growing up?

I consulted the *FirstMe;* perhaps she knew what brighter future was in store for me. *"What had the FirstMe loved to do as a little girl? What had she come up with all on her own? What had she gotten in trouble for?"* More guiding memories surfaced, with astounding results.

·CHAPTER 23·

Garbagegems, Dollishops & Pioneergypsy

- Mom's *Jug Tug*
- Remembering my **Dollishops**
- A Pioneering Frontier

The power of my old beliefs proved fascinating. By convincing myself I couldn't write, I'd sidetracked a big part of myself that could help me live my light and find joy in my life's reinvention. How many other forgotten yet integral parts of me needed to be rediscovered and refined as my *reVirement* journey unfolded?

What else had I unlearned that was essential to my reinvention? What were the things the *FirstMe* loved — the things that no one suggested to me? I searched for the purity of previous inspirations. I also considered what I got in trouble for, since this had curbed my natural inclinations. These investigations held rich clues for finding buried inner treasure.

When I was growing up, taking care of our garbage was very different from what it is today. We burned our trash. There was a concrete incinerator in the backyard to burn combustibles; all other trash required a weekly visit to the local garbage dump. One indelible story from a garbage trip with Mom and Julie shed light on another deeper truth about myself.

After we unloaded the pungent grass clippings from the back of the Scoutie-outie, Mom yelled out, "Oh, look girls!" She then scrambled over mounds of garbage in her beige Keds and red peddle-pushers (ankle-high pants from the fifties).

·203·

In short order, Mom lugged something down the mountain of discarded rubbish. Julie and I leaned in to examine her trash-treasure. My five-year-old brain couldn't understand why Mom was so excited.

It was a hefty ceramic jug like ones that moonshiners used in the 1930s for their prohibition brew. At that moment Mom imprinted upon me a Thornton trait that would contribute to my lifetime panache for trash.

By the time Dad came home from work that night, Mom had already scoured the jug clean with steel wool. He joined in her enthusiasm over her thrilling find. I remember still wondering what the heck I was missing. To me, it was just an old, brown jug from the garbage dump!

After dinner, Dad disappeared into his workshop in the basement. At bedtime he hurried upstairs cradling the jug, which he'd transformed with copper tubing and wiring. Mom jumped with glee when the jug was placed on the coffee table next to the couch.

Dad screwed in a lightbulb, and Mom ceremoniously plugged the jug-light into the living room's electrical socket. Shouts of *Hurray!* and *Wow!* filled the room as the light was lit. Later that week Mom would make a bell-curved lampshade for the jug-lamp and place a brown velvet bow around the shades' hour-glass middle.

This story, along with others, became a conversation piece that lit up my parents' eyes in the telling. Dad also made a coffee table out of one of Grandpa Byron's wagon wheels, and Mom reinvented "first-day-of-school" dresses for Julie and me from Aunt Vida's hand-me-downs.

When Dad and I began inventing our creative words, **garbagegems** (gar•bage•gems; gems from garbage) would be the **Thornism** for all of our trash-treasures. **Garbagegems** captured the Thorntons' knack for recycling, repurposing, revamping and renovating almost anything into treasures.

Not only did my mom's *jug tug* become one of the family's recycled stories, it epitomized our **garbagegem** genes. This re-purposing tenacity would become the theme for the reinvention and innovation that was my new *song* to *sing* for my life's second-half.

Another of my old **MyStories** changed. The historical **roughStuff** I'd deemed to be my life's "garbage" now held the gems that allowed me to stay steady on my high way toward a revamped **innerstate**.

To this day, I can't drive past a pile of interesting garbage without slowing down to gaze. My "dumpster DNA" considers all the creative possibilities of treasure in what is often discarded or judged as trash.

As my *reVirement* unfolded, I saw there were untold gems of possibility hidden within the previous trials of my life. Like Mom's *jug tug*, rediscoveries and illuminations could be found there, along with my *right* to uncover the *light* of who I truly came here to *BE*.

My flair for thrifty scavenging in secondhand stores brought a jewel of a clue to yet another hidden reclamation within me. Twenty bucks and a trip to the thrift store led to a greater inner truth about my endless passion for transformation.

Remembering my **Dollishops**

In the midst of mining my mind for my original inspirations, I remembered another long-forgotten childhood joy. At the age of five, I invented something I called my **Dollishops** (doll•i•shops; beauty shop makeovers for dolls). Inspired by Grandma Beulah's beauty shop, I enjoyed a nonstop enthusiasm for dolling up dolls.

One summer I became bored with re-fixing my doll's hairstyles, which were close to worn off from my constant recurling, retwirling and restyling. So I took to the streets—the neighborhood streets. Dad painted **A M Y** in black letters on the back of my red Radio Flyer wagon, which soon became a taxi for dolls. I pulled it along as I went from door to door, asking for tired, old dolls that needed some fixing up.

When the wagon was full of sad, worn-out dolls, I pulled them up our steep driveway and brought them into the basement laundry room, where my transforming **Dollishops** began.

I scrubbed, curled, trimmed and sewed until new hairstyles and wardrobes adorned the dolls. Renovated, transformed, and ready for return to their respective homes, they were piled back into the wagon-taxi and delivered to delighted owners.

Julie and me with our dolls and my **AMY** *doll taxi.*

This occurred years before reality television popularized makeovers and well before spas became mainstream. Where did I get the idea for my **Dollishops**? Not from my super-clean mom, clever renovator though she was; she certainly wasn't thrilled about me dragging those germy, dirty dolls into her sparkly, clean laundry room.

No one told me to do this. No one suggested, *"Hey, Amy, why don't you go out and get all the messed-up dolls and fix 'em up?!"* I came up with it on my own and found such joy in it. What had that been about?

During one of the first weekends into my *liTe* to *liVe* quest, I found out. I reenacted one of my **Dollishops**—as the grown-up *NewMe*.

I took a twenty-dollar bill and visited a local thrift shop to buy as many dolls as I could find. I hit the store on half-price Saturday to maximize my spending. The cheaper and more beat-up the doll, the better it would be for testing my makeover abilities.

Out came the Comet cleanser, iron, glue gun and box of sewing supplies. I spread the sorry-looking dolls out on my dining table.

*"Amy, what are you doing? Are you crazy? You're over fifty! You are going stark, raving, **thornallistic**! Has it come to playing with dolls? You really need to go out on a date!"* My sarcastic Brain Bandits pelted me with all sorts of doubts, determined to maintain the status quo.

I swatted these thoughts away with conviction: *"I'm trying something out; why not? This was something I loved to do!"* Without any more thought, I launched into my reenacted **Dollishop**.

After two hours of combing, washing and fixing, I lost all sense of time. I continued for another two hours, and a very interesting thing happened. As each doll got cleaned up, combed out and dressed up, they seemed to sparkle with a new light. Was it the dolls who were changing or was it me?

Witnessing this simple transformation evoked feelings of deep joy and satisfaction within me. I'd helped these dolls find their original light.

*Before and after dolls get a **Dollishop** makeover.*

Lined up for a final photo shoot, they were remade celebrities in my eyes.

Those dolls helped me realize a big truth about myself. Not only did I love the whole reinvention process, but I was passionate about helping others find their own transformations. Could I help others reclaim their original light and joy? Was this the key to why I came here to *BE?*

Later, I thought about how much I loved my dolls as a child. They were there for me when my family was not. There was some sort of magic in what I transferred to them. That day, the renovated dolls delivered to me the same **soulace** I'd felt decades earlier.

The next week I met up with one of my friends and mentors, Cynthia James. I enjoyed many of her transformative classes, and she was starting one in two weeks. I shared the story of my weekend **Dollishop** experiment. Cynthia loved it and asked me to lead a "live" **Dollishop** as part of her workshop. Its success inspired more.

During the workshop's doll experiences, the women shared stories that were extraordinary. Many had found a reconnection with lost treasure buried within them, gems hidden beneath adult veils. The simplicity of allowing the dolls to bridge a deeper wisdom about our original *liTe* we came here to *liVe* was awe-inspiring. How could something as simple as revisiting my childhood joy of **Dollishops** help me turn about my life towards an inspired second-half?

What I discovered was almost too dang simple; it was *right-in-front-of-me*: Explore the things I loved to do before I squelched them and seek the essential ingredient in those things. Then infuse that essence into the qualities of my life's reinvention. This simple strategy would bookend my second half of life with my first half in ways I'm still uncovering.

A Pioneering Frontier

Childhood brought another realization for reclaiming my *liTe* to *liVe*. Inspired by television shows such as *Rawhide* and *Bonanza*, I loved to play **pioneergypsy** (pi•on•eer•gyp•sy; a pioneer-gypsy combination).

This playful persona was a combination of independent trailblazer and free-spirited, wild gypsy who traveled the Western frontier on imaginary wagon trains in our backyard. From our suburban home west of Denver, I climbed to the middle of our large cottonwood tree, captivated by the expansive range of the Rocky Mountains just twenty miles away. This easily set the stage for my **pioneergypsy** escapades.

A green tin box with handles that stored our dress-up clothes became a perfect covered wagon cargo chest. Flowing skirts, felt hats and layers of scarves adorned my **pioneergypsy** character.

Unlimited imaginary characters flowed from the green tin dress-up box.

A rickety, weather-beaten table Mom used for transplanting plants on our back porch was pushed and dragged into position under the lowest hanging bough of the cottonwood tree.

From Dad's lawn-mowing shed, I found the triangle of a nylon parachute Dad had bought at the Army Surplus store for fifty cents. He used it for collecting grass clippings when Julie and I weren't concocting adventures with it. It was only a third of the size of an original army parachute, but it was huge.

I shook out the white nylon and draped it over the tree limb to create the perfect canopy for my adventure. When my **pioneergypsy**'s wagon was set, I centered myself on the edge of the table and yelled out to my imaginary horse brigade, *"Yee-Hahhh! Rollin' rollin' rollin'...."* That was followed by a cracking-the-whip sound, which I'd mastered with a dramatic flourish.

Rocking back and forth on the edge of the table, which was close to falling apart, I replicated what I fancied as crossing the prairie to a new frontier. If attacked by hostiles, I would *shake-rattle-and-roll* the whole caper with creative vengeance.

When I wasn't imagining myself as this trail-blazin' pioneer-gal, I was adding layers of colored skirts from the dress-up box to my outfit so I could be a gypsy.

Dad fashioned a pair of two-inch hoop earrings out of lightweight curtain rings. They were spray-painted gold and had tiny eye-hooks on top with big rubber bands threaded through them. This provided the perfect (and comfortable) means for looping them around my tiny ears for some fantastic gypsy-hoop earrings.

I danced wildly about and ran up and down our two back hills. Cavorting in a series of imaginary, close escapes from certain captivity by a wild band of bandits, I always triumphed.

Fast forward to my *reVirement* journey. I realized that, in their essence, these games clearly reflected the spirit of independence and creative exuberance that is quintessential to my soul.

Even more surprising was the discovery that – hidden within the life I'd built – an unacknowledged **pioneergypsy** faced challenges with the same *shake-rattle-and-roll* of inventiveness.

I began to consider the things that got me into trouble. Again, I was led to some surprising clues for reclaiming my *liTe* to *liVe*.

In fifth grade, a year after my *AsIF* decision to become the perfect student, I got into trouble at school. On this day, I couldn't contain my excitement about art. Before class, I gathered a group of fellow students around me and, with nonstop enthusiasm, regaled them with my insights.

I was promptly asked by Mr. Teacher to stand in the corner due to my inability to suppress my enthusiasm.

It was a real shocker. I thought I was _supposed_ to be excited about what I was learning. Had I been too enthusiastic? What was "too much"? I didn't know. In the corner that day, I decided to tone myself down, dim my excitement. I certainly didn't want to get in trouble anymore.

If only I'd known then what I do now about my enoughness, I might not have spent years installing and operating my inner-light dimmer switch. This was one story of many when, although innocent enough, early decisions had the power to direct life-altering consequences.

Yet this story also held a gem. It revealed an inherent enthusiasm for sharing and involving others in my insights. It was clearly no coincidence that this trait followed me throughout my life. And, it held no surprise that I now hoped to passionately share my _JOLLI_ inspirations and enthusiasm with others!

Birthed from stories like these, a host of renewed perspectives influenced my thinking about how and where to reshape and repurpose my life's second-half.

There were _LoveIT_-gems throughout my history to be found and reconsidered. Even from later adulthood, classics were brushed off and brought to life for my renaissance. The path broadened, providing a shift that included more pivoting potential for my reinvention.

From the best parts of my past I pondered a plethora of principles, practices and paradigms that provided permission for me to plow forward. The path of the V was surprisingly filled with a preponderance of P-words that helped me describe principles I found to be inspiring.

SUMMARY> **Garbagegems, Dollishops & Pioneergypsy**

♦ The knack for finding gems in garbage inspired reinvention.

♦ Joyful **Dollishops** revealed more of who I truly am.

♦ *Old* ideas, stored in stories, dimmed my *bold* light.

CHAPTER 24

Top Three P's

- Pretending My Intending
- Prevailing Perception Insights
- Meeting My **Playright**

When I piled a big stack of writings together, over half a dozen concepts competed for a place in this chapter. There played an uncanny recurring theme. I found myself toying with "P" names to describe these poignant paragraphs. At one precipice in the process, I named this chapter "P's for V" as there were so many P-principles to share, but my dear friend Sue gently pointed out, "Amy, is your book about the P or the V?!?"

I settled on sharing the top three P-principles that I'd adapted to support my pivotal journey to authentic living. Although I'd learned about them in workshops led by mentors, they took on new layers of meaning when I renovated and expanded their original lessons to the increasing wisdom I'd gained. The first of the three required brushing up on a childhood mindset and skill I'd once been really good at ... pretending.

When I was a kid playing **pioneergypsy**, my imagination and ability to pretend was at its peak. Not every kid has crossed an entire frontier to escape invading hostiles while riding on a rickety old table under a parachuted tree bough. Pretending my intending provided one surefire way for me to enhance any *inTent* to *inVent*. In fact, now I could petend with an adult-sized life arena, which provided a whole new array of skills to play with.

Tending to my pretending gave my newly-hatched intentions a jumpstart. A perfect opportunity to practice them occurred during the year I devoted to painting my artwork full time and creating my **artIT**.

I participated in a women's workshop about manifesting lifelong dreams. During the morning session, the other women and I made two lists: one was our unfulfilled bucket-dream list and the other was a list of our blocks—stories about why our dreams couldn't happen.

Then, it was time to knock down our mental blocks. After the lunch break, we were guided to shift our pretending skills into high gear. Referring to our lists, we were to pretend none of our mental blocks existed. We brushed off our imaginations and directed our inner-actresses to live out everything on our bucket-dream lists.

Mild groans of trepidation spread across the room; this required stepping over many of the inner barricades we'd spent the morning discussing. But then something happened. When the background music signaled the start of our pretending-play, the energy in the room shifted from caution to exhilaration. Quickly, I unleashed a new role for my *AsIF* Amy to play to her heart's content. The phrase "act *AsIF*" took on an immediate sensation of new meaning.

I practically skipped over to my friend and exclaimed about my "pretend dream" *AsIF* it were already true. "Hi, Karyn Ruth. I just got back from Hawaii, where I installed one of my art commissions in Wayne Dyer's home. He LOVED it! I'm off tomorrow with my awesome husband on a New York trip to install more of my paintings, and ...."

My dream story went on and on. Soon my arms shivered with the realization that, in just moments, I'd became my own Ms. Had*IT*all!

With visceral sensation from deep within, my whole body, mind and spirit aligned with my dream *LoveIT* life, and it felt completely real. The power of my pretending, like the Opposites Game, gave me a simple, painless way to turn about my old mental blocks with new tangible realism. My mind didn't have to believe any of it; if I pretended long enough, I would soon shift closer to it. Once I could start *SEEING* from a new perspective, the *DOING* and *BEING* didn't seem so out of reach.

The momentum from this simple exercise led me to take some novel actions after the workshop ended. When I returned home, I went into my art studio to create an imaginary *AsIF* check for $5,000.

With a bold purple pen, I playfully signed the check with an *AsIF* signature by Dr. Dyer. Then I wrapped it in a handwritten *AsIF* note in make-believe Dyer-penmanship. I wrote *AsIF* he were thanking me for the newly installed painting in his Hawaii home. Then I mocked up a purple envelope and attached a pretend Dr. W. Dyer return address label in the far left corner. The next morning before I could talk myself out of it, I addressed the envelope to myself at my current address and slid the pretend letter with its check into a local mailbox.

Playful and fun as it was, my *AsIF* letter started a brave, inner momentum. That week I was inspired to take steps towards actually making my *AsIF* dream happen. Through a fascinating synchronicity of events, I was led to an associate of Dr. Dyer. I mailed a letter to her asking her about making my dream a reality. This real letter was more challenging to write and mail, but what did I have to lose? A momentum had started, I made a decision and, without hesitation, went for it.

A couple days later, I received the purple envelope in the mail and opened it with pretend excitement. I gushed at receiving the *AsIF* check for $5,000—*AsIF* it were genuine. I set the check next to my little altar for added spiritual mojo. I returned to my busy life, soon forgetting about both letters.

A few weeks later, I came home and found tucked into my front door's gate a Fed Ex packet. I was expecting some art supplies so I didn't give it a lot of thought, until I checked the small return address label.

It was a tiny, unpretentious label with Dr. Dyer's name on it from a Hawaii address. Instantly I thought of Karyn Ruth White, my friend from the workshop. She's a hilarious professional speaker who sometimes uses outrageous props in her talks. I thought, "*Okay, Karyn Ruth, you got me; I'm officially punked from pretending my intending.*"

I went inside, thinking of ways to play along with her joke. I tossed the package aside to fix lunch. Later, I casually opened it to find that, indeed, it was a *RealDeal* letter from Dr. Dyer. He'd received my request and followed up with a handwritten, personal note. I was **amyazed**!

A wonderful and generous surprise from Dr. WAYne Dyer

By tending to my pretending, I'd allowed a whole stream of events to unfold, all of which I could never have imagined ahead of time.

What became the grand finale to this story? I did create some artwork for Dr. Dyer, but that seemed minor compared to the gifts I gained from pretending. I realized just how transforming passionate, make-believe powers could be.

I'd gained irrefutable evidence for enhancing my abilities for my *inTentions* to actualize *inVentions*.

Pretending my intending allowed me to pursue more than just *reVirement*-ripe ideas. It could actually enhance and expand many of the life-long dreams I hoped to create.

Prevailing Perception Insight

The second P of my top three was the principle of Prevailing Perception, a basic concept I'd also learned in a workshop. With a creative "P-spin", however, I renovated its basic concept for a *reVirement*-strength *life-lift*. The pivotal possibilities it provides for finding greater compassion and understanding can't be overestated.

It works like this: My Prevailing Perception is the sum total of five other P's that combine to influence the unique filter of interpretation I possess. This one-of-a-kind perception prevails in any given instant, until one of the P's changes.

Any new choice I make instantly creates a new Prevailing Perception, which, in turn, impacts future choices. I perceive my life and others through this filter that is unique only unto me. No one else can possibly know what I perceive.

P's that combine to create my Prevailing Perception include my PAST (genetics plus parents), my PERSONALITY (personal qualities), my PURSUITS (life experiences), my PREFERENCES (choices I make) and my PATTERNS (whatever I repeat over and over).

In any given moment, I can't possibly *SEE, DO* or *BE* anything beyond my current Prevailing Perception's combination of those five P's. Until something happens and I experience a shift involving a different choice or life experience, I can't change my perceptions.

I further discerned that everyone else lives and makes choices from their own unique Prevailing Perceptions. I can never truly know anyone else's, only my own. This awareness has increased my ability to find fascination and freedom versus judgment and limitation within disagreements with others.

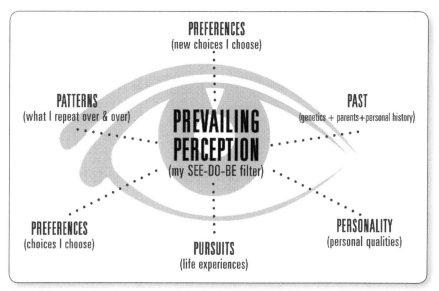

The filter of Prevailing Perception.

What a great pivoting practice it became to accept that, in any given moment, I operated at my very best based on my Prevailing Perception — unless, of course, something happened and my *SEEING* changed, which then gave me the chance to reinvent my Prevailing Perception.

In my pre-V days, I'd raced from *IT* to *IT*, searching to find answers. My Prevailing Perception was convinced I had to figure *IT* all out and make *IT* all happen. This created *old* patterns of limitation that kept *bold* choices out of reach. But now all that was changing. Living a life of turning-about required changing my Prevailing Perception, sometimes several times a day.

Meeting My **Playright**

The last of my top three P's resulted from another revelation I experienced during a two-day workshop. I'll call it the *"You're Right!"* weekend. Our instructions were simple, but implicit.

We were guided to tell the other participants anything we wished; our life's story, current challenges — anything and everything. As half of us went on and on with our details, the classmates who listened were only allowed one brief reply. No matter what story or drama was being told, those listening could only reply with a resounding *"You're Right!"*

Over and over, while detailing **MyStories**, without any sympathies or agreements came the same response: *"Amy, You're Right!"* It soon became a challenge to persuade the listeners to respond with anything other than *"You're Right!"* But they stood firm.

We spent the entire Saturday in this exchange. After about five hours, an indelible impression was etched into my psyche that returned with richer depth during my reinvention.

No matter what my mind made up or tried to figure out about life, I was always right, or so my limited mind thought. The script my mind wrote was always the result of my inner **playright** (play•right; my inner playwright who always gets to be right). If my inner **playright** was writing stories that insisted I was always right about whatever happened, then I _really_ needed to *check-out-the-data*. I could easily be thinking about an upside-down script!

What happened when I combined the top three P's into one final expansion? It resulted in an experience described with another great word that also begins with the letter P ... paradigm.

 paradigm a typical pattern of something; the collection of assumptions about any given subject.

During the course of finishing this book, many of my previous assumptions turned about and I experienced multiple paradigm shifts.

For a couple of years I passionately tended to my intentions to *WRITE THE BOOK!* During that process, I rewrote the draft into at least thirty alternate versions of its final edition. The homestretch finally arrived; I reached the final, Final, FINAL rewrite.

I decided to create a *JOLLI* writing refuge called my *White Write* retreat. I draped white sheets over my furniture and wore only white. This was my signal to Providence that I was serious about my decision to commit; this was my final *White Write!*

A white-write *rewrite retreat.*

For the first couple of days, once again, my *concepts* came together in *concerts* of melodic understanding. Then, with only six chapters to go, I hit a thick wall of writer's block.

Resistance flooded in and I turned things upside down to find my way through the block. It's interesting to note that writing a book about the *chance* to *change* can be quite challenging. I'd often complete a chapter or section only to have life and unforeseen changes require an adjustment to my theories and a flood of revisions.

I was in the middle of this P-chapter, fine-tuning my Prevailing Perception diagram, when I realized that everything I'd written sounded a bit like *selling* rather than *telling*. I asked myself to find a new kind of angle to the chapter. But wait! Why was I finding an angle instead of writing what was real for me? Old ways sometimes died hard.

A mini-meltdown occurred as my struggling old mindset held on for dear life, convincing me, *"Amy, you've got a schedule to keep; you can't rewrite this chapter now. You've got to figure this out! What is going on?!"* After a few hours, my *trying, prying* and *crying* brought no solutions. I collapsed on the couch to watch the lengthy, director's cut of the film *Robin Hood*.

After three hours of watching twelfth-century battles over ownership and territories, I realized that my mind's Prevailing Perception was doing the same. Refusing to give up its mental territory, my mind was fighting back. It refused to change anything in which I was deeply invested.

Loyalty to old ideas triggered an inner battle. With six chapters to go, why was this happening? My mind held on tight, locked in a battle of resistance on my internal battlefield.

Resistance, based on a myriad of fears, remained the biggest tyrant to all chances for turning about. And, like *Robin Hood*'s stingy bad guy, my inner Sheriff of Nottingham vied for all mental holdings. My mind did not want to budge and give up some of its hard-earned perceptions, and my **playright** had to be *right* and was putting up one heck of a *fight*.

Her plight to be *right* was dimming my *light* exponentially.

In a flash of realization, I saw what was going on with my thinking. My perceptions about Prevailing Perceptions no longer prevailed!

Finally the wall of writer's block I'd faced crumbled, exposing the needed revisions. All my frustration had been just the **overIT** momentum needed for a paradigm shift. I aligned with a spiritual realization that had unraveled throughout the years of my *JOLLI* jaunt.

I no longer lived a life that relied solely on my Prevailing Perception filter. Over and over, I ventured to keep my eyes peeled for upside-down stories. My **playright**'s script-writing most often proved limited. Even the intentions I thought I *should* be pretending were, more often than not, turned in another direction by unexpected incoming data. My mind was no longer in charge, and being right no longer held the same intrigue.

I couldn't pinpoint exactly when it occurred, but the idea that my mind knew best was a paradigm that shifted dramatically. I googled the phrase "paradigm shift" and, sure enough, discovered a parallel.

A scientist named Thomas Kuhn described paradigm shifts in relation to scientific revolution. Although he wrote his theories in 1962, his definitions described exactly how I'd lived over several years while going through the **innervention** of my own **innerstate**.

Kuhn argued that scientific advancement is not evolutionary but, rather, a "series of peaceful interludes punctuated by intellectually violent revolutions." In those revolutions, "one conceptual world view is replaced by another."

This is exactly what was happening to my mind's territory. My conceptual views were being replaced by others, sometimes peacefully and, at other times, quite abruptly—as a violent revolution. The way I thought and lived my life had undergone a dramatic paradigm shift.

My entire relationship to *DOING* had been turned upside down. In the past, after *SEEING* what needed to be done, I'd set about *DOING* all manner of things to create a new state of *BEING*.

But now the opposite was happening. My state of *BEING* took priority over all forms of *DOING*. Before *DOING* anything, my first priority became my sense of *BEING*.

I no longer relied on **nexITs** to find answers. My *IT*-focused life almost disappeared completely. I connected with aspects of myself and all of life, finding a greater nexus. My **nexIT** had found a **nexUS** (nex•us; spelling of word nexus to stress "US") paradigm shift.

 nexus a connection or series of connections linking two or more things. A connected group. The central and most important point or place.

It became an undeniable fact that something greater than my own Prevailing Perception now ran the Amy show. A **nexUS** had occurred that was more reliable, sustainable and dependable. This unification transcended my very best thinking from the past. A series of **nexUS** connections now linked together to guide my life.

A surge of information and insights – along with people, places and things – continued to take me towards a greater sense of *BEING*. In the **Amyzone**, I found an alliance much greater than my **playright**'s limited scripts. It seemed as though everything now happened for my greater good from a collective source greater than my own mind.

I reflected: *"What if it's all good? What if it all happens for a reason? What if it's all more than good? What if ... ?"*

SUMMARY>Top Three P's

◆ Tending to *inTentions* sped up their *inVentions*.

◆ My prevailing perception created a one-of-a-kind filter.

◆ A paradigm shift arrived for a timely **nexUs** revelation.

CHAPTER 25

It's All Go(o)d

- The **PreSCRIPTion** Theory
- Three Good Things
- It All Counts!

I could no longer diminish the divine-like timing of everything that had happened throughout my life. All the heartaches, headaches and backaches from my desire to travel the right *road* were just the *load* I needed to turn my life about.

Through the wisdom of retrospect, it became very clear that everything that occurred in my life delivered the **preSCRIPTion** (pre•scrip•tion; a pre-SCRIPT providing a healing prescription) necessary for me to find my *RealDeal* heal. What I'd previously thought was my quirky *odyssey* was now becoming a ***godyssey*** with a godly twist.

This was a precarious topic to include in my book. Defining and discussing that one simple word, God, is a debatable endeavor. Millenniums and millions surround the simple God-word, from inspired revolutions to deadly battles and more. In my **Amynation** alone, I'd traversed vast territories and dived to my own depths in efforts to define God, a three-letter word packed with meaning.

Defining or discussing God could easily become a complex task wrought with contentions. There are as many Prevailing Perceptions about God as there are people with perceptions!

Once again, my **typoknackabilities** and **grammaring** came to the rescue. By adding *just-one-little-letter*, an "o" with a couple of parentheses, the discussion of God took on an easier dimension. No longer part of a religious or spiritual discussion, it simply considered what's **Go(o)d** (good {or god}: parenthetical blend of God with good).

The following three accounts encouraged my beliefs in the conviction that everything I'd lived and all that happens were truly, all **Go(o)d**.

This first story provided the perfect script for me to *SEE* the irony of my **playright**'s inability to get the story right. Sometimes the worst things bring about the best prescribed outcomes. This story occurred shortly after my first **vepiphany**, when I began writing a book solely about *reVirement*.

Convinced I was going to change the world with my *JOLLI* revolution to turn about the **tiredword**, I launched into writing and researching. A plan was hatched whereby I would write a brilliant proposal and convince a publisher to fund the writing of my book.

Thornton gumption took hold and I was blinded in my naiveté by unbridled enthusiasm. I could clearly *SEE* the potential for the book and composed a multi-paged folder complete with sections on my competition and market research. Unfortunately, I avoided one minor detail ... I hadn't written the book yet!

A colleague agreed to look over my proposal and give me feedback. She was a savvy editor and we'd worked together on several book projects. Convinced I would win over Ms. Editor, I surged forward with my enthusiastic V-vision.

I designed a beautiful packet and dropped it off on a Friday afternoon at Ms. Editor's home for her weekend review. I was terrified but proud that I'd accomplished one leg of the journey to getting published. I headed home, exhausted and full of expectation.

By the next evening, I was beside myself. Why hadn't I heard from her? Did she hate the book? No, it was too good of an idea for that. Maybe she was editing my proposal with some of her own ideas. My mind wrote an entire script about my hopes for the project.

By Sunday night, I called Ms. Editor and cautiously inquired, "Well—what do you think?" I was not prepared for her response. After a gap of silence that spoke volumes, Ms. Editor stumbled and then said, "Amy—I just don't think there is enough here for a book."

I gripped the phone, devastated. My worst doubts had been right. *"Who was I to write a book about the V? I'm a terrible writer!"* I quickly got off the phone and launched a massive **blamestorming** (blame•storm•ing; a storm of *lame blame)* session that went on for days.

I tried to let myself just be *AsIS* with my disappointment, but I was angry, tired, frustrated and ashamed. The worst blame was directed right at me, *"REALLY Amy, who do you think you are?! You're not a good writer, nor will you ever be a published author; time to put away this whole V-idea!"*

On the third day, I sat thinking about what happened and all that had led to that moment. I was at a fork in my mental road. I could lose another day in my *Not-OK Corral*, or I could consider changing directions. I made a new decision: *"I am NOW turning this about!"*

Considering the ideas *"It's all good"* and *"I'm always right,"* I thought, *"What happens when what I think is right turns out to be wrong?"*

A playful thought came to mind:*"Amy, how would your **playright** pre-write the script?"* I smiled, thinking, *"If only I'd given Ms. Editor a pre-SCRIPT to follow, I wouldn't have this sinking thinking!"*

Then I wondered, *"What SCRIPT would have presented the right healing* **preSCRIPTion**?" I grabbed my *Streams* journal and wrote out the script I thought Ms. Editor should have followed.

In playful detail, I rewrote the events of the last few days. Then, the oddest thing happened. At the end of my pre-script, a powerful awareness swept in. Alternate understanding flowed from the inside out.

If Ms. Editor had followed my pre-script, or even half of it, I would never have arrived at the momentum that built inside me over her rejection. I would never have experienced how truly passionate I was about writing the book. It's important to note that her dismissal would fuel my insistence to *WRITE THE BOOK!* for the next few years.

Her rejection was perfection! It was the **preSCRIPTion** I needed to turn in a new direction. Further, if that book proposal had been a success, I would have neither discovered my other two **vepiphanies**, nor experienced the profound opportunities that evolved over the next few years.

The wisdom of retrospect, once again, delivered a great truth with more evidence that everyone and everything really is always right, and *it's-all-**Go(o)d**!*

Then I wondered if this **preSCRIPTion** might apply to the other things that had gone "wrong" with my life. Daring thoughts followed. *"Amy, what if every aspect of life, including every dark corner, was the right* **preSCRIPTion** *to heal your life and reach your liTe to liVe? Could it all be part of an unfolding* **Go(o)d** *plan?"*

What if it all counted? What if everything was exactly what was needed in order to arrive at my truth? I considered some of the worst tragedies of my life; could those pass my **preSCRIPTion** theory?

Over and over, as I considered the greatest trials of my life, I realized that every one of them had forged a unique aspect of me. The darkest things that had happened were the exact **preSCRIPTion** needed to arrive in the present moment, where I'd finally found my *liTe* to *liVe*.

A deep and quiet reminder came through: It really was all **Go(o)d**. All my apparent "garbage" contained the gems I needed to become the *ME* I came here to *BE*. Without betrayal, I would not have transcended. Without fear, I would not have found faith. Without *pain*, there would not be *gain*. My life's masterpiece, filled with its layers of contrast, was perfect for me.

Three Good Things

In retracing some of the worst things that had occurred in my life, I recalled this second story of a robbery that occurred just after I'd returned from Manhattan to live in Denver.

In the years I'd lived in the often-perceived "dangerous" city of New

York, I was never involved in any sort of robbery; yet, within one week of returning to Denver, someone broke into my home and stole a lifetime collection of jewelry.

I was devastated. After the police left, I read an article by Dr. Norman Vincent Peale, who suggested that at least three good things could come from every tragedy.

At the time I thought, *"Three good things could come from this robbery?!? You've got to be kidding."* I challenged the universe to show me these three things and, within a short time:

1. I realized that I didn't need all my jewelry to be attractive.

2. I met an insightful detective who taught me some great safety tips to create a secure home—tips I would practice for decades.

3. I learned about the three-good-things list, which I also continued to use for years in the face of seemingly bad things.

Could my **preSCRIPTion** be combined with the pivoting possibilities of uncovering just three good things on the other side of challenging **LifeStuff**? I ran my theory through one of the more significant tragedies of my life: Mom dying from breast cancer.

Three good things that came of it:

1. A strict Lutheran and Sunday school teacher, Mom probably would have struggled over the years with my many differing views, and I might've reacted by "giving in" in order to please her.

2. The depth of empathy and compassion I feel for anyone going through a severe illness or tragic loss would never have evolved had I not gone through that difficult trial.

3. I learned to survive some very rough things at an early age and gained the stamina I would need to cope with many other hardships.

*Extra credit: I learned how very precious and vulnerable life can be, which has enhanced my conviction to *live life* with deep appreciation.

I considered my pains and betrayals and, within each one, found a treasure, a **garbagegem** each had forged deep within my character.

I increasingly embraced the idea that some redeeming order existed in the worst of things, often in the form of unexplainable divinity and timing. It surely seemed like *"It's-all-***Go(o)d***."*

"But what about all those terrible, tragic things that happen every day in the world?" I could hear my inner skeptics when I suggested living by this *It's-all-***Go(o)d*** insight. I considered a possible answer.

I might not have answers to why bad things happen, but what if each contains the exact momentum of **NecessaryStuff** needed for a **quantumesque** turnabout to happen and something good to arrive?

It All Counts!

A third story confirmed my ideas. Once again my friend Ted and I wound our way along the Apex trail to our favorite overlook. It was time to put my *It's-all-***Go(o)d*** theory to a Ted-test.

I asked Ted if he'd be willing to consider some of his worst life-trials from a new perspective.

"Sure," Ted agreed, looking a tad nervous.

To ease him into my theory, I asked Ted what he had _loved_ to do as a kid. What were his early childhood *LoveITs?* What were the things he came up with on his own that brought him joy? What were the things he got in trouble for?

"Oh, that's easy!" Ted lit up. "I grew up back East in a house surrounded by woods. I built forts, explored the woods, tumbled and fought with my brother and always came home battered and bruised.

"My father never gave me much attention; blood and bruises simply showed him that I played hard and won hard. But my mom would get so mad when I kept getting messed up. To me, the more beat-up I was, the harder I'd played the game and the better adventurer I was."

Ted took on the same lightness of step and inner luster that emerged whenever I asked my friends about their childhood *LoveITs*. Even friends with tragic or abusive childhoods found something that their *FirstMe* genius used to bring them comfort or joy.

I shifted the topic and brought Ted's attention to my three-good-things and *It's-all-**Go(o)d*** theories. I asked him a tough question, "Ted, what's one of the biggest betrayals that ever happened to you?"

Ted didn't skip a beat. "That's a no-brainer," he said, "the horrible split I had with Ms. BadBreakup."

He launched into a detailed description of his **traumadrama** with Ms. BadBreakup. He concluded by telling me that, at the end of their relationship, his whole reputation had been on the line. Lawyers were involved with a lawsuit so thick he landed in court in front of a judge who held the future of Ted's career in his hands. It wasn't until the judge hit the gavel and pronounced Ted's innocence that the ordeal was resolved.

When he'd finished, Ted looked at me, miserable from reliving the drama, and said, "Now, Amy, don't tell me there were three good things in that. I would have done *ANYTHING* not to have gone through that horrible nightmare!"

"Okay, Ted, I won't go there ... not yet, anyway. I'm almost done with my Ted-test. Pretend that you are a **playright** and could write the right **preSCRIPTion** for how it all *should* have happened."

Ted balked a bit, defending with great detail how none of this mattered now that it was over. I could see that Ted was committed to his **blamestorming** and hoped to convince me he was the victim and Ms. Badbreakup was the bad apple who'd spoiled everything.

I urged him to rewrite the script (whether he believed it or not). He started linking his thinking and rewrote the script of the painful event.

A fascinating thing happened as Ted recited his pre-script. Memories collided with the rough childhood he'd survived. We landed on a **garbagegem**: Ted had always succeeded despite horrendous obstacles. With his own wisdom of retrospect, he soon saw the correlation. The greater the pain, the better he "played the game" of winning at life.

Then his AHA arrived, the moment of insight-opportunity knocking. Ted got it. He stopped in his tracks along the trail and blurted, "Amy! You mean ... it all counts?!?"

Ted's big grin said it all. "It's all part of my personal puzzle, isn't it? It's exactly what I needed to get me to right here. Now I *SEE* what you're saying. I'm always right when I look at it from that **preSCRIPTion** perspective!"

Instead of blaming Ms. BadBreakup for her bad behavior, Ted saw she'd actually read her lines perfectly as the live-film played out on Ted's life-movie screen.

We reached our favorite overlook and found at least four or five good things that had come from Ted's ordeal. Then we turned and headed back down the trail. When we arrived at the paved parking lot, Ted challenged me with my own theory.

He knew all about my breakup with Mr. Farmile and was curious to see if he could break my three-good-things code. But, alas, I was getting good at my theory and responded without skipping a step:

1. I got to experience a level of love with Mr. Farmile that I never thought possible; although it had not worked out, it was worth it.

2. If we hadn't split up, I would not have bought my little home, experienced my dreams as an artist or met the friends I now have in my life. I might not have landed in my *Not-OK Corral* and my whole *reVirement* revolution might never have occurred!

In a global summary, I listed number three:

3. I would <u>never</u> have become who I am today if we'd stayed together. I would have lived an entirely different life.

A rinse of clarity and brilliance washed over me. Goose bumps shot up my right arm, signaling I was right-ON. A wave of gratitude swept through me. I hugged Ted goodbye and got in my car.

While VIDA's engine warmed up, I suddenly made another connection with what Ted and I discussed. Three childhood **traumadramas** came to mind, priming me to dive in even deeper.

At around age five, I was inseparable from one of my dolls, a troll doll whose hair I trimmed to match my own brown, pixie haircut. My fearless confidant, she was always with me. Our bond was so sacred I shared everything with her, and she allowed my full *AsIS* Amy to be exactly who I was: *sad, mad* or *bad*.

On a family outing, she accidently fell out of my pocket, and I didn't discover this until we returned to the car after a four-hour hike. I was inconsolable and a part of me never got over the loss. It was my first visceral experience of death—even if it was just the death of a doll.

Within a year, I'd bonded with another doll: a Chatty Cathy talking doll. Once again, my doll and I became inseparable. I pulled one of her front teeth to match mine and she'd taken so many baths with me that her talking voice-box no longer worked. I didn't care because my imaginative **playright** always scripted the perfect lines for her anyway.

My parents convinced me she was pretty beaten up and broken, so we shipped her off to the Mattel factory to get her voice box and tooth repaired. I'll never forget what happened when we picked her up. I ripped open the box, only to find they had sent me a brand new doll.

Mom was overjoyed. I was grief-stricken. I attempted to tuck the pain deep beneath my **sureface**, but I never played with another doll— and I'm the inventor of **Dollishops**!

Recalling these two doll stories triggered a soft but deep pain in my chest. They'd both been true friends and unconditional companions who'd died quickly and unexpectedly. My little heart was broken and I buried the pain deep within my core for years.

At age eight, I turned from my dolls to love our second Siamese **supercata**. He had such a sweet and loyal disposition that I considered him my baby. I dressed him in Chatty Cathy's clothes and he returned unconditional love.

Then he got sick and developed severe pains. My parents took him to the vet for some medicine and returned without him. He had swallowed a bone and there was nothing to be done. They'd made the only difficult choice they could. And I buried my grief deep, for years.

The hike with Ted led me to explore more about those three deaths. I applied my *It's-all-**Go(o)d*** overview.

1. Perhaps those three losses had prepared me for the difficult deaths of Julie, Mom and Dad.

2. My childlike capacity to love deeply had been there all along. I could now reach back and bring more of that love into life now.

3. I now could *SEE* how an early decision to protect myself from ever loving so deeply again eventually became an *issue* in my heart *tissue* that would impact all my close relationships.

Supercata, *my baby.*

With flooding insight, a stream of questions reached back through those roots, cracking my heart wide open. *"Amy, is this why you hold yourself back from loving too much? Is this an old script about loving that needs a bold turnabout? Could I now love without limits?"*

While driving home, I considered how powerful the re-telling of my history was. Without anything to *DO* about it, I could just let my unique story *BE*. In telling the truth, without any *lame blame* towards both myself or others, I was setting myself free. I pulled into the driveway and looked at myself in the rearview mirror and thought, *"Amy, I love you. I love everything that ever happened to you. I love your failings and your triumphs. I love all of you ... AsIS. I love you without limits!"*

I shook my head in **amyazement**. I'd just landed on perhaps the greatest *JOLLI* role for my life's second half. *"Amy, from now on, it's all about shining your liTe to liVe ... as loVe!"*

Within weeks, the V delivered a vision of love so big, it could only be described as **vastronomical** (vast•ro•nom•i•cal; astronomically V-sized).

Chapter 26

A V.O.D. Experience

- A Visceral ExtraVaganza
- Indisputable Graphic **Vevidance**
- The Divine Feminine

Shortly after my hike with Ted, I experienced a mind-altering encounter I described as a **V.O.D.** (v•o•d; acronym for V-Over-Dose, overdose on the letter V). It convinced me beyond doubt there exists something supernatural and influential about this one simple letter.

Midway through one of the earlier drafts of this book, I ventured again to New York for a week's writing retreat. A friend recommended a small motel named The Born Free Motel a block off the beach in the southernmost village of the Hamptons on Montauk, Long Island.

I landed at LaGuardia Airport, rented a small red Honda and picked up a few groceries. While driving along the Sunshine Highway, I imagined the next five days of doing nothing but write, Write, WRITE!

The broad horizon of the highway narrowed to a point up ahead, illustrating the classic **vhorizon** V—it was a simple reminder to align my *inTent* with what I wished to *inVent*. I reviewed my V-inspired revolution and remained passionate about telling my *JOLLI* story.

When the highway curved, leading the Honda directly into the bright sun, I shielded my eyes from the glare. As if on cue to get my attention, a conductor of natural phenomenon, the V, began orchestrating a visual extraVaganza that induced nothing short of a spiritual **aVakening** (a•vak•en•ing; awakened by the letter V).

As I adjusted my sights to the blinding light coming through the window, the glare softened, allowing my focus to sharpen on the surrounding trees hugging the highway. Suddenly I saw limbs in all shapes and sizes reaching out to me in an applause of V's. I entered a movie backlit by the brilliant indigo sky and framed with the gold-to-red spectrum of the autumn canopy.

How could I have missed the vast array of V's inherent in trees before? In my art school days, I'd painted hundreds of trees, but I'd

Tree limbs reached out with all variations of the V.

failed to overlay the V to their structural shapes. A multi-experiential perspective unfolded before me: I literally saw V's eVerywhere. It proved so distracting I slowed the car, reminding myself to drive carefully.

A strange power enveloped me. I became transfixed and was brought to tears at the vast variety of beauty and wonder of these V's extending out to me. The kaleidoscopic perspective of V's amidst the rustling leaves and tree limbs completely interrupted my driving.

I stopped the car on a favorite lane leading to a nature trail I'd enjoyed a decade earlier. I needed to get some air and stretch. I glanced in the rearview mirror to wipe off my runny mascara. Before swiping my cheeks clean, soft streams of grey lines etched V crow's-feet from the outside edges of my eyes. The sides of my face radiated with V's.

I shook my head in disbelief, not sure if I wanted to clean them or photograph their beauty. I'd never considered my wrinkles beautiful, yet now they opened my eyes, radiating—like the V-principles of perspective.

Grabbing the roll of paper towels I'd picked up at the store, I stopped short. The bold typography of the brand, VIVA, blasted a graphic confirmation; the V wasn't only evident in nature all around me. I'd used VIVA brand paper towels for years (they have excellent absorbency for artists' paints) but this was the first time I linked the brand name with the Spanish celebratory toast of "Long life!"

I flashed on the *JOLLI* phrase I'd coined a few weeks earlier: "My *liTe* to *liVe* is *loVe!*" With amplified fusion, my "*Viva the V!*" salute intensified, confirming I was on to something vaster than I'd imagined.

Cleaning my face became fruitless as more tears flowed. I reached down to tighten my V-laced running shoes, and the veins on the tops of my hands raised in delicate, olive-green V-veins. I dove into a state of V-verklempt, the Yiddish word meaning "overcome with emotion".

I tried to calm down, thinking, *"Keep it together,* **Amyzon**. *You're on a bizarre V-edge. It's either fatigue or someone is really trying to get your attention!"*

I opened the car door and stepped onto a V-planet. From a heightened state of **aVareness** (a•vare•ness; aware of V), I looked down and noticed a recent rainstorm had fissured the dirt road in odd V's. Cracked rivers of V's were embossed in the dried mud beneath the Honda's tires, leaving a pattern of intricate V-tracks in their path.

At the side of the road, a wave of beautiful tall grasses sprouted from the earth; shapes of V's swayed to the rhythm of the wind. The V's

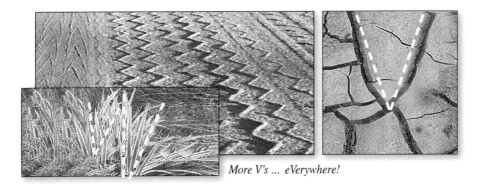

More V's ... eVerywhere!

seemed to be proclaiming their connection to Mother Earth. I swooned, **enVraptured** (en•vrap•tured; enraptured by the V)!

The small nature trail greeted me with a pathway of greenery that displayed a plethora of V's throughout their infrastructure.

A jagged oak limb arched low across the trail's path, and I bowed to go under it. I clasped the branch, which was filled with pentagonal-shaped leaves, to see a limitless tally of V-veins within each leaf.

I was outside of myself, *SEEING* with V-shaped glasses. In classic *right-in-front-of-me* form, the Olympian goddess of nature revealed yet another of her many best-kept secrets—all encrypted by the V.

More tears blurred my vision and I stumbled slightly over a sprawling V-shaped root from the overhead oak tree. I sat down on a fallen limb, deciding that it was official: I'd succumbed to my first verifiable overdose induced by the letter V. I was indeed **V.O.D.ing**!

Every botanical nuance my eyes landed on appeared etched, carved, or branded with some iteration of the V. A daddy longlegs spider squiggled across the bark beside my foot. His legs sprouted from his body in thread-like V-angles as he ventured along the path with kinetic V-movements.

Even the tiniest of grasses lining the trail joined together, sprouting arms of multiple V's. This audience of V's confirmed that I was not hallucinating but, indeed was seeing something extraordinary.

At this point, I needed another kind of **innerVention**, but I didn't know a soul who could have **innerVened** (in•ner•ven•ed; intervened between the inner me and the V). Nature called out to me, *"Amy, it's all about the V! Pay attention to what the V-path is teaching you. This is all about who you came here to BE!"*

Was Mother Nature reminding me of the pivotal path that was always available if only I opened my eyes to *SEE* it? How many answers were so simple I missed them? How many times had I unintentionally ignored the most important things that were *right-in-front-of-me?*

I sat blinking, attempting to absorb what was happening when, above and to the left, a choir of honking geese in full formation passed overhead. Heralding in a grand finale, the ultimate sign of the V, their intuitive flight path dotted across the arching sky in a dancing V shape.

My heart raced. I shook my head in disbelief, hearing my grandmother's excited voice from my memory banks. Upon witnessing a breathtaking sunset, she would exclaim *"For the love of God!"* Was this V-inspired spectacle *ALL* about the *LoVe of Go(o)d?* In that moment, as eVerything connected with unwavering love—it was *ALL-Go(o)d.*

The V engulfed me with a symphony of visceral notes that united my physical, emotional and spiritual *BEING.* And, for a **V.O.D.** finish, V's burst across the sky when the sun's rays flashed through the white clouds, creating the most vibrantly-defined V-beams imaginable.

I jumped up, raising my arms and spreading my fingers as I stretched out in a V-stance. My own body held thousands of its own V's. I'd experienced paradigm shifts and rebirths before, but nothing in my past compared to this life-

EnVraptured, in a state of oneness with the V.

aligning moment. I merged with the V, at one with it.

How could this life-changing experience transpire, literally, from one old word ... the **tiredword**? I practically floated during the rest of the drive through Montauk, where I checked into the Born Free Motel.

When I opened my *Streams* journal to record my **V.O.D.** and further explore all that had happened that afternoon, I started doodling with the shapes of V and was swept away in another tidal wave of visual V-connections inspired from my years of creating graphics.

Indisputable Graphic **Vevidance**

My professional life in graphic design began the day Dad brought home a Chandler & Price antique letterpress along with several cabinets of wooden type. We quickly turned half of his art studio into a print shop.

I learned to hand set type and lock rows of letters into a frame called a chase before the rollers pressed on the ink. Placing individual letters to make a sentence seemed archaic to me back then, yet I loved printing colorful wedding napkins, programs and flyers for all occasions. This was long before computers revolutionized the graphic design scene.

When I entered art school, I spent two semesters learning about fonts and the anatomy of letters. This type-anatomy, like physical anatomy, has corresponding Latin names.

Intrigued by my *T-to-V* **vepiphanies**, I pulled out my laptop to research the type-anatomy of the letters "T" and "V", thinking I might uncover more hidden V-clues.

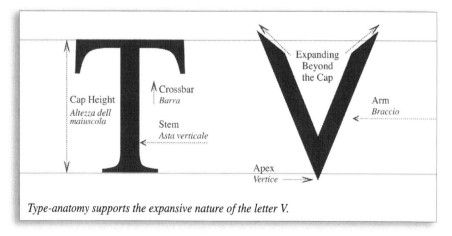

Type-anatomy supports the expansive nature of the letter V.

Fascinated by the graphic **vevidance** I'd uncovered, I sketched signatures to my **V.O.D.** day. Presented below are my favorite two.

The verbal descriptions of the V's anatomy confirmed its inspiring powers. Not only is the "V" composed of two arms extending from its central apex, but its arms reach out into infinity. The "V" is an open-ended triangle with a spacious gateway to limitless extension at the top.

In geometry, the apex is defined as the highest point in a plane or solid figure. In botany, the apex is the growing end of a shoot. In vocabulary the verb "to apex" means to reach a point or towering edge.

In contrast, the top of the "T" is defined as a crossbar that rests on a stem. Crossbar, as a noun, is defined as a horizontal bar fixed across another. Nothing too inspiring about that.

It was getting late, but I was on a *T-to-V* roll. I applied various fonts to my graphical play with the letters T and V.

Looking at the letter "T" again, I considered its lower-case version: "t". With its crossbar moved down on its stem, the letter now closely resembled a cross, a powerful symbol in existence for thousands of years. I considered its symbolism in relation to my *T-to-V* revelations.

This ancient symbol—so often associated with pain and suffering—delivered a new **Amyalogy**. Had not all my pain and suffering landed me in a midlife *Not-OK Corral?*

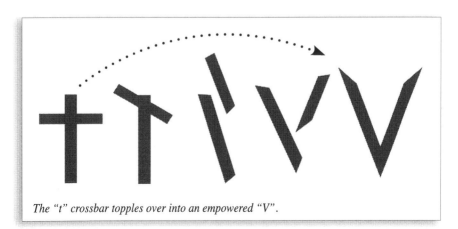

The "t" crossbar topples over into an empowered "V".

I now saw a parallel between me and the letter "t". I created a quick sketch wherein the "t" opened up into an ever-expansive "V".

Hadn't the **tiredword** become my own cross to bear? Only after banning its exhaustion from my vocabulary had I been able to open up like an ever-expansive "V". Throughout my *reVirement*, I would release many *old* crosses as I embraced the *bold* path of V. I recalled my Sunday school classes and thought, *"Amy, surely Jesus would want you to get off the* old *crosses you bear and embrace a* bold life *to* live!"

The Divine Feminine

I was too **envraptured** to fall asleep and continued my creative V-venture. I searched the internet, perusing a variety of fonts and symbols—something graphic designers love to do. I stumbled across a font of universal symbols and was just about ready to call it a night when one last graphic insight came.

As my eyes landed upon the international symbol for a female, my mouth fell open and I thought, *"Seriously? How did the international symbol for female end up with a crossbar for a body? Who walks around like that? Maybe the inventor of that symbol was some mad-male scientist determined to keep women in their place. Who knows?!"*

Immediately I created a revised symbol for "woman". Doesn't this new universal symbol—the one in the middle—make more sense?

Universal symbol for Female   *ReVised symbol for Female*   *Universal symbol for Male*

I emailed the new symbol to Melm, who responded with a *"LoveIT"* text. When we spoke the next morning she would say some Native American legends state women get their power from the earth while men get theirs from the sky. The V's in my new symbols confirmed this.

While brushing my teeth before bed, I mulled over an emerging possibility. *"Amy, maybe Mother Nature and the V are all about a divine feminine power?"* That thought was answered immediately when I climbed into bed and started reading Dr. Dyer's book on the *Tao Te Ching*. An inspired interpretation from the ancient text by Lao-Tzu, a Chinese philosopher and poet, Dr. Dyer's words provided a massive, poetical-exclamation point to end my day.

The poignancy of the sixth verse brought tears to my eyes. I sat up in bed and read it twice, soaking it in. The verse encapsulated the magic of my **V.O.D.** experience and introduced even more for me to consider.

Sixth Verse of the *Tao Te Ching*

The spirit that never dies
   is called the mysterious feminine.
Although she becomes the whole universe,
   her immaculate purity is never lost.
Although she assumes countless forms,
   her true identity remains intact.

The gateway to the mysterious female
   is called the root of creation.
Listen to her voice,
   hear it echo through creation.
Without fail, she reveals her presence.

Without fail, she brings us to our own perfection.
Although it is invisible, it endures;
   it will never end.

      — *Lao-Tzu*, Chinese sage

I searched through the words again, considering all my V-**vevidance**. I paraphrased Lao Tzu's sixth verse with a slight V-twist:

"Although the V assumes countless forms, her true identity remains ... the gateway to the mysterious female ... the root of creation. Listen to her V-voice echo. Without fail, she reVeals her presence ... she brings us to our own perfection. The V endures ... it will neVer end!"

Through my **V.O.D.** extravaganza, had the V been encouraging me to explore a greater, diVine energy – in countless forms – at the foundation of eVerything? Had the oneness I'd experienced with the V contained an undeniable hint that eVerything was connected? Had I been granted an experience of unity that only my quirky fascination with the V could produce?

My writing retreat had just begun and already I was contemplating too much to condense into words. I stayed up, making notes, not sure how these new insights would fit into my book's current content. My newest discoveries would turn about several concepts and add at least another chapter. Oh well, that's what writing about change often entails—more change!

I fell fast asleep in a blissful state of wonder over what had happened that day. I felt more spiritually tuned-in than I could remember ever *BEING* before. My poor, little ole' mind struggled to figure it all out. I felt humbled and inspired at the same time.

The following morning, I arose to an emerging dawn. Rays of sunlight peeked through the motel room's corduroy curtains; daybreak called. With four more days to explore my reVelations, I fixed a cup of tea and packed up for the beach.

Filled with reinvigorated curiosity, I looked forward to my next discoveries. What more did the V have to show me? Could the mysterious feminine be beckoning me to align with my own diVinity? Was there more of her presence to be reVealed that day?

The *Tao Te Ching* described the Divine Feminine as bringing us to our own perfection—was this a new destiny for me to discover? Indeed, I was about to uncover the final answer to my life-long *IT* search.

SUMMARY> A V.O.D. Experience

- ◆ A writing retreat provided a mind-blowing extraVaganza.

- ◆ Graphical **vevidance** supported my enigmatic V-theories.

- ◆ Lao-Tzu's ancient verse suggested a diVine destiny.

CHAPTER 27

Finding *IT IS*

- Knowing My **Nowing**
- Letting *IT* Go
- So it *IS!*

I headed down the front stairs of the Born Free Motel with a vigorous skip. On a **soulular** (soul•u•lar; beyond a cellular level, in one's soul) level, I anticipated some time journaling and beach exploring to let my **V.O.D** extraVaganza really soak in.

A brilliant blue sky held the diamond of an incandescent sun. As I stepped onto the crunchy gravel of the parking lot, I paused for a stunning 360-degree spin to take in my surroundings. I breathed in the fresh sea air and heard seagulls greeting the day.

The wooden sign of the Born Free Motel resembled those atop Colorado's many mountain passes. As I flashed back to my family's campfire singing, I began humming the adapted version of my revised favorite, *"This inner light of mine, I'm gonna let it shine."*

I hummed the tune, anticipating my day. I felt truly "born free" with a daily – moment-by-moment – *chance* to *change*.

A sandy path led to the beach, where only a few silhouettes strolled up ahead. The arching tufts of swaying V-grasses dotted the shoreline. The scent of the ocean breeze filled my senses as I sank my toes into the warm loose sand. Soon I was jogging to the foamy edge of breaking waves, following a trail of sandpiper tracks on the hard-packed sand that led the way to the shoreline.

Of course! A combination of V's formed each of the sandpiper's prints.

The sea's expanse stretched beyond the horizon. I arched my head back, taking in the magnificent moment of freedom and fresh air. Anchoring myself into the earth, I recalled Melm's morning reference to women receiving their power from earth while men received theirs from the sky.

Smiling, I thought of myself in the shape of my revised symbol for female. I imagined a future male partner linked with me under the sun. The sea washed up, cooling the warm sand at my feet, as a radiant heat blended the moment all together and the oneness feelings of my **V.O.D.** returned.

I softly began singing a Native American chant I'd learned years earlier to an audience of seagulls and dancing sandpipers:

> *"Oh Great Spirit, Earth, Sun, Sky and Sea,*
> *You are inside and all around me."*

Gentle waves swept up around my feet, settling me further into the warm beach. The words of my chant sank in at a **soulular** level. Was there a deeper message in this simple chant that I'd overlooked?

The words christened a **wholographic** sense of connection with everything in and around me in that moment. I locked into its rhythm while chanting and gliding down the beach:

> *"You are inside and all around me.*
> *Oh Great Spirit, Earth, Sun, Sky and Sea,*
> *You are inside and all around me."*

I embraced a state of oneness with time, space and nature as a unity of **nexUS** – the connection linking me with everything – arrived. *"Amy, this is truly* BEING *here ... now."*

Swept away and without thinking, I danced along with the sandpipers, adding my own creative footprints to the many etched along the shoreline's sandy tracks. I chanted to the great Mother Earth Spirit – the Divine Feminine – who supported billions of footprints. Ever-sustaining, she held immeasurable wonder. Oh how often I took her for granted. A **greatfull** moment of **greatitude** (great•i•tude; great gratitude) passed through me. I felt one with everything happening in that moment.

I once heard a great description for the moment of now, and recalled it then as the only way I could describe the peaceful moments I was embracing: *"The eternal flow of whatever is happening right NOW."* For years, I read works by Eckhart Tolle on his teachings about the power of "now." Suddenly, I understood the endless stream – the eternal flow – of brilliance the now could be.

I felt the morning's stream of moving moments strung together in a *new now*-sensation. In fact, being in the flow of whatever was happening right now was more like a verb, something like **nowing** (now•ing; experiencing the string of *now* moments). I thought to myself in that glorious moment: I must be *knowing* my ***nowing***. To celebrate, I assumed the V-position and asked a fellow beachcomber to take my photo.

A playful momentum kicked in with my **Thornism** and I picked up the pace to trot along the beach. Inspired by the spirit of earth, sun, sky and sea flowing around me, I rode a wave of **nowing**. I felt a great sense of oneness, an alignment within my whole *BEING*, though I couldn't define *IT* or translate *IT*.

The ***nowing*** sense of *knowing IT* transcended all seeing *IT*, doing *IT*, feeling *IT*, hearing *IT*, tasting *IT*, knowing *IT* or sensing *IT* – whatever that glorious *IT* was. I found myself totally absorbed in the full *BEING* of *IT*.

I left the sea's edge to *capture* my *rapture* and located a rise of sand surrounded by tall dancing grasses. Plopping down into a cross-legged position, I paused to take *IT* in again, but then realized *IT* wasn't anything to "take". I recognized another paradigm shift. *IT* was no longer outside of me – as something to "take or get" – *IT* was within me and through eVerything. Surely, I'd arrived at bliss. This state of *BEING* brought me completely into the eternal and internal flow of *knowing* my ***nowing***.

Letting *IT* Go

In that moment of bliss, I marveled at life's journey. The metaphor of my life as a collection of books merged and I sensed all of them uniting inside of me. The *NewMe* had become a *NowMe* and the many faces of me flashed by in a seamless review.

An unexpected wave of bittersweetness flushed through me as I reflected on the first half of my life. What price had I paid in my plight of trying to get life right? How much time had I spent spinning on the outside track in a futile search for an *IT* that had never come close to the peace I felt right now?

I wrapped my warm arms around me and gently rocked with sweet compassion as I consoled the past. My *AsIF* Amy and her **sureface** had brought contrasting dark depths to the light of this moment of sweet success. I retraced the melting of my **viceberg** and the living death of my life of many *ITs*.

Mother Earth's warm sand held me steady so I could take this in. I sensed a final farewell. I took a deep breath and made another committed decision to let *IT* all go.

As the sun moved behind some billowy clouds, radiating V shadows beamed towards me with variegated hues of light. I witnessed my V's visual reassurance and received its message of *"All is well, Amy, all is well."* Rocking back and forth I calmed my mind, repeating, *"All is well."*

I picked up a bleached, blonde piece of driftwood and sketched over one of the sun's V-rays in the sand. I perceived the V's as **varrows**, directing me to live in the present, away from past *pain* to the *gain* of now. It had taken all my *ITs* to arrive at last.

I reminded myself: This *is* the *NowMe*. There is nothing else to *SEE* or *DO*. There is only this moment to *BE*.

From that peaceful place I found a *haven* of *heaven* on the inside. Yet, at the same time, I seemed to stretch beyond the confines of my limited self into a limitless expression. A united sense of *BEING* radiated both in and out.

"Amy, this *IS IT!* This *IS* the *IT* that you've been searching and waiting for. This *IS* the *RealDeal* of *AsIS* living."

My *JOLLI*-joy signaled another dramatic insight ... my *IT* was *IS!* I drew the word *"IS"* into the sand. How often did I race from the *IS* of a moment to grasp another *IT?* Maybe my *liTe* to *liVe* is *loVe* statement was really all about the *IS* word before *loVe!*

IS was so simple—like many of my other life-changing AHAs. I recalled my **artIT**, which had forgotten the all important "S." There was that *"IS"* again. Was practicing the art of *IS* the new v*IS*ion for my **Art*IS*t**?

So *IT IS*

I spent the rest of that morning on Montauk's beach reviewing my *T-to-V* journey. I'd need to make adjustments to my book in light of my recent **aVakenings**. The culminating *IT*-to-*IS JOLLI* embodied my *RealDeal* journey with a profound *NowMe* realization.

I thought about Mile Hi Church in Denver, where I'd enjoyed years of classes, retreats, workshops, concerts and lectures. I loved my membership at this dynamic spiritual center for inspired living. Mile Hi friends would delight in hearing about my Montauk insights. I flashed on the phrase used at the end of our affirmative prayers: *"And so IT IS!"*

How could I have missed seeing this *JOLLI* before? My *IT* and *IS* – so simple – had been *right-in-front-of-me* all along!

My **nowing** continued with exhilaration. I lay on the warm blanket of fine sand, stretched out my arms and legs and sculpted a sand angel like the snow angels I made as a kid.

Shaking off the sand, I looked down at the sweeping V shapes that met in the middle of my sand angel, pointing to my heart. They formed yet another reminder — to *liVe* as *loVe*.

I retraced my steps to the Born Free Motel, singing a playfully revised *IS* version of my chant:

> *"Oh Great Spirit, Earth, Sun, Sky and Sea,*
> *You IS ... inside and all around me."*

After a quick shower, I opened my *Streams* journal to record the day's insights and write out my revised chant. Another *IT IS* clue leapt from the page as I highlighted the "I" and "S" of *IS* with capital letters: InSights were building an Inner Strength from InSide me.

I considered more phrases and found a host of I and S combinations that linked words with the power of *IS*. A brilliant **ISessence** (is•es•sense; essence of *IS)* was hidden within the *I* and *S* letters of certain words. Like a puzzle suggesting the power of now, the words with **ISessence** brought me to a summation based on the day's revelations. There was an Infinite Source surrounding me. It revealed ItSelf to me as an Inner Strength — changing my InSides via all of my InSights.

I searched through phrases I'd written and selected my favorite three. The word pairings fit together in a culminating realization that linked them with my third *T-to-V* switch, *liTe* to *liVe*.

> An Infinite Source provides Inner Strength from
> the InSide and grants me the *liTe* to *liVe* as *loVe*.

This was more than *Good*, th*IS* might just be *God* ...

... and so IT IS!

SUMMARY> Finding *IT IS*

◆ Living the moment became *knowing* my ***nowing***.

◆ My elusive *IT* transformed into the *JOLLI* giant *IS*.

◆ **ISessence** showed up in hidden words and phrases.

CHAPTER 28

Vow to Wow

- Here's Higher Love
- *Amistad* and Ancestors
- My Resurrecting Right

As my Montauk writing retreat continued, I became more InSpired. One late afternoon, I drove around the tip of the island. Dusk loomed on the horizon and I hoped to catch the vista of a vibrant sunset.

I'd spent the day writing and kiting on the beach. A fierce wind had blown my butterfly kite about with fury. Several times I lay down flat on the warm beach to rest my neck while my butterfly kite danced freely across a backdrop of blue, its dancing wings of freedom yet another metaphor for my trip.

It was almost sundown when I packed the rental car and took off, keeping my eyes peeled for a spectacular sunset. Casually flipping on the radio, I dialed through the static and landed on a music station that played classics from the 1980s.

At the top of a great hill, I parked the Honda and set out for a grassy overlook. I assumed a V stance and stretched out, breathing the view in. I sent out thoughts of appreciation to Mother Nature's beauty so easily found in the Hamptons. I walked closer to the edge of the hilltop, where a solitary bench provided prime viewing. A spectacular sun-setting drama was about to begin.

An array of salmon-pinks, golds, blues and purples merged into one another as the light made a slow descent behind the water's horizon. A quiet exhilaration infused my spirits from the magnificent sight.

Unexpectedly, a wave of fatigue swept over me as the sun disappeared. Time to head back for a warm dinner.

I returned to the Honda and turned on the ignition. A classic rock station blasted one of my all-time favorite songs from the eighties, Steve Winwood's "Higher Love". I rolled down the windows, turned up the volume and unabashedly sang out the words as I hastened along the winding highway back to the Born Free Motel. The song refreshed my weariness and I found a smooth high way along my revitalized **innerstate**.

I pulled into the gravel parking lot of the motel, belting out the last line of the song: "Where's that higher love I keep thinkin' of?"

"Hmmm ...." I paused, clicking off the engine, and wondered about that last line. While humming the tune, I bundled my things back into my room and dumped them on the dining table.

The next day would be my last before returning to Denver. With each day's insights, I'd found a greater sense of the *NewMe* emerging, a *NowMe*. My rapture was thrilling, though somewhat exhausting. I might soon need a vacation from my vacation.

I kept humming the "Higher Love" song and heated up some soup in the tiny microwave. Curious about the last line, I hit the space bar on my laptop to wake it up so I could locate the lyrics.

Words from the song reflected and accentuated the story emerging from my Montauk retreat. It was easy to link the synchronicity between this song and the higher love I'd experienced since pulling into the Born Free Motel a few days earlier.

As if hearing the lyrics for the first time, I realized they described much of my journey—except for *just-one-little-letter* that needed fixing in the last line of the song: *Where's that higher love I keep thinking of?*

I flipped open my journal and jotted down the last line, omitting the "*W*" in *Where* for a revised line. I scurried about, dishing up my soup, and chirped the new ending to the song: <u>*Here's*</u> *that higher love I keep thinking of!* ~ Thanks, Mr. Winwood.

Amistad and Ancestors

Across the room, a small video cassette player sat atop a small television. A movie would be a welcome break from all my reVelations. I viewed the collection of alphabetized videos that stood in a bookcase.

Third in the top row was the film *Amistad*. I smiled, remembering that I'd been deeply moved by Steven Spielberg's 1997 film. The historical drama chronicled the true story of an uprising aboard the slave-trade ship, La Amistad. Sengbe Pieh, the primary character, endures capture; he fights his way towards freedom despite insurmountable odds.

I popped the video into the slot, grabbed the VCR remote and hit play. Then I plunked down on the couch with my bowl of soup and let out a long sigh. I was ready for a break.

About an hour into the movie, however, I felt a sudden wave of negativity surface in my thoughts. Weary from either the retreat or the disheartening slavery theme of the movie or a combination of the two, I sank into a wave of sinking thinking.

A sudden spell of loneliness hit as I considered all the time I'd spent on my solo-writing retreat. A mini-mental-meltdown commenced, providing the perfect opening for some Brain Bandits to amp up their negative ammunition. The mental shots started: *"Amy, what are you DOING?!? Really? Do you think this book is going to make sense to anyone but you? Who's going to read a book about YOU?! All these JOLLI ideas are making you a little* **vrazy***!"*

Those dang internal hijackers paid close attention; they'd collected **Amy-intel** the whole time I was having my spiritual **aVakenings** in Montauk, and now they were using it against me. Their inner attack got so loud, I pushed the pause button on the remote.

I got up to make some tea. Shocked and surprised at the level of sudden pain I felt in my chest from just a few seconds of thought bombing, I wondered, *"What's this all about?"*

I glanced over the notes I'd made about allowing myself to just *BE* myself ... *AsIS*. Could my newly acquired **ISessence** allow me to *BE AsIS*, even through the *mad, sad, bad* parts of life?

Time for a self-test for some of my own medicine. I breathed in slowly to calm my negative thoughts, then returned to the couch with the tea to sit with my mental thought-bombers and just let them *BE*.

"Fascinating!" I thought, realizing that this alone was a huge leap for my **Amynation**. In the past, I might have spent considerable time *stalking* my *talking* or playing the Opposites Game with my mind's talk.

Instead I pondered, *"Hmmm, sinking thinking. Fascinating! Hmmm, well, I'm just gonna let these thoughts be AsIS for now. Remember, Amy, we're okay. You're just a little tired. I'm here for you. I love you AsIS, no matter what your thinking may think!"*

I sipped my tea, already feeling lighter from my turned-about thinking. My old negative thought tribes were slightly outraged that they'd been so easily dismissed. I returned to watching the movie, holding the negative thoughts in pause mode, off to the side of my thinking. Soon I became so engaged with the *Amistad* drama, I forgot to think about them.

Towards the end of the film a debated drama played out over the ownership and rights of the *Amistad* captives. The final trial before the Supreme Court depicted John Quincy Adams, played by Anthony Hopkins, preparing Sengbe for the courtroom battle. Adams implied that the verdict might not be favorable.

Instead of reacting with fear, Sengbe Pieh said something profound. I hit rewind and replayed the scene several times so I could write the quote in my journal verbatim. It moved me to tears.

Sengbe looked deep into his lawyer's eyes. With piercing focus he said, "Mr. Adams, we won't be going in there alone." Adams responded with confusion; their counsel was limited to two.

Sengbe continued, "I meant my ancestors. I will call into the past, far back to the beginning of time, and beg them to come and help me at this judgment. I will reach back and draw them in to me. And they MUST come. For at this moment I am the whole reason they existed at all."

Emotions swept in as I recalled the passing of my ancestors. Yet, thanks to Sengbe's words, I felt a renewed sense of fortitude and courage to forge ahead on my path.

John Adams, inspired by Pieh Sengbe's proclamation, said, "... we must embrace the understanding that who we are, *IS* who we were."

This unforgettable exchange reassured me that _all_ I had _been_ contributed to what I had become—and it was all **Go(o)d**. After the film, I lit a candle to reflect more. A calming aura filled the room, as if my ancestors had arrived. I sensed the important message they carried: *I was the very reason they had come.*

Was it now up to me to turn about any ancestral karma of hiding the *liTe* that is within to *liVe* as *loVe?* As the last Thornton in my lineage, did my vow to *liVe* my *liTe* as *loVe* make all the past count?

I pulled out Marianne Williamson's quote, which I used as a bookmark in *Streams*, and remembered, *"Who was I NOT to be talented, gorgeous, InSpired and in love with myself and my life? Who am I NOT to BE this? ISn't this what my ancestors wanted? I have a bold song to sing; it's filled with a bright, inner light of mine, and I'm gonna let it shine!"*

With a deep decision, I recommitted with *JOLLI* joy: I *vow* to find the *wow* in my life. I would make my life count because, as Ted said, "It _all_ counts!" I opened my *Streams* journal to a fresh page and wrote out a *JOLLI* roll to close the day:

I Vow to Wow in Now!

Our deepest fear is not that we are inadequate. Our deepest fear is that we are powerful beyond measure. It is our light, not our darkness, that most frightens us. We ask ourselves, Who am I to be brilliant, gorgeous, talented, fabulous? Actually, who are you NOT to be? You are a child of God. Your playing small does not serve the world. There is nothing enlightening about shrinking so that other people will not feel insecure around you. We are all meant to shine, as children do. We are born to make manifest, on earth, the glory of God that is within us. It is not just in some of us. It is in everyone. And as we let our own light shine, we unconsciously give other people permission to do the same. As we are liberated from our own fear, our presence automatically liberates others.

I sank into the cozy bed and felt a renewed sense of loving energy around me; maybe it was my ancestors confirming my renewed understanding to love all of me, *AsIS*. ~ Thank you, Ancestors!

My Resurrecting Right

Upon awakening the next morning I felt refreshed and reinvigorated. My *vow* to *wow* in *now* was bright and fresh on my mental page. I puttered around, fixing tea and breakfast, looking forward to one last morning jog along Montauk's incredible beach.

While rewinding the *Amistad* videotape, I sent a **greatfull** thought to Mr. Spielberg for delivering such a provoking story.

I glanced through the motel room's collection of books. There was a green leather Bible like the one my folks had given me in grade school. It was years since I'd cracked open a Bible.

In the past, I'd harbored many internal debates about the Bible's deeper meanings. But that morning, I felt completely neutral and open. In a playful challenge, I wondered what passage I would land on when I randomly opened this Bible.

My eyes rested on the verse John 11:25: *"Jesus said to her, 'I am the resurrection and the life ....'"*

"Hmmm. Resurrection and life," I thought while munching on an orange. I flipped open my laptop and looked up the word "resurrection."

The definition seemed almost too simple for a word packed with so much meaning.

 resurrection the revitalization or revival of something.

I switched to the thesaurus to find similar words and found a stream of verbal invigoration.

resurrection resurrect, revive, restore, regenerate, revitalize, breathe new life into, bring back to life, reinvigorate, resuscitate, rejuvenate, stimulate, re-establish, relaunch, restore to life, revive.

I responded with a, *"wow, Wow, WOW! Every one of those words describes my* reVirement *to a T (or should I say V?!?)."*

If one word could epitomize the *evolution* of my inner *revolution,* this was it. I was now living out my own midlife resurrection!

The day had barely begun and, once again, I'd gotten signs that I was right on track. My *JOLLI* expedition had led to a culmination of rejuvenation that was nothing short of personal resurrection.

Resurrection. I considered the word again. Such a powerful word for multiple associations and possible debate. Did I dare use the word in my book? I mulled the concern in my mind. A resounding *"Yes!"* replied, for I had *r**IS**en* from my own living-*IT* death and found the peace of resurrected understanding.

If the *inTent* of my book was to *inVent* the *right* to find my *light* and manifest the glory that *IS* within me, then I would tell *IT* like it *IS.*

Was this a resurrecting right that's here for everyone? A *right* to the rebirth of the original *light* that we all came here to shine? Was this light our essential birthright? I answered again with a conclusive *"Yes!"*

Before heading to the beach, I tucked the bookmark back into my *Streams* journal and mentally repeated to myself:

I AM born to make manifest on earth the glory of God that IS within me. It IS not just in some of us; it IS in eVeryone ...

... and so it really IS!

◆ A new *JOLLI* came from *where's* love to *here's* love.

◆ Spielberg's film, *Amistad*, revealed ancestral messages.

◆ I possessed the resurrecting *right* to my own inner *light*.

·Chapter 29·

I AM Ammo

- I *AM Amy*
- Memory-Lane Pain
- An Ammo Victory

I walked down the motel's wooden porch, smiling back at the sign on the stairway. Those two words, born free, not only branded my Montauk montage of insights, but epitomized all my *reVirement* reversals. The Born Free Motel had given me the opportunity to bring eVerything all together, from a rendezvous with **MyStuff** through a renaissance of refining previous classic principles to a culminating resurrection. ~ Thanks, Born Free Motel!

Walking across the beach to the shoreline, I looked back, noticing the trail of woven V-tracks my Nike running shoes had pressed into the sand. *"But, of course!"* I thought. Jogging my way towards the deserted end of the sea line, I jumped foam hurdles along the water's edge. Up ahead, a curious glob of dark driftwood sat beyond the sea a few yards. I made my way towards it, thinking it might be a washed-up **garbagegem**.

A mass of driftwood, shells and seaweed formed a towering altar in a collective art piece created by hundreds of beachcombers. All sorts of washed-up gems were woven into the altar. It was quite a marvel and stood about five feet high.

My dumpster DNA leapt for joy at the sight of this glorious, beach-trash artistry. Taking it in, I wanted to make my own artistic contribution. Combing through the morning's tidal wash-up, I searched for a V-symbol to thank Montauk for my many **aVakenings**.

Under a clump of seaweed bulbs, I spotted a broken piece of white Styrofoam and immediately noticed two letters, "A" and "M", pressing up from the flat bumpy surface. I thought of Marianne Williamson's quote that began "I AM born to make manifest" and realized that I'd just found a gem imprinted with these important two letters.

Then a *JOLLI* jolt flashed. How many years had I been signing "Amy" as my first name? Why hadn't I considered this massive *JOLLI* hidden within my own name? There it was, *AM* and *AMY*. How beautifully this supported my newly inspired *IS* thoughts. I considered the short, power-packed phrase, *I AM AMY*. My commitment to living an *AsIS* life aligned with this new insight, and an idea formed.

"Wow, Amy, this says it all. Allow your AsIS Amy to BE who I AM. After all, I AM AMY. Simple, and it only took five decades to SEE it!" This invited in a simplicity of *BEING* that embraced all that *I AM*. What a jolly "I *am*" to *aim* for in my life's second half.

The light around the beach shifted as the sun tucked under a mountain of dramatic grey clouds. Only a few rays cast spotlights on the beach-altar piece. A small rosary swung in the wind, casting a cross-shadow in the sand. I flashed on my typographical **vevidance** for letting go of the crosses I'd been bearing.

My retreat had provided a unifying experience launched by a **V.O.D.** The Great Spirit of earth, sun, sky and sea had birthed a spiritual awareness within me that inspired a **godyssey** of greater understanding.

Even the film, *Amistad*, helped me embrace the understanding that all that I am *IS* all that I was. This *I AM AMY* affirmation was a culminating signature to anchor my *vow* to *wow* in *now*.

I tucked the white piece of Styrofoam into my pocket to display on my small altar at home. Then I found a driftwood V-branch to place high atop the beach altar before turning about and heading back to Colorado.

On my United flight home, I felt as if all the parts of me had indeed united into another **nexUS**. My writing retreat had been a resurrecting experience filled with off-the-charts synchronicities. So much happened, it would take some time to absorb.

Memory-Lane Pain

For the next few weeks, I rode the waves of enthusiasm I'd found on the shores of Montauk's beach.

Then, it was tax time. I prepared for my yearly visit with Randy, my accountant, whose office is located in the Denver suburb where I grew up. The drive to my appointment took me through many memory lanes from the first seventeen years of my life.

I drove past the church where our **Easterescapade** egg tree still stood. Twenty feet away was the evergreen under which I'd buried some of Mom's and Dad's ashes. Randy lives one block from my high school. After our meeting, I meandered home, driving through streets full of memories that replayed like a living movie.

The last street I took curved up the neighborhood where I'd pulled my red Radio Flyer wagon to get dolls for my **Dollishops**. At the top of the hill sat our small, red brick house. The towering cottonwood tree in the backyard now shaded three neighbors' yards. Memories of my **Pioneergypsy** travels had dimmed after so many seasons of change.

By the time I returned home, the combination of taxes and memories I'd experienced stirred up a taxing *motion* of *emotion*. While preparing dinner, I felt increasing uneasiness escalate into an all-out, bona fide thought-bombing session.

I started to blame the IRS, the house chores that needed to be done and a few other choice *lame-blame* victims. When I ran out of those, I turned to the one person I could always blame for feeling bad ... myself.

By the time my inner **Amyrant** ended, I'd wrestled with all-out despair. Then I remembered to ask, *"Amy, what's the thinking?! What are you telling yourself? Remember the* Opposites Game. *Do you have your inner story upside down?"* I reached for *Streams* and began to **nagivate** the internal rapids that were washing over me.

Here are just five sinking thoughts out of the hundreds I had negatively entertained:

1. Your book is never going to get finished.
2. The V is a joke; you can't turn anything around.
3. No one cares about you.
4. You are all alone; no one loves you.
5. It's all over; you should just end it all now.

Shocked, I couldn't believe my inner guerilla terrorists, whom I'd thought were locked up, had launched such an all-out nuclear attack on my **Amynation**. I felt as if the brightest and best parts of me had become contraband to make thought grenades for my own destruction. I faced my own **Amygeddon** (amy•ge•den; Armageddon of Amy, total destruction). The force of this interior negativity baffled me.

"What is going on? How could I have experienced a resurrection just weeks prior and now have this kind of thinking still sinking inside of me? How can I know what I know and still be thinking like this? Even worse, how can I be writing a book about this and still entertain these thoughts? What is wrong with me?!?"

I needed some inner ammo, and fast. I grabbed for my best defense to turn about my thoughts. I replayed the day, realizing all the historic pain my trip down memory lane had triggered. While driving past my *past*, I'd attempted to *pass* on my old pain. My hysterical *lame blame* was more historical than it was about anything happening in my current life.

I sat down, doubling over in a wave of pain. As I let the feelings wash over me, my thinking changed. I came to my own rescue. I breathed into the ache, assuring myself, *"Amy, go* in *to* win. *It's okay; these are the* issues *in your* tissues. *This is the past that you need to pass through. It's okay; you're okay; let it all BE ... AsIS, no matter how it feels. You don't have to DO anything right now."*

As the wave of feelings crashed, a soothing release followed. I looked at the open pages of my journal and the negative list of sinking thinking. Months earlier, Melm had taught me an advanced level of the Opposites Game. I'd learned to convert my stalked-talk list into powerful *I AM* statements. It was the most powerful form of inner-ammunition around, and I called it *I AM* Ammo. I was ready to turn those thoughts around and transcend them.

An Ammo Victory

The first step was going through the messy *stalk*-my-*talk* list with a bold pen and changing the operative words from negative to positive.

1. Your book is <u>going</u> to get finished.
2. The V is <u>no</u> joke; you can turn anything around.
3. <u>Many</u> care about you.
4. You are <u>never</u> all alone; <u>many</u> love you.
5. It's all <u>starting</u>; you should just <u>begin</u> it all now.

My list was now ready for the advanced levels of the Opposites Game that turned the positive list into *I AM* affirmations. I wrote a custom-tailored list of my thoughts in my exact Amy inner-language.

1. *I AM* finished with my book!
2. *I AM* turning anything around!
3. *I AM* cared about!
4. *I AM* connected and loved!
5. *I AM* my greatest yet-to-*BE!*

Voilá! A minor mental miracle had taken place. By taking the time to *pause* the *cause* of my *pain*, I'd received the *gain* of insight to turn it all about. Armed with *I AM* Ammo, I'd transcended some of the most negative *issues* in my *tissues* with internal artillery to blast the negatives out. In amplifying each positive with an *I AM* statement, I returned full circle on what could have been hours, days or weeks worth of internal **turbulations** in order to turn them all about.

The force and cumulative effects of <u>all</u> my past had been exactly what I needed to find the **quantumesque** leap into a *RealDeal* moment of resurrection and light. I was living my *liTe* to *liVe* as *loVe* from a rich compassion resting deep within.

As I linked my *I AM* Ammo with my *I AM AMY JOLLI*, a powerful inner dialogue amped up. In facing down my historical pain and allowing it to wash through me as *part* of my *past*, *AsIS*, I found my way back to the **ISessence** that anchored and united the **Amyalgamation** of me.

> An Infinite Source
> brings me Inner Strength
> from the InSide.
>   ~ Thank you, *IS!*

SUMMARY> I AM Ammo

◆ I discovered an obvious life-long *JOLLI* ... I *Am Amy.*

◆ Historical *pain* from memory lane delivered great *gain.*

◆ The Opposites Game created the *I AM* Ammo I needed.

CHAPTER 30

A *JOLLI* Finale

- Celebrating the V-journey
- *Me-We* Reflection
- Last Two Words

A *Just-One-Little-Letter-Insight* led me out of my *Not-OK Corral* onto a journey to where all was *Now-OK*. The V continued to provide stimulating insights for changing directions. My *SEEING* led me towards the turning-about apex of *DOING*, which had pivoted toward greater states of *BEING*.

Much had occurred in the expanse of over half a decade. To summarize within this grand finale, I sketched out my V-journey on a big letter V. Around its open arms, I highlighted my three **vepiphanies**: *ReTirement* to *ReVirement*, *InTent* to *InVent* and *LiTe* to *LiVe*. It astounded me to review all the V had inspired.

Before the V arrived, I'd seriously considered suicide from the despair of midlife. But the V catapulted me into a new realm of limitless possibilities. I found *AsIS* freedom away from the rat-race of an *IT*-focused life. The revolutionary power of *reVirement* started it all.

A committed decision to ban the **tiredword** from my inner kingdom instigated a revitalized turnabout. The V inspired an inside lane, a path, to shift from the inside out. Gloria Steinem led me to consider how powerful a one-letter revolution could be. She also inspired the *JOLLI* suggestion that change could come from *your word* to *our worlds* and *old* to *bold*.

I grabbed hold of my mental steering wheel and pulled onto the inside track to uncover an entirely new direction with my thinking. By

linking my sinking thinking with all that *ailed* and *failed* me, I began to *stalk* my *talk*. All manner of unforeseen opportunities came as I pulled into the inside lane, where *RealDeal* authenticity was possible.

I uncovered the secret identities of my inner guerilla terrorists, who'd spent years launching thought-bombs in efforts to bring me down.

My **overITs** and **nexITs** loosened my internal grip on an *IT*-focused life, and I learned that I could change directions to travel a new **innerstate** with **quantumesque** speed.

From all my *SEEING*, I moved into *DOING*, where the V stretched out before me with renewed perspectives, pointing me to **vhorizons** ahead. As invisible **varrows**, the V continued to show up out of *no-where* to keep my attention on *now-here*. This opened my eyes around all my stuff and I aimed headfirst through the land-o-**MyStuff**.

My second **vepiphany** revealed a link between *InTentions* and *InVentions*. The *DOING* process of my expedition began; I went *in* to *win*. When the haze of physical **MyStuff** cleared, I traversed the boundaries of my **InnerStuff**. There I met the *AsIF* Amy who'd perfected a **sureface** life — a cover-up for the hidden **viceberg** floating below the surface of my life's historic trials.

Previous perceptions expanded – via the V – as I disclosed the stories I was storing. Diving deep to the center of my core, I melted the layers of frozen pain and shame embedded as the *issues* in my *tissues*.

Many passes through the past took me to this core. I learned the difference between historical truth and the hysterical stories I made up to avoid painful feelings. This blew apart many of the paradigms upon which I'd built the first half of my life.

As I bared all and came round 'n' round the **InnerStuff** on my **innervention**, a revitalized compassion for all the parts of me emerged. At a friend's suggestion to fall madly in love with myself, I discovered a series of pivotal steps to help *inVent* the *inTent* for a *RealDeal* genuine life.

Pivotal practices were engaged to find my enoughness, know my *NOs* and clarify my personal policies. I came to understand my *delay* in *relay* and recommitted to *telling* my truth versus *selling* it.

A renovated *AsIS* Amy arrived in the **Amyzone** at peace with my out-of-balance **Amyzon** past. A revitalized equanimity emerged from within. All my *SEEING* and busy *DOING* culminated in a process that continued to produce the genuine *BEING* I'd always longed to experience.

The process involved a living death that allowed me to replace the center of my *IT* target with the true essence of what I sought. *IT* was *I*.

When my third **vepiphany** inspired a reinvigorated *liTe* to *liVe*, I met the brilliance from within that had been born in the *FirstMe*. I wondered if the emerging *NewMe* could tap the glory of my original light in order to shine light on the true direction of my unfolding reinvention.

Clues merged as I remembered childhood joys and sorrows and strove to solve more of the *mysteries* of **MyStories**.

P-principles widened my perspectives, and the scope of the journey expanded as I considered the power of pretending my intending, the filter of Prevailing Perception and the scripting of my inner **playright**.

I found a new *kind* of *mind*. My misdirected thoughts no longer ran the Amy show. Something greater delivered outcomes beyond my **playright**'s limited abilities. I could *SEE* just how **Go(o)d** it *all* was and how it *all* counted. With growing conviction, I knew a divine order must *BE* in and through everything.

As though to confirm this, a **V.O.D.** experience cracked open my body, mind and spirit. A blazing, V-extraVaganza confirmed the magical, yet mysterious, *godyssey* of my V-inspired *odyssey*.

On my Long Island, Born Free retreat, an **ISessence** came into full view. A *vow* to *wow* anchored my commitment to *liVe* my *liTe* in honor of my ancestors—for I was the very reason they had existed.

Had I reached a V-version of enlightenment? The resurrecting path of the V certainly guided me to find *"in-light-I'm-meant"* to live.

I embraced the I *AM* of being *AMY*. The V had shaken me up, turned me upside down and inside out. The V pointed to a finish line at the other end of the *IT* rat-race to a vital victory. The V became my valiant heroine of a divine nature. My **greatitude** soared to new heights.

Finding the **ISessence** in a stream of phrases secured my turning about from all the *ITs* out *there*, leading me to relish the *IS* that was in *here*. I loved *knowing* the ***nowing*** of an ever-flowing Infinite Source that provided endless InSights to replenish my Inner Strength. Truly my thankfulness *IS* beyond measure. ~ Thank you, my vital V!

To conclude this book, I searched through photos to illustrate this last chapter. I found a photo taken of me at age 49, just prior to the Arizona trip that started this journey. The camera had accidently clicked an unflattering and revealing photo of myself while I rushed to pack.

A tired photo reveals my old self.

As I reviewed the photo, post *reVirement* and my *JOLLI* expedition, I was stunned to see an image of the woman I once was. Exhausted and bewildered and constantly in search of worldly *IT* success, I had allowed my true light to disappear. I'd forgotten I possessed a *right* to let my divine *light* shine from within.

Unexpectedly and with great compassion, I realized that I deeply loved my *NowMe*. In fact, I wouldn't ever think of calling myself old or fat on the other side of my V-path. Truly, outside changes could transpire from the inside out. I've heard that the body's cells completely regenerate themselves every seven years—was it any coincidence that I'd celebrate age 57 by the time my book went to press? My seven-year-*IT*-itch would finally be quelled.

To celebrate the completion of my writing escapade, Melm took some lively photos of me in my favorite red cowgirl hat. During our photo shoot, she directed my **pioneergypsy** persona to shine through as she yelled out, "Ride 'em, *Cowgirl!*"

I laughed and quickly amended this with a *JOLLI* twist: "Ride 'em, *Wowgirl!*" Placing the *NowMe* photo close to the *old*, it was **amyazing** to see all the *bold* that *just-one-little-letter* had generated. The V had ignited a *liTe* to *liVe* in me; I'd never be the same again.

And, just when I thought my fascinating V-tale had come to its final ending, yet another reVelation crossed my path that seemed better than them all.

New insides find a new outside.

ME-WE Reflection

One afternoon during my *White Write* retreat, I took a nature walk along a path parallel to a small neighborhood creek.

Off to the side of the brook, a quiet pool reflected the image of a lush evergreen in the shape of an upside-down V. The mirror image brought the tree to me even though, physically, it towered blocks away. My shoes touched the reflection of the fifty-foot tree at the pools' edge, inspiring a new thought. I was ready to *SEE* a revealing secret.

I thought, *"That huge tree is right here at the tips of my toes. How could this little pond have so much power? What's happening with the power of reflection?"*

I reached down, placing my finger on the tree's top in the water. Ripples of radiating halos undulated out in concentric circles that spread wide across the pool in seconds. Another metaphor came to mind.

What if I'm like this reflecting pool of water? What if all day, every day, I'm radiating ripple effects out to the world? Considering that now my *liTe* to *liVe* was to *loVe* both myself and others, I stumbled upon another mega-metaphor for metamorphosis. As an easy graphic reflection flashed in my mind's eye, I grabbed a stick to draw it.

Into the dirt along the side of the creek bank, I etched out the word *ME*. Then I hopped over to the other side of the small creek and looked at the word upside down. Eureka! My turned-about idea reflected a *JOLLI* treasure back at me—my *ME* had become a *WE*.

Flooded with a familiar rush of affirmation, I raced down the path to get home to my Mac and create some typographical proof for this fascinating one-eighty insight.

Sure enough, this was one of those hidden *JOLLIs* filled with **metaphormorphosis** from its sheer simplicity. I absolutely loved its reference to the inseparable connection between *ME* and *WE*. What a uniting concept for many more **nexUS** contemplations!

In respect to the concept of *"your-word* to *our-world"*, maybe this was another reminder to inspire worldly shifts on our planet. An imperceptible line of separation linked the *ME* with the *WE*. Did this suggest that the same interdependence rippled back and forth from the reflecting energy of *ME* into the bigger *WE?*

Limitless possibilities and ideas gushed forth, including a logo that

captured the exact essence of the powerful concept. The idea of a worldwide *ME-WE* revolution took *hold* with *gold* proportions. Maybe this two-letter theme could encourage a greater unity within *ME* to influence a greater *WE?* It was undeniable that, by becoming a better *ME*, I was finding my greater yet-to-*BE*.

With **Amyzon** enthusiasm, I considered this one-eighty flip to ignite another *chance* to *change*. I mocked up a book cover and started sketching out possible chapters. Its working title:

ME-WE Reflection
OUR GREATER YET-TO-BE

Then another synchronicity arrived. The reflecting nature photography I was compiling for the summary pages of this book included photos that were not only inspired by the V, but embodied the beauty of reflection. Within the center of each photograph was a corridor of V paths. All sides came together in a visual confirmation of my resurrecting path of V.

Two Final Words

At the end of my twenty-one-day *White Write* retreat, I emerged from the silence to some intense world news. Faced by the juxtaposition of biochemical warfare in Syria and severe flooding in Colorado, I wondered, once again, what difference could I really make in our world?

How could my *reVirement* message really make a dent with so many challenges going on? Did I really believe *it's all Go(o)d?* Were my V-inspired ideas viable in a world laced with seemingly insurmountable problems? A few mental clouds of doubt rolled in and, along with them, a stream of questions.

Are the answers to our world's problems really out there in some *IT* we've yet to tap? Are our individual challenges the result of someone else and their *IT?* Could our collective consciousness be blinded by the hidden ripples of frozen shame at the hub of our individual issues?

If my thinking was powerful enough to destroy my peace of mind, what universal thinking was destroying our collective minds?

Every day I can choose the path of inner-revolution from the inside out. I can take the chance to *liVe* my *liTe*, no matter what prevailing perception is shaping the outer world. There seems to be one answer, and it all rests on *ME*. If I remain willing to go through any **RoughStuff** to get to the other side while keeping my eyes peeled on the destination, a high way will come.

A committed hope now lives deep in the InnerStrength I found along my V-journey. It assures me that there is always a *chance* to *change*.

One morning I awoke to finish writing these final paragraphs. I hoped to uncover one last *JOLLI* to end my saga, but none arrived. While lying quietly, I asked the V for one last insight, one missed along the way. What two-word message could bring it all together?

Almost as soon as I'd asked, a quiet answer from deep within came. True to form, rich and simple, it said,

"Live love, Amy. *Live love."*

Surprised, I sat up and jotted down the *JOLLI*, shaking my head. *"No way, that's too simple, too cliche! That message has been around for eons of time — it's overused. Everyone is* **overIT**!" My thoughts rejected the phrase, but then I reconsidered, *"Overused, or just under-lived?"*

Soon the sheer simplicity of this final *JOLLI* brought tears of awareness and **greatitude**. Even though it's been said over and over, wasn't love one of the greatest commandments religions profess? Again, I recalled from my upbringing the simple phrase, "Love one another."

As teenagers, Julie and I memorized the Dionne Warwick song "What the World Needs Now Is Love" ... sweet love. This one simple idea consistently provides a final answer to any problem imaginable.

Not only was *"live love"* the most brilliant *JOLLI* ever, typographic **vevidance** confirmed the V's approval. Two big V's rested smack dab in the middle of both words: *liVe* and *loVe*. It was the perfect signature for my verbal heroine's story.

The next day, I celebrated the completion of my manuscript over lunch with my artist friend, Kate Kennedy. Enraptured with my saga, she shared many insights from her own second-half reinvention. She grabbed her phone to show me a quote she'd found that embodied all we'd shared in one simple sentence.

> There is only one journey, going inside yourself.
>
> – Rainer Maria Rilke

My journey of living from the inside out proceeds to reveal a greater love of life that I continue to explore. The puzzling picture of my midlife muddle is now glued together. And, like the many jigsaw puzzles done at my grandparents' *Holiday Cabin*, the colorful stories and adventures told throughout this book have found fusion in its pages. **MyStory** is finally worthy of framing and passing along to my many friends.

May we all shine *bright* with our *right* to express our greatest *light*.

Peace, blessings and *JOLLI* joy to all.

~ Viva the V!

- ◆ Celebrating the Path of V produced a grand summation.

- ◆ A greater yet-to-*BE* was reflected in a *ME-WE* reflection.

- ◆ The simplicity of *LiVe LoVe* said it all ... and so it *IS!*

Living Life *AsIS*

At the time of this book's completion, all of the insights and ideas presented here were tested in a painful *RealDeal* application. Without warning, yet another tragedy hit. My lovely niece, Heather, and her French husband, Jacques, died in a tragic murder-suicide.

Jacques struggled for years with debilitating cluster headaches. They are often coined "suicide headaches" because they incapacitate one through engulfing pain. Jacques had turned to drugs for relief. In an LSD trip gone terribly bad, he carried out the events that ended both their young lives. This challenged all my abilities to *walk* my *talk* and continue to embrace life—good, bad and sometimes ... very, very ugly.

Throughout the horror of piecing together what had happened, I received significant support from the practices and insights contained in the book I'd just written.

"Three good things will come of this, Amy" and *"It's-all-**Go(o)d**"* gave way to a gripping real-life test. Could I truly find something good in this horrific tragedy? An immediate three came to mind:

1. Jacques and Heather were now relieved of years of suffering induced by this incurable illness.

2. My **Stuffology** degree expanded to the complete dispersal of an entire household of **TheirStuff**—my *LoveITs* and *LoseITs* process had never been more needed.

3. I accessed untapped spiritual reserves, found forgiveness and discovered a *live-love* spirit beyond anything I'd ever experienced.

Could I truly *live love* throughout the stress and strain of this event? Would I remain present and authentic in the face of a **tsunamic** (tsu•na•mic; overwhelming, like a tsunami) range of feelings? Could I allow myself the full spectrum of grief and allow it to *BE AsIS?* Could I honor the *"what's real for me"* truth? Would I stay in the **Amyzone**, or turn to the default settings of my **Amyzon** past? Would I turn to previous *additions* or *addictions* in order to *delay* the *relay* of pain and sorrow?

And, perhaps the most important test of all, could I hold my own hand in self-love, trusting an InnerStrength would be supplied from an Infinite Source? When landing in this very *Not-OK* place, could I continue my practices of turning about and changing directions towards *Now-OK?*

What transpired was indeed remarkable. Throughout the weeks of grief and resolution, little by little, all my insights worked! I came to find a peace that far surpassed all my previous understandings.

I remembered my three *T-to-V's: reVirement* (turn about); what's my *InTent* to *InVent*; and where's my *liTe* to *liVe?* These three tenets, along with my *JOLLI* mindset, continued to anchor me and inspire further transformation. Any need to act *AsIF* could finally be left behind.

Heather and Jacques in France

Many blessings to you, dearest Heather and Jacques. May your expanded journey be filled with the eternal *flight* of *light*. I love you.

What Happens Now?

Discovering hidden powers in *Just-One-Little-Letter-Insights* continues to fascinate me. One of the most common *JOLLIs* I watch out for is: I *can* or I *can't*. These two words are too easily interchanged, with "can't" inhibiting countless acts of creativity and reinvention.

As the speeding world zips by, I'm encouraged more and more to keep things simple. *JOLLIs* help me do just that.

With steadfast practice, I challenge untrue neural ruts as I strive to *check-out-the-data* and get **MyStories** straight. *Stalking* my *talking* keeps me on alert for those clever Brain Bandits, who constantly collect more **Amy-intel** for unexpected thought-bombings.

When I'm missing my **ISessence** – that place of being *Now OK* with whatever *IS* – I run a mental checklist of *IS* questions to realign.

- *IS* my thinking sinking? What am I telling myself?

- *IS* this *(whatever I'm making-up)* what's *really* going on? *IS* my **playright** getting the story upside down?

- *IS* an **overIT** on the horizon? *IS* it time to turn about?

- *IS* there acceptance for whatever *IS* going on, or have I pulled on my *AsIF* **sureface** mask and re-entered the outside *IT* rat-race?

- *IS* it all **Go(o)d**? What are three good things?

- *IS* **MyStuff** or **TheirStuff** threatening to take over? *IS* it time for a *LiveIT*, *LoveIT* or *LoseIT* review?

- *IS* my faith in an Infinite Source bringing me InSights that increase my Inner Strength?

Most importantly … am I living from the InSide out?

These queries lead back to the *in*-to-*win* path, where my answers *live* and where my best *life* truly *IS*.

As I embrace the greater yet-to-*BE* of *ME*, the reflection of our greater *WE* arrives. Living life with love brings the everlasting hope that I'm part of the world's ongoing *chance* to *change*.

· Acknowledgments ·

This book celebrates the courageous journey to embrace change in many forms. Without the exceptional friendship and support hundreds have given me, it would not have found its published voice.

To the friends and family who grace these pages, I owe gratitude beyond measure. In addition, there remain dozens to thank, including those whose names I may have regrettably but unintentionally omitted.

Many patiently reviewed this manuscript in part or in its entirety and inspired my vision at different stages as it evolved from a flurry of V-excitement to a cohesive story. Annie, Amy, Bliss, Debra, Debbie A., Debbie T., Diane, Dr. Roger, Carl, Cathy, Christen, Cynthia, Erica, Frosty, Gay, Ger, Grace, Heidi, Jason, Julie, Kathy H., Kathy W., Karen, Mariah, Mary, Michael, Michelle, Otha, Sandy, Sara, Scott, Sue, Suzanne, Trish, Tom and Tracy ~ Thank you so very much!

For scores of literary and professional acuity I received from sources too numerous to list, I'm deeply appreciative. For editorial patience, shaping and publication refinement, I thank Ann Douden, Gail Nelson and, most profoundly, Karen Carter.

Thanks for supporting me in all ways!

Few could experience the endless inspiration and joy I receive while participating in the enthusiastic discussions of my JavaBookChat book group. Beautiful ladies, you absolutely rock and give me more than you will ever know.

A deeply personal thanks to Dr. Don Hemerson, Michael O'Rourke and Michelle Elm for their generous energy, fortitude and encouragement. To Dr. WAYne Dyer and Gloria Steinem, thank you for the personal touches and broader contributions you've brought to me and countless others.

And, lastly, to millions of comrades in recovery fellowships across the world, I thank you for all the stories and experiences that continue to inspire hope and inner strength. For over three decades, you've saved my life and given me ongoing courage to trudge the path of going *in* to *win*.

Great eternal Spirit that breathes in and through us all, to you I give my complete devotion and gratitude; for without you there is no *love* to *live*.

· ABOUT AMY THORNTON ·

Amy Thornton writes, paints and designs for a better world. In the same way she creates artwork that explodes with color and movement, Ms. Thornton paints with words to shape illuminated stories packed with meaning. She believes the power of *words* can change *worlds*.

Committed to reinventing all that is *old* and turning it to *gold*, she has invented *JOLLIs*, **Thornisms** and **typoknackabilities** that deliver refreshing insights with simplicity and candor. *Chance to Change*, her first foray into creative nonfiction, expands upon themes found in her popular *Stalk Your Talk* and *Dollishop* transformational experiences.

Ms. Thornton's passion for artistic innovation began early under the influence of both her creative parents. At age twelve, she learned from her artist father how to hand set type on the family's antique letterpress, and her zeal for creating graphics and publications took flight.

Through the past thirty years of professional artistry both as an internationally-collected fine artist and award-winning creative director, Amy has lived and worked in London, Manhattan and Denver.

With an impressive list of clientele and collectors that include Fortune 500 companies and pro athletes, she has also had artwork installed at Trump International Hotel & Tower New York in Manhattan. Amy is passionate about her contributions, whether they are made via a paintbrush or a computer keyboard.

Her many accolades include: The Gold Award, Book Design, Independent Publishers Association; First place, Annual Report Design, Silver Peak Awards; Pride Award, Selected for National Tour, Appleton Papers; Outstanding Guidebooks, American Association of Museums; Finalist, Children's Books of Distinction, *Hungry Mind Review*; Pick of the List, American Booksellers Association.

Ms. Thornton lives with her verbal heroine, the V, and her harem of Macs in Denver, Colorado. There, she practices her daily destiny of *BEING* in a *DOING* world.

· To Connect ·

Amy facilitates frequently on a range of topics including: turning about negative self-talk, transformation, personal inspiration and practical *AsIS* living. She loves to deliver keynotes and half-day or full-day versions of this content, depending on the needs and focus of an organization.

All inquiries are welcomed; please email:
amythorntonartworks@gmail.com

To share your own inspirations and to find more to explore, visit:
AmyThornton.com

You can also connect with Amy here:
Twitter: *twitter.com/amythorntonart*
Facebook: *facebook.com/amythornton*

· GLOSSARY ·

Thanks to my dad, John Thornton – the ever-illustrative creative spark – for inspiring my journey into creative word painting. The list below offers a quick reference to the **Thornisms** and terms that helped shape my *chance* to *change*.

A

AHA (a•ha; acronym for Awareness Has Amazement)
Amy-intel (am•y•in•tel; highly classified Amy-intelligence)
Amyalgamation (am•y•al•ga•ma•tion; amalgamation of Amy, uniting of all parts)
Amyalogies (am•y•al•o•gies; analogies by Amy)
Amyammo (am•y•am•mo; Amy's mental ammunition)
amyazed (am•y•azed; Amy is amazed)
amyazing (am•y•a•zing; Amy finds something amazing)
Amygeddon (am•y•ged•don; Armageddon of Amy, total destruction)
amylyzing (am•y•ly•zing; Amy over-analyzing)
Amynation (am•y•na•tion; the nation living within Amy)
Amyrant (am•y•rant; when Amy goes on a rant)
Amytoo (am•y•too; nickname for Amy Kendall)
Amyzon (am•y•zon; an Amy nickname inspired by the Amazon; the name aptly describes the over-excited momentum that can run me at times)
Amyzone (am•y•zone; the zone of Amy in balance)
amyzonian (am•y•zon•i•an; Amy gets the size of the Amazon)
artIT (art•IT; turning art into an *IT* to get)
artobiography (art•o•bi•og•ra•phy; life biography via art)
AsIF (as•if; an alter ego of acting "as if")
AsIS (as•is; being with whatever is, "as is")
aVakening (a•vak•en•ing; awakened by the letter V)
aVareness (a•vare•ness; aware of V)

B

Boomer (Short for Baby Boomers)
Bhahkti (Nickname for laptop; Sanskrit for "to share in, to love, to worship with")
Beetlebug (Car nickname for red Volkswagen vehicle)
blamestorming (blame•storm•ing; a storm of *lame blame*)
Blanca (Car nickname for white Subaru vehicle; Spanish word for "white")

D

d'illusion (dil•lu•sion; the delusion of an illusion)
Dad-elation (dad•e•la•tion; Dad's unbridled elation)
de'Nile (de•nile; denial as long as the river Nile)
Dollishops (doll•i•shops; beauty shop makeovers for dolls)
dynomantics (dy•no•man•tics; the dynamite antics of our family dynamics)

E

Easterescapade (eas•ter•es•ca•pade; escapade around Easter)
enVraptured (en•vrap•tured; enraptured by the V)
Explority (Name of my college folk-singing duet)

F

FirstMe (Nickname for my original self)
fragilistic (fra•gil•is•tic; description for Dad's fragile antiques)

G

garbagegems (gar•bage•gems; gems from garbage)

Go(o)d (good or {god}; parenthetical blend of God with good)

godyssey (god•ys•sey; an odyssey to finding my own version of God)

grammarring (gram•mar•ing; marring grammar)

greatitude (great•i•tude; great gratitude)

greatfull (great•full; full of great gratefulness)

H

Hamptonesque (hamp•ton•esque; a unique beauty unto the Hamptons)

I

imperfectionoughta (im•per•fec•tion•ought•ta; ought to be imperfect)

inCASEitis (in•case•i•tis; justifying symptom of **stuffonia**, holding on in case)

innerstate (in•ner•state; interstate of my inner mind)

innerVened (in•ner•ven•ed; intervened between the inner me and the V)

innervention (in•ner•ven•tion; intervening on the inside to get help)

ISessence (is•es•sense; essence of *IS)*

J

JOLLI (jol•li; acronym for *Just-One-Little-Letter-Insight)*

K

knackability (knack•a•bil•i•ty; a knack for expanded ability)

L

*LiveIT, LoveIT, LoseIT (JOLLI*s used to sort stuff into three categories)

M

M'or (mor; Nickname for Michael O'Rourke)

Melm (melm; Nickname for Michelle Elm)

metaphormorphosis (met•a•phor•mor•pho•sis; a metaphor for a metamorphosis)

Mona Lisamy *(*mo•na•lis•amy; Mona Lisa-inspired Amy)

MyStory (my•sto•ry; the story[ies] I'm making up)

MyStuff (my•stuff; my vast collections of stuff, worthy of its own word)

N

nagivate (nag•i•vate; navigate nagging aggravation)

NewMe (Nickname for my new self)

nexIT (nex•it; the need to exit before any next *IT* can begin)

nexUS (nex•us; spelling to stress "US"; nexus: a connection of two or more things)

nowing (now•ing; experiencing the string of *now* moments)

NowMe (Nickname for my now self)

O

O.P.T. (o•p•t•; acronym for *On-Purpose-Typo)*

obstackle (ob•stack•le; obstacle to be tackled*)*

overIT (over•it; the state of being over an *IT)*

overITness (o•ver•it•ness; noun for state of **overIT**)

P

peacing (peac•ing; the peace of piecing together)

perfectionoughta (per•fec•tion•ought•a; ought to be perfect)

pioneergypsy (pi•on•eer•gyp•sy; a pioneer-gypsy combination)

playright (play•right; my inner playwright who always gets to be right)

preSCRIPTion (pre•scrip•tion; a pre-SCRIPT providing a healing prescription)

Q

quantumesque (quan•tum•esque; with the quality of quantum leaps)

R

RealDeal (Noun or adjective combining the *JOLLI real* and *deal* for authenticity)

reverbalations (re•ver•bal•a•tions; revelations of a verbal nature)

reVirement (re•vire•ment; French word for a turnabout, change of direction, revolution)

reVirementality (re•vire•men•tal•i•ty; having a *reVirement* mentality)

S

S.M.D. (Acronym for Stuff Management Degree)

Scoutie-outie (Nickname for four-wheel-drive Scout vehicle)

shero (she•ro; she version of hero)

soulace (soul•ace; solace for my soul)

soulular (soul•u•lar; beyond a cellular level, in one's soul)

Streams (Nickname for my *Streams of My Mind* journals)

Stuffology (stuff•ol•o•gy; study of stuff)

stuffonia (stuff•o•nia; disease of too much stuff; sounds like pneumonia)

supercatas (Nickname for the Thorntons' Siamese cats)

sureface (sure•face; the surface face of being sure)

switcheroo (switch•e•roo; switch in awareness; inspired by Amytoo)

T

theremometer (there•mom•eter; an inner-gauge determining inner-esteem measured by something "out there")

thornistic (thorn•is•tic; having Thornton tendencies)

thornallistic (thorn•al•lis•tic; when a Thornton goes ballistic)

Thornisms (thorn•isms; Thornton-invented words)

thorntonesque (thorn•ton•esque; with the flair of a Thornton)

tiredword (tired•word; **Thornism** for the word retirement)

traumadrama (trau•ma•dra•ma; additional trauma added to a drama)

tsunamic (tsu•na•mic; overwhelming, like a tsunami)

turbulations (turb•u•la•tions; a turbulent flow of tribulations)

typoknackabilities (typ•o•knack•a•bil•i•ties; the knack for typos)

V

V.O.D. (v•o•d; acronym for V-Over-Dose, over-dose induced by the letter V)

varrow (var•row; V-inspired arrow)

vastronomical (vast•ro•nom•i•cal; astronomically V-sized)

velights (ve•lights; delights of the V)

vepiphany (ve•pi•phan•y; V-inspired epiphany in a moment of sudden awareness)

verbalation (ver•bal•a•tion; verbal elation)

vevidance (vev•i•dance; dance of V-evidence)

vhorizon (vhor•i•zon; V-inspired horizon)

viceberg (vice•berg; an invisible iceberg of vices)

VIDA (Nickname for gold Subaru vehicle; Spanish word for life)

viology (vi•ol•ogy; biology of letter V)

vortext (vor•text; whirling vortex of text)

vortextology (vor•text•o•logy; textual study of V)

vrazy (v•raz•y; V-crazy)

W

wholographic (whole•o•graphic; a holographically inspired wholeness)

writobiography (write•o•bi•og•ra•phy; biography of writing)

In the Works ... COMING SOON

Join Amy for more JOLLI insights. Three new publications guide you IN to WIN and find your LITE to LIVE!

A Guidebook ...
Old to *Gold*
Hands-on Tips for Change

Put insights into action with this companion to **Chance to Change: A Midlife Resurrection**

- *Packed with easy-to-follow guides.*
- *Simple, quick tips that work!*
- *Large, open format for writing.*

The Sequel ...
ME-WE Reflection
Finding a Greater Yet-to-*BE*

More explorations continue the journey from the inside out for a better world.

- *Includes practical guides to becoming the best you.*
- *More metaphors for metamorphosis!*
- *Stories to inspire change — from YOUR to OUR world.*

Text Tonic ...
JOLLI Dolli
The Healing Magic of Dolls

*Based on popular **Dollishops**, a storybook journal to help you align with your original spark of genius.*

- *Self-discovery games for all ages.*
- *Bring out the true you with play.*
- *Perfect for parents and grandparents.*

Visit AmyThornton.com for more JOLLI joy.